Producing
Teaching
Materials

Producing Teaching Materials

SECOND EDITION

A HANDBOOK FOR TEACHERS AND TRAINERS

Henry Ellington and Phil Race

Illustrated by Stan Keir

NICHOLS/GP PUBLISHING

Kogan Page Ltd, London
Nichols Publishing Company,
New Jersey

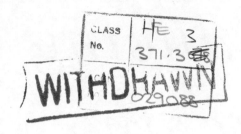
First published in 1985 by Kogan Page.
This second edition first published in 1993 by Kogan Page.
Apart from any fair dealing for the purposes of research or private study,
or criticism or review, as permitted under the Copyright, Designs and
Patents Act, 1988, this publication may only be reproduced, stored or
transmitted, in any form or by any means, with the prior permission in
writing of the publishers, or in the case of reprographic reproduction in
accordance with the terms of licences issued by the Copyright Licensing
Agency. Enquiries concerning reproduction outside those terms should
be sent to the publishers at the undermentioned address:

Kogan Page Limited
120 Pentonville Road
London N1 9JN

Reprinted 1994

British Library Cataloguing in Publication Data
A CIP record for this book is available from the British Library.

ISBN 0 7494 0393 4

Published in the United States of America by Nichols Publishing,
P.O. Box 6036, East Brunswick, New Jersey 08816

A CIP record for this book is available from the Library of Congress.

ISBN 0-89397-418-8

Typeset by Spectrum Typesetting Ltd, London
Printed and bound in Great Britain by Clays Ltd, St Ives plc

Contents

Acknowledgements

We are pleased to acknowledge the valuable assistance we have received from the following people in preparing the respective editions of this book: Eric Addinall for constructive criticism and general advice, Stuart Allan for technical advice particularly relating to audio recording, Bill Black for technical advice on photography and for providing photographs, Margaret Geddes and Doreen Alexander for typing parts of the manuscript, Anne Howe for advice at the planning stage of the first edition, Stan Keir for producing most of the illustrations, Robert Edwards and students at the University of Glamorgan for contributions to the computer conferencing case study, and many colleagues within and outwith The Robert Gordon University and the University of Glamorgan for information and advice on many topics. We are also very grateful to Dolores Black, Helen Carley and Robert Jones (Kogan Page Limited) for their expert help and advice in bringing this second edition of the book to fruition.

November 1992

Professor Henry Ellington	Professor Phil Race
Educational Development Unit	Educational Development
The Robert Gordon University	University of Glamorgan
Aberdeen	Pontypridd

The authors and publisher also gratefully acknowledge the co-operation of the following organizations regarding the publication of copyright materials:

- The Association for Science Education and the Institution of Electrical Engineers (Figure 2.3)

- The Scottish Council for Educational Technology and Nuclear Electric (Figure 2.8)

- SEDCO and Omnitechnology Ltd (Figure 6.2)

- Mast Learning Systems for extracts from 'Secrets of Study' (Chapter 8)

- Professor Philip Barker, and Robert Hall, and The Association for Educational and Training Technology (AETT) for the respective extracts from the Proceedings of the 1991 Conference (Chapter 8).

Introduction

Since the first edition of this book was published in 1985, the world of educational and training technology has been changing very rapidly. There are many visible manifestations of this change, including the everyday use of video (and the virtual disappearance of cine film), the proliferation of open and flexible learning resources (often using a variety of media), and even the tendency for chalkboards to be replaced by overhead projectors – or at least by markerboards. Something that has changed little – if at all – is the range of processes by which people learn (even though the resources from which they learn have changed, as, indeed, have the attitudes and expectations of learners and trainees). In other words, the systematic approach used for instructional strategies is just as relevant today as it was in 1985 (even if some of the terminology used in the approach has changed somewhat – with competence statements, learning outcomes and performance indicators being modern educational terminology for what used to be described as instructional objectives).

This book is primarily written as a handbook for practising educators and trainers. Practitioners should find it of considerable help regarding the design and production of support materials to use in their everyday work. The book should also be useful to trainee lecturers, teachers and instructors, and to anyone involved in educational and training technology – whether as a practitioner or as a student.

Since the book is not set in any one particular educational or cultural context, and covers the various topics in broad terms, it is hoped it will prove as useful for practitioners in the United States, Australasia, and other English-speaking countries, as for those in Britain.

In updating this book for the 1990s, we have faced a dilemma – what to leave out. It was easy enough to decide on the new things which we needed to bring in, such as information on word-processing, open learning modules, greater detail on uses of video technology, camcorders, and a taste of the massive advances made in computer-assisted learning. However, it was more difficult to decide what to discard from the earlier edition of the book. After all, chalkboards are still in use in much of the world, including in most schools and colleges in Britain. In general, therefore, we decided to leave in material relating to those older technologies which are still in fairly common use (with the exception of cine, which video has so largely swept aside), so that practitioners who still find the older technologies useful will find relevant advice in the book.

The main text of the book is divided into eight chapters. The first sets the scene for what is to follow by outlining the main types of teaching/learning situation in which instructional and support materials can be used. This chapter gives a general review of the different kinds of material which are available, and provides general guidance on how to select suitable materials for particular purposes and when to decide to produce your own materials. The remaining seven chapters deal in turn with specific classes of instructional materials, offering detailed guidance on *when to use* the materials, *how to design* the materials, and, in most cases, *how to produce* the actual materials.

Chapter 2 deals with what are still the most important kind of educational and training materials, namely, those based on print. These include handout materials, worksheets, resource sheets, and open and flexible learning modules. The instructional situations in which such materials prove useful are discussed, and basic guidance is provided on the educational design, composition and layout of the materials. The chapter also examines the different methods which may be used to produce multiple copies of printed materials.

Chapter 3 covers the general field of non-projected display materials, dealing in turn with chalkboards, markerboards, and other display media of this type.

Chapter 4 deals with the various types of still projected display materials, looking in some detail at the most common form – overhead projection transparencies – and offering guidance on how to make the most of such media. The chapter also provides advice on producing photographic slides.

Chapter 5 discusses simple audio materials, and includes a basic introduction to sound recording and editing.

Chapter 6 examines various ways in which audio materials can be linked with still visual materials, dealing first with systems that link tape with textual and photographic materials, then with less well known combinations such as tape-model and tape-realia.

Chapter 7 is devoted to a study of educational and training uses of video, which, since the first edition of this book was published, has all but superseded what then was the other primary moving-visual medium – cine. In particular, this chapter examines the reasons for choosing to use video as a teaching/learning medium, and suggests ways of ensuring that the learning outcomes arising from the use of video are made explicit and tangible. The chapter includes an introduction to the various new, relatively low-cost sorts of equipment (such as camcorders) now used in video production and provides some tips on using these.

Chapter 8 represents the area where things have moved on most dramatically since the publication of the first edition of this book: computer-assisted learning. It would now be quite impossible to give an adequate review of the massive field of computer-assisted learning in a single chapter in a book of this size. Nevertheless, we have attempted to give a perspective of the power of computer-mediated learning by including basic case study details of two particular applications: computer conferencing, and interactive video. However, our illustrations, being confined to the medium of print, can only serve to give you a basic impression of the sophistication and user-interaction that is now possible in highly-colourful multimedia learning packages. We have also included an extended bibliography incorporating a list of relevant journals.

For the most part, rather than break up the flow of the text with frequent references to other work (which would also reduce our attempt to make this book as self-sufficient as possible) we have provided bibliographies at the end of each chapter, listing reference materials for readers who wish to go deeper into particular areas. We have also added a fairly-detailed keyword index which we hope will help readers to track down any topics that particularly interest them.

Chapter One

A Guide to the Selection of Instructional Materials

INTRODUCTION

The first step in any systematic approach to course or curriculum design should be to establish a clear picture of the learning outcomes that it is intended should be achieved. This can be achieved by working out appropriate instructional objectives, or statements of competence, specifying exactly what it is intended that learners should become able to do. Once these learning outcomes are established, teachers, instructors and trainers need to examine the various instructional methods (and the various learning situations) to become able to select the most appropriate method (or combination of methods) to use. As part of this analysis, it is particularly important to keep the target audience of learners firmly in mind, so that learning situations can be as appropriate and relevant as possible for different groups of learners.

Next, teachers, trainers and instructors need to decide what supportive or illustrative materials they will need to enhance the quality and effectiveness of learning. They need to be able to select suitable materials from those already available, and more important, to design their own materials to be particularly relevant to individual learning programmes and objectives. This book has been written to help teachers, instructors and trainers acquire the knowledge – and develop the skills – necessary to carry out such choosing, developing and using of instructional materials.

When first planning the original edition of this book, it was intended to limit it to seven chapters, each dealing with the design and production of one particular group of instructional materials. However, it was decided that the usefulness of the book would be greatly increased by adding an opening chapter that would place the following chapters in a logical educational context, by providing a broad view of the way in which well-chosen instructional materials can enhance the effectiveness of teaching and learning processes. We will therefore begin by examining the different roles of instructional materials in various teaching/learning situations, reviewing the range of such materials which are available to the modern teacher or trainer, and offering guidance on how to set about selecting materials for specific purposes.

The remaining chapters will then offer detailed information and advice on how to acquire, develop, produce and use the various sorts of instructional materials.

THE VARIOUS ROLES OF INSTRUCTIONAL MATERIALS IN DIFFERENT TEACHING/LEARNING SYSTEMS

Since this is a practical book on producing teaching materials rather than a treatise on the theory of learning, we will resist the temptation to begin this section by discussing Skinner's stimulus/response model, Gilbert's mathetics, Gagné's categories of learning, the taxonomies of learning objectives proposed by Bloom, Krathwohl and Harrow, and so on. Readers who are unfamiliar with the basic ideas of these various workers, and who feel that it is necessary for them to acquire such familiarity before proceeding further, are referred to any basic text on the subject. The opening chapter of Romiszowski's *The Selection and Use of Instructional Media*, for example, provides an excellent introduction to the field (see Bibliography).

Rather, we will proceed directly to a discussion of the different types of teaching/learning systems as seen from the point of view of the practising teacher or trainer rather than the educational theorist, using a classification that we have found particularly useful. This classification, which was first introduced by Professor Lewis Elton of the University of Surrey in a seminal paper that he presented at the 1977 ETIC Conference (see Bibliography), was subsequently used by Fred Percival and Henry Ellington in *A Handbook of Educational Technology*. It divides all teaching/learning systems into three broad groups, which may be loosely described as mass instruction techniques, individualized instruction techniques and group learning techniques (see Figure 1.1). Let us now examine these in more detail, and see what role instructional materials are capable of playing in each.

Class of techniques	Examples	Role of teacher/ instructor/trainer
Mass instruction	Conventional lectures and expository lessons; television and radio broadcasts; cable television; films.	Traditional expository role; controller of instruction process.
Individualized instruction	Directed study; open learning; distance learning; programmed learning; mediated self-instruction; computer-based learning (CBL).	Producer/manager of learning resources; tutor and guide.

Class of techniques	Examples	Role of teacher/instructor/trainer
Group learning	Tutorials; seminars; group exercises and projects, games and simulations; self-help groups	Organizer and facilitator.

Figure 1.1 **The three basic classes of instruction methods**

Mass Instruction Techniques

This group encompasses all techniques that involve expository teaching of a class of students or trainees by a teacher or instructor, either directly (via a lecture or taught lesson of some sort) or indirectly (via an audiovisual medium such as film, closed-circuit TV, broadcast TV or radio). It places the teacher or instructor in his traditional role, namely, that of a source of information and controller of the teaching/learning process, with the learner being restricted to a more-or-less passive role and having to work at a rate that is entirely determined by the instructor.

Although there has been a considerable move away from the former near total reliance on this mode of instruction over the last 20 or 30 years, it is still a commonly used method in most educational and training establishments. The reasons for this are many. First, it is the method with which the great majority of teachers and trainers are most familiar and feel most comfortable, probably because they are 'in control' and do not have their authority challenged. Second, it is generally popular with students and trainees, probably because they, too, are familiar with the method and feel comfortable and 'secure' with it; most students, after all, are perfectly happy to be placed in a passive role that makes no great demands on them. Third, it can be extremely cost-effective (at least in purely logistical terms) enabling large numbers of students or trainees to be taught by a single teacher or instructor. This is particularly relevant in the early 1990s, with increasing numbers of students entering higher education in the United Kingdom. Fourth, it makes timetabling relatively simple and straightforward – a feature that endears it to educational administrators who, in many cases, seem more concerned with the smooth running of their establishments than with the quality of the learning process that takes place therein. Thus, despite its many educational shortcomings (inability to accommodate different student learning styles and learning rates, unsuitability for achieving many higher cognitive and non-cognitive objectives, and so on) mass instruction will almost certainly continue to play a major role in formal education and training for many years to come. It is therefore up to the average 'coal-face' teacher or trainer to try to use the method as effec-

Figure 1.2 (a) **A pharmacy lecture at The Robert Gordon University**

(b) **A typical taught lesson in a secondary school**

tively as possible, something that can only be done (we would submit) if systematic use is made of appropriate supportive instructional materials.

Within the context of the various techniques that can be employed as vehicles for mass instruction, audiovisual and other instructional materials can play a number of roles. In some cases (eg the use of visual aids, handouts or worksheets in a lecture or taught lesson) their role will probably be mainly supportive; in others (eg film or video presentations or off-air broadcasts) they can constitute the essence of the method itself. In both cases, however, it is important that the materials be chosen because of their suitability for achieving the desired learning objectives, and not merely because they 'happen to be available' or because the teacher or instructor wants to 'fill in time'. Some of the ways in which instructional materials can be used in mass instruction are given below.

- Forming an integral part of the main exposition by providing 'sign-posts' and 'links', guidance for note-taking, illustrative material, worksheets, etc.

- Providing supplementary material (background reading, remedial or extension material, enrichment material, and so on).

- Increasing student motivation by introducing visually attractive, interesting or simply 'different' material into an otherwise routine lesson.

- Illustrating applications, relations, integration of one topic with another, and so on.

As we will see later, a large number of different materials can be used to fulfil these various functions.

Individual Instruction Techniques: Open and Flexible Learning

Whereas conventional mass instructional teaching strategies are dominated by the teacher or instructor and by constraints imposed by the institution or system within which he operates, the various techniques and systems that fall into the class of 'individualized learning methods' are much more learner-centred in their approach. These are designed to cope with the needs of individual learners, who can differ greatly in such things as preferred learning style and natural pace of learning. A wide range of individualized learning techniques has been developed over the years, from text-based methods of the type used in traditional correspondence courses to the latest audiovisual and computer-mediated techniques. The educational and training contexts within which such techniques are used also vary greatly, ranging from the incorporation of specific elements of individualized or resource-based learning into conventional teacher/institution-centred systems to systems where practically all the conventional barriers to educational or training opportunities have been removed, so that a potential learner can be of any age or background and can study in places, and at times, which suit the individual rather than the host institution.

Although individualized learning, in the form of correspondence courses and similar systems, also has a long tradition of use in education, it was only comparatively recently that it started to become an integral part of mainstream education and training. The catalyst for this develop-

Figure 1.3 (a) **A student engaged in individualized learning**

(b) **Students engaged in individualized learning using networked PCs**

(c) **A group of primary school children working on individualized learning materials, supervised by their teacher**

ment was Skinner's work on behavioural psychology and the stimulus-response model of learning during the 1950s. In many people's view, the latter constituted the first truly 'scientific' theory of learning, and triggered off the bandwagon programmed learning movement that so dominated progressive educational thinking during the 1960s. Indeed, while at Aberdeen College of Education in 1966, one of us remembers being told by one programmed learning enthusiast on the staff that the traditional classroom teacher would soon become obsolete, being replaced by the wonderful new 'teaching machines' that were being developed as delivery systems for learning programmes. As it turned out, however, these teaching machines proved to be the biggest non-event in the history of education, partly because of their high cost and the failure of their manufacturers to produce high-quality associated courseware in the quantities that would have been needed to enable them to make any real impact, and partly because of the increasing realization that there was much more to education than the mere teaching of facts and principles (which was basically all that such machines could do). Nevertheless, the programmed learning movement has had a tremendous – and beneficial – influence on educational thinking, and has certainly led to a more widespread use of individualized learning techniques such as tape-slide programmes and computer-based learning, as well as to the development of fully integrated self-instruction systems such as the Keller Plan and Open University systems. Certainly, no progressive teacher or trainer can really afford to ignore individualized learning any more, since it constitutes one of the most powerful groups of techniques in the modern educational armoury

– especially as a means of covering objectives in the lower-to-middle region of the cognitive domain and teaching certain basic psychomotor skills.

As shown in Figure 1.1, the role of the teacher, instructor or trainer in an individualized learning system is completely different from the traditional role as a presenter of information and controller of the instructional process. Rather, the role is that of a producer/manager of learning resources and a tutor and guide to the learner. Needless to say, some teachers and trainers – especially the older or more conservative ones – find it very difficult or even impossible to reconcile themselves to such a role. Also, the role of the actual instructional materials in an individualized instruction system is radically different from that in a mass-instruction system. In the latter, their role is generally supportive, with the main vehicle of instruction being the teacher or trainer in control of the class; in an individualized instruction system, on the other hand, the materials themselves constitute the vehicle whereby instruction takes place. Thus, it is particularly important that such materials should be designed and produced with the greatest care: if they are not, the system could at best fail to achieve all its instructional objectives and at worst break down completely. Much of the remainder of this book will be devoted to helping readers to make sure that this does not happen with any self-instructional materials that they produce.

Group Learning Techniques

While mass instruction and individualized instruction can be used to overtake a wide range of educational and training objectives, there are, in fact, a number of definite limitations to both approaches. For example, neither is suitable for achieving the full range of higher cognitive objectives that are coming to be regarded as so important in today's education, and neither can be used to develop the various communication and interpersonal skills that a person needs in order to function effectively as part of a group. This has led to an increasing realization in recent years that the various activities that come under the general heading of group learning have a very important role to play in modern education and training. In Britain, for example, the Government has spent large sums of money promoting the wider use of such techniques through the 'Enterprise' Programme that it launched in 1988 (our own colleges were each awarded £1 million under this programme).

The theoretical basis of much of the current interest in group learning is the humanistic psychology that was developed by people such as Carl Rogers during the 1960s – a totally different type of psychology from the highly mechanistic behavioural psychology which formed the basis of the programmed learning movement. Humanistic psychology is concerned with how people interact with and learn from one another in small-group situations, and involves the use of the techniques of group dynamics. When used in an instructional situation, such techniques

Figure 1.4 (a) **Business students in a small-group seminar**

(b) **Secondary school pupils working on a group project**

Figure 1.4 (c) **Secondary school pupils playing an educational card game designed to reinforce their knowledge of basic chemistry**

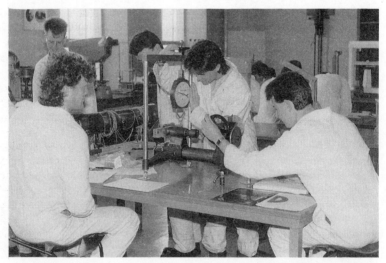

(d) **Pharmacy students at The Robert Gordon University carrying out laboratory work collaboratively**

generally require no specialized hardware, and, in many cases, very little in the way of courseware other than textual materials (booklets, briefing sheets, worksheets, etc); indeed, the emphasis is usually on the approach or technique rather than a reliance on specific types of hardware or courseware. Nevertheless, it is vitally important that any courseware that is required for such an exercise should be very carefully designed, since it can play a key role in making sure that the exercise runs smoothly – as we know from our own work on educational games and simulations. Some of the ways in which such courseware can be used in group learning activities are given below.

- Forming an integral part of the group-learning process by providing background information, information about roles, instructions, and so on.

- Providing supplementary or enrichment material.

- Increasing student motivation through visually attractive or intrinsically interesting materials.

As in the case of mass instruction, a large number of different types of materials can be used to fulfil these various functions.

THE DIFFERENT TYPES OF INSTRUCTIONAL MATERIALS THAT ARE AVAILABLE TODAY

Compared with their counterparts of 30 or 40 years ago, modern teachers or trainers have a vast and often bewildering range of instructional materials at their disposal. When we were at school during the late 1940s and 1950s, practically the only teaching aids that were in regular use (apart from textbooks and specialized laboratory and workshop equipment) were chalkboards, wallcharts, posters and realia like geological and biological specimens, backed up by the (very) occasional use of slides, filmstrips, films, gramophone records and radio broadcasts, and (in the case of one art teacher) a somewhat antique opaque projector. We do not remember duplicated materials like worksheets and handout notes being used to any great extent; tape recorders were extremely rare; there were no overhead projectors or television sets (at least, not in our schools); resource-based and mediated learning had still to be invented; and there were, of course, no video recorders, electronic calculators or computers. Indeed, it is only during the last fifteen years or so that the overhead projector (surely now the most basic and essential of all teaching aids) has become a standard fitting in teaching rooms in our own colleges.

   In order to help readers to become familiar with the main characteristics of the various types of instructional materials that are currently available – and give this book a workable structure – we have divided them into seven broad groups, in order of increasing technical sophistication.

These groups are:

1. printed and duplicated materials;
2. non-projected display materials;
3. still projected display materials;
4. audio materials;
5. linked audio and still visual materials;
6. video materials;
7. computer-mediated materials.

Let us now take a broad look at these various groups and identify the general characteristics of the materials that compose them.

Printed and Duplicated Materials

These comprise all textual and handout materials to be used by students or trainees which can be run off in large numbers by printing machines, photocopiers and duplicators. Facilities for the production of such materials are now available in practically every school, college and training establishment, and they have become the most basic and widely used of all educational tools. Some of the more important types are listed below.

Handouts:	These comprise all the different types of information-providing materials that are given out to students or trainees, usually in connection with a taught lesson or programme of some sort. They include sets of notes (either complete or in skeleton form), tables, diagrams, maps and illustrative or extension material.
Assignment sheets:	These include such things as problem sheets, reading lists, lab sheets, briefing sheets for projects and seminars, worksheets, etc. They can be used in practically all types of instructional situations.
Individualized study materials:	These comprise all the different types of textual materials that are used in connection with individualized learning. They include open learning modules, study guides, structured notes, textual programmed materials and textual support materials for mediated learning systems.
Resource materials for group exercises:	These comprise all the various printed and duplicated materials that are used in connection with group learning exercises. They include background reading material, briefing material, role sheets, instruction sheets, data sheets, open learning packages and so on.

Non-Projected Display Materials

As its name suggests, this category includes all visual display materials that can be shown to a class, small group or individual student without the use of an optical or electronic projector of any sort. It includes a number of the most basic – and most useful – visual aids that are available to teachers and trainers, some of the more important of which are listed below.

Chalkboard displays: Displays that are written, printed or drawn on a dark-coloured surface using chalk; still one of the most widely used of all visual aids, despite the fact that practically everything that can be done using a chalkboard can be done more easily, less messily, and (in most cases) more effectively using the overhead projector. Probably they are most useful for displaying impromptu 'sign-posts' and 'links', notes and diagrams during a taught lesson and for working through calculations and similar exercises in front of a class.

Markerboard displays: Displays that are written, printed or drawn on a light-coloured surface using felt pens or other wet markers of some sort. These can be used in the same ways as chalkboard displays and have the advantage of being less messy and offering a wider range of colours; also a markerboard can double up as a projection screen if necessary.

Feltboard displays: Movable displays that are produced by sticking shapes cut out of or backed with felt or some similar material to a board covered with felt, or to a sheet of felt pinned on to a wall. This is a comparatively cheap, highly portable and extremely useful display technique, especially in situations that require the movement or re-arrangement of pieces (demonstrating table settings, carrying out sports coaching, etc).

Hook-and-loop board displays: Similar to feltboard displays, except that the backing material on the display items possesses large numbers of tiny hooks that engage loops on the surface of the display board. These are suitable for displaying heavier items than feltboards.

Magnetic board displays: Displays consisting of items that are made of or backed with magnetic material or fitted with small magnets so that they stick to a ferro-magnetic display board. These can be used in much the same way as feltboard and hook-and-loop displays.

Flipchart displays: Large sheets of paper hung from an easel of some sort so that they can be flipped forwards or backwards in order to reveal the information on a particular sheet or produce a fresh blank sheet on which impromptu information can be written or drawn.

Charts and wallcharts: Large sheets of paper, carrying pre-prepared textual and/or graphical and/or pictorial information. Such charts can either be used to display information during the course of a lesson or can be pinned to the wall of a classroom in order to be studied by the students in their own time. Wallcharts, in particular, can be extremely useful for providing supplementary material or acting as a permanent *aide-mémoire* or reference system for learners (eg the periodic tables of the elements that are prominently displayed in practically all chemistry classrooms).

Posters: Similar to wallcharts, but generally containing less information – often simply a single dramatic image. They are useful for creating atmosphere in a classroom.

Photographic prints: Enlarged prints made from photographic negatives may be incorporated into textual materials, wallcharts, etc and, in linked sequences with suitable captions, can form a useful instructional medium in their own right. Such sequences are particularly suitable for use in programmes designed for individual study.

Mobiles: Systems of two- or three-dimensional objects that are hung from the roof of a class by thread, thus producing a visually attractive display whose shape is constantly changing due to air currents. These are particularly useful for creating interest among younger children.

Models: Useful in cases where three-dimensional representation is necessary (eg crystal structures, animal skeletons, etc) or where movement has to be demonstrated.

Dioramas: Static displays that combine a three-dimensional foreground (eg a model landscape of some sort) with a two-dimensional background, thus creating an aura of solidity and realism.

Realia: Displays of real items (eg geological or biological specimens) as opposed to models or representations thereof. These are extremely useful if such materials are readily available and easily displayed.

Still Projected Display Materials

This category includes all visual display materials which do not incorporate movement and which require an optical projector of some sort in order to show them to a class or group or enable them to be studied by an individual learner. It again includes some of the most useful visual aids that are available to teachers, instructors and trainers, the most important of which are listed below.

Overhead projector transparencies and similar materials: Textual or graphical images on large acetate sheets that can either be displayed to a class or group using an overhead projector or viewed by individuals or small groups using a light box of some sort. These are probably the most useful and versatile visual aid that can be used to support mass instruction methods in the modern classroom, as we will see later.

Slides: Single frames of 35mm photographic film mounted in cardboard, plastic or metal binders, often between twin sheets of glass (compact slides), or larger images roughly $3\frac{1}{4}$ inches square (lantern slides – now largely obsolete). These are one of the most useful methods of displaying photographic or graphic images to a class, small group or individual student using a suitable front or back projector or viewer – either singly or in linked sequences.

Filmstrips: These are simply strips of 35mm film carrying linked sequences of positive images, each usually half the size of a standard 35mm frame (half-frame or single-frame filmstrips) but sometimes the full size (full-frame or double-frame filmstrips). They are a convenient and, when purchased commercially, comparatively cheap alternative to slide sequences and can be used in much the same ways, using suitable filmstrip projectors or viewers for display or study.

Microforms: Microform is a general term for any medium that is used to carry micro-images, ie photographically reduced images of pages of text, graphic materials, etc. The most common types are microfilms (rolls or strips of photographic film carrying a linear sequence of such images), microfiches (transparent sheets of photographic film carrying a matrix of such images) and microcards (opaque sheets carrying similar matrices of micro-images). All such microforms can be used to carry the frames of instructional programmes (eg programmed learning sequences), to act as highly compact databanks, etc, and can be studied using special magnifying viewers or projectors.

Audio Materials

This category includes all the various systems whereby straightforward audio signals can be played to or listened to by a class, group or individual. It includes a number of extremely useful – albeit often neglected – instructional aids, some of the most important of which are described below.

Radio broadcasts: Educational radio broadcasts constitute an extremely useful resource for teachers and trainers and, although they are often difficult to incorporate into the timetable if listened to at the time they are actually transmitted, this can easily be overcome by recording them for later playback. Note, however, that it is only certain designated educational broadcasts that can be so used without infringing the copyright laws.

Audio discs: Recordings of music, plays, etc on vinyl or compact discs constitute a relatively inexpensive and readily available instructional resource in certain subject areas. They are suitable both for playing to a class or group and for private listening by individuals.

Audiotapes: Audio material recorded on open-reel tape or tape cassette constitutes one of the most useful resources at the disposal of the modern teacher or trainer, and can be used in a wide range of instructional situations, either on its own or in conjunction with visual materials of some sort.

Linked Audio and Still Visual Materials

This is the first of the three classes in which audio and visual materials are combined to form integrated instructional systems, and includes a number of media that are particularly suitable for use in individualized instruction. Some of the most commonly used systems are listed below.

Tape-slide programmes: Audiotape recordings (usually on compact cassettes) synchronized with linked sequences of slides constitute one of the most useful and commonly used integrated audiovisual media. They can be used in a wide range of instructional situations, particularly individualized instruction.

Tape-photograph programmes: These are basically the same as tape-slide programmes, except that sequences of photographic prints are used instead of sequences of slides. Their range of applications is not as great, however, being largely restricted to individualized learning situations.

Filmstrips with sound: These are simply filmstrips that have an accompanying sound commentary, usually on a compact tape cassette. They can be used in much the same way as tape-slide programmes.

Radio-vision programmes: This is a technique pioneered by the British Broadcasting Corporation whereby still filmstrips are produced to accompany educational radio programmes. The filmstrips can either be shown to a class during the actual broadcast or used with a recording of the programme.

Tape-text: Combinations of printed or duplicated materials with audio recordings constitute an extremely useful individualized instruction technique. The audio component can either be carried on a separate audiotape (usually a compact cassette) or carried on a special strip or sheet that is incorporated in the medium that carries the text; the latter systems (known as audiocards, audio pages, talking pages, etc) require specialized equipment to use them.

Tape-model, tape realia, etc: Combinations of audiotapes (usually compact cassettes) and other still visual display materials such as three-dimensional models, collections of realia (eg geological and biological specimens) and microscope slides. Such hybrid systems can prove extremely useful vehicles for individual-ized instruction, as we will see in Chapter 6.

Video Materials

This class includes media that enable audio signals to be combined with *moving* visual sequences, thus enabling a further dimension to be added to integrated audiovisual presentations. The main systems that are cur-rently available are as follows.

Tape-film programmes: These are highly sophisticated integrated sys-tems that enable audio material to be combined with sequences of still and moving pictures. Most systems of this type use separate cassettes or cartridges to carry the audio and video components, and obviously require specialized equipment to show or view them.

Television broadcasts: As in the case of educational radio broadcasts, educational television broadcasts constitute an extremely useful free resource for teachers and trainers. Like the former, they are not usually transmitted at convenient times, but, thanks to the development of relatively cheap video-recorders, this limitation can now be easily overcome. Readers should again note, however, that it is only certain designated educational television programmes that can legally be re-corded for subsequent educational use, and that an appropriate licence is usually required even for this.

Videotape recordings: Television sequences or programmes recorded on videotape now contribute one of the most useful and powerful instructional media at the disposal of teachers and trainers, and can be used in a wide range of teaching/learning situa-tions as we will see later.

Videodisc recordings: Although not yet as widely used as videotapes and videocassettes, videodiscs (in which the signal is recorded optically or electronically on the surface of a special disc, in the form of a spiral track similar to that on a gramophone record) have tremendous potential in education and training as we will see in Chapter 8.

Computer-Mediated Materials

This final category includes all the various materials that require a computer of some sort to enable them to be displayed, studied or used. Arguably, the computer constitutes the most important single resource ever to become available to teachers and trainers since the invention of the printing press and may well have a similar revolutionary effect on the way education and training are carried out, bringing about the massive shift from conventional expository teaching to mediated individualized learning that some commentators have recently predicted (see, for example, Hawkridge's book *New Information Technology in Education* and the book on *The Interactive Learning Revolution* by Barker and Tucker). Whether or not this happens, there is no doubt that appropriate use of computers can be of tremendous assistance to the practising teacher or trainer. Some of the main types of computer-mediated systems are listed below.

'Number crunching' and data-processing packages: One of the most obvious uses of the computer in education and training is as a 'super-calculator' or data processor. It is now possible to acquire or produce software packages that enable virtually any calculation or data-processing task to be carried out automatically on the computer and, when appropriately used, such packages can be of tremendous help to both teachers and learners.

'Substitute tutor' packages: Another obvious use of the computer is as a vehicle for administering individualized learning, since it has the potential to provide a degree of interaction and feedback that no other system possesses. Thus 'substitute tutor' computer-based learning packages seem certain to become one of the most important tools available to teachers and trainers.

'Substitute laboratory' packages: A third important instructional application of the computer is as a vehicle for providing, through computer-based simulations, access to a far wider range of educational and training experiences than has ever been possible before. Again, such 'substitute laboratory' packages seem certain to become increasingly important tools for teachers and trainers of all types.

Database systems: As well as being used to process information, the computer can be used to store it and to help retrieve it when required. Thus teachers and trainers can now use computers to create

Type of materials	Instructional mode(s) for which materials are most suitable	Can materials be produced on-site by teachers and trainers?
Printed and duplicated materials	All modes	Yes
Chalkboard and marker-board displays	Mass instruction; group learning	Yes
Feltboard and similar materials	Mass instruction; group learning	Yes
Magnetic board materials	Mass instruction; group learning	Yes
Flipchart displays	Mass instruction; group learning	Yes
Wallcharts and posters	Mass instruction; group learning	Yes
Photographic prints	Mass instruction; learning	Yes
Mobiles, models, etc	All modes	Yes
Realia	All modes	Yes
OHP transparencies	Mass instruction; group learning	Yes
Slides	All modes	Yes, but technical support may be needed
Filmstrips	All modes	Not easily
Microforms	Individualized instruction	Not easily
Radio programmes	All modes	Not without professional support
Audio discs	All modes	No
Audio tapes	All modes	Yes
Tape-slide programmes	All modes, especially individualized instruction	Yes, but technical support may be needed
Tape-photo programmes	All modes, especially individualized instruction	Yes, but technical support may be needed
Sound filmstrips	All modes	Not easily
Radio-vision programmes	All modes	Not without professional support
Tape-text programmes	Individualized instruction	Yes
Tape-model and similar materials	Individualized instruction	Yes
Tape-film programmes	All modes, especially individualized instruction	Yes, but external support required
TV broadcast programmes	All modes	Not without professional support
Video materials (on videotape)	All modes	Yes, but technical support may be needed
Video materials (on videodisc)	All modes	No
Conventional CBL materials	All modes, especially individualized instruction	Yes
Interactive video and multimedia materials	All modes, especially individualized instruction	Only if specialized facilities are available

Figure 1.5 **Summary of characteristics of different instructional materials**

Type of materials	Does production of materials require any specialized skill(s) other than instructional design skills?	Does production of materials require any specialized equipment?	Is any specialized equipment needed to use the materials?
Printed and duplicated materials	Basic graphic skills	Printing or duplicating equipment	No
Chalkboard and marker-board displays	Basic graphic skills	Chalkboard or markerboard	Chalkboard or markerboard
Feltboard and similar materials	Basic graphic and craft skills	No	Suitable display surface
Magnetic board materials	Basic graphic and craft skills	No	Suitable display surface
Flipchart displays	Basic graphic skills	No	Suitable support system
Wallcharts and posters	Basic graphic skills	Not necessarily	No
Photographic prints	Basic photographic skills	Appropriate photographic equipment	No
Mobiles, models, etc	Appropriate craft skills	Not necessarily	No
Realia	No	No	No
OHP transparencies	Basic graphic skills	No	Projector and screen, or light box
Slides	Basic photographic and graphic skills	Appropriate photographic equipment	Projector and screen, or viewer
Filmstrips	Specialized photographic skills	Appropriate photographic equipment	Projector and screen, or viewer
Microforms	Appropriate photographic skills	Appropriate photographic equipment	Suitable viewer
Radio programmes	Professional production skills	Studio equipment	Radio receiver
Audio discs	External support required	Studio and manufac-turing equipment	Record player
Audio tapes	Basic recording and editing skills	Basic recording and editing equipment	Audiotape player
Tape-slide programmes	As for slides and audiotapes	As for slides and audiotapes	Audiotape player and projector or viewer
Tape-photo programmes	As for photographs and audiotapes	As for photographs and audiotapes	Audiotape player
Sound filmstrips	As for filmstrips and audiotapes	As for filmstrips and audiotapes	As for filmstrips and audiotapes
Radio-vision programmes	Professional production skills	As for filmstrips and radio	As for filmstrips and radio
Tape-text programmes	As for textual materials and audiotapes	As for text materials and audiotapes	Audiotape player
Tape-model and similar materials	As for models, etc and audiotapes	As for models, etc and audiotapes	Audiotape player
Tape-film programmes	As for cine film, slides and audiotapes	Special equipment required	Special projector/player
TV broadcast programmes	Professional production skills	TV studio facilities	TV receiver
Video materials (on videotape)	Basic TV production skills	Basic video production facilities	Videotape player and TV monitor
Video materials (on videodisc)	External support required	Highly specialized equipment	Videodisc player and TV monitor
Conventional CBL materials	Basic programming skills*	Access to suitable computer or authoring system	Suitable computer
Interactive video and multimedia materials	Programming skills;* video production and other appropriate skills	Video production and other appropriate skills facilities; CBL authoring and interface facilities	Computer and other appropriate hardware

*Not needed if authoring system used

databases that can be used in a whole range of instructional situations.

Computer-managed learning systems: A fifth major application of computers in education and training is their use in an administrative or managerial role, eg in the overall administration of the system, timetable planning, budgetary control, and the management of the actual teaching/learning process. Here again, software packages that enable these various things to be done are likely to become increasingly widely used.

Interactive video systems: Such systems, which constitute one of the most powerful and potentially useful vehicles for mediated instruction yet developed, use a computer to gain access to video material stored in a videodisc or random access video recorder in the context of a fully interactive computer-based learning programme. They can be used in a wide range of individualized and group learning situations, and are achieving increasingly widespread use now that 'off the shelf' courseware is starting to appear at reasonable prices.

Multimedia interactive systems: Such systems, which constitute the most recent addition to the educational armoury, use a computer to enable the user to gain access to and (in some cases) combine, edit and orchestrate a wide range of media, including text, computer courseware, sounds, still graphic and pictorial material, and video material. They are increasingly becoming known by the generic title *hypermedia*, and constitute an even more powerful and potentially useful instructional vehicle than interactive video.

A summary of the main characteristics of all these various materials, considered from the point of view of the user and would-be producer, is given in Figure 1.5 on pages 32 and 33.

SELECTING SUITABLE MATERIALS FOR SPECIFIC PURPOSES

Let us now consider some of the factors that should be taken into consideration by a practising teacher or trainer when choosing materials for some specific instructional purpose. In many cases, such selection is made purely on a basis of personal preference and availability, with little or no thought being given to the suitability of the materials for helping to achieve the desired instructional objectives. Inevitably this often leads to the use of inappropriate materials, with a resulting reduction in the effectiveness of the instructional process.

A large amount of basic research has been carried out on the relative effectiveness of different types of materials in different instructional situations. This shows that most media can perform most instructional functions to a certain extent, but that some are better at doing certain things than others, with no single medium being best for all purposes. Thus it is possible to adopt what is at least a semi-objective approach to the selection of instructional materials, based on consideration of the particular instructional strategy that is to be employed, the specific tactical methods to be used within that strategy, and the characteristics of the materials that can be used to support or implement these methods. Using such an approach, we have developed the algorithm given in Figure 1.6, which we hope readers will find helpful. This should be used to identify possible materials for achieving specific objectives, with the final selection being made after other factors such as availability or ease of production, availability of necessary equipment, cost, convenience and personal preference have been taken into account.

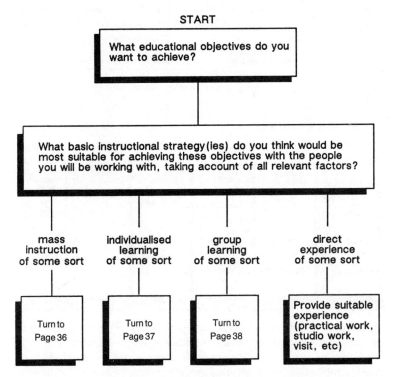

START

What educational objectives do you want to achieve?

What basic instructional strategy(ies) do you think would be most suitable for achieving these objectives with the people you will be working with, taking account of all relevant factors?

| mass instruction of some sort | individualised learning of some sort | group learning of some sort | direct experience of some sort |

Turn to Page 36

Turn to Page 37

Turn to Page 38

Provide suitable experience (practical work, studio work, visit, etc)

Figure 1.6 **Algorithm for selection of instructional materials**

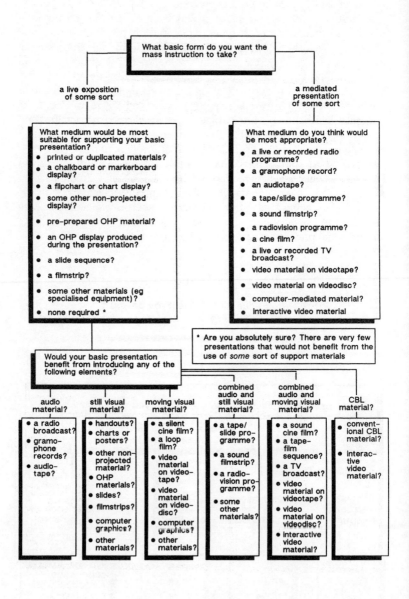

Figure 1.6 (continued) **Choosing materials for mass instruction**

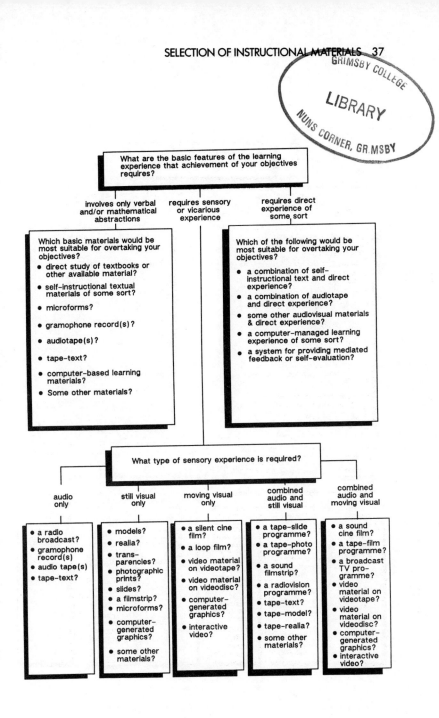

What are the basic features of the learning experience that achievement of your objectives requires?

involves only verbal and/or mathematical abstractions

requires sensory or vicarious experience

requires direct experience of some sort

Which basic materials would be most suitable for overtaking your objectives?
- direct study of textbooks or other available material?
- self-instructional textual materials of some sort?
- microforms?
- gramophone record(s)?
- audiotape(s)?
- tape-text?
- computer-based learning materials?
- Some other materials?

Which of the following would be most suitable for overtaking your objectives?
- a combination of self-instructional text and direct experience?
- a combination of audiotape and direct experience?
- some other audiovisual materials & direct experience?
- a computer-managed learning experience of some sort?
- a system for providing mediated feedback or self-evaluation?

What type of sensory experience is required?

audio only
- a radio broadcast?
- gramophone record(s)
- audio tape(s)
- tape-text?

still visual only
- models?
- realia?
- transparencies?
- photographic prints?
- slides?
- a filmstrip?
- microforms?
- computer-generated graphics?
- some other materials?

moving visual only
- a silent cine film?
- a loop film?
- video material on videotape?
- video material on videodisc?
- computer-generated graphics?
- interactive video?

combined audio and still visual
- a tape-slide programme?
- a tape-photo programme?
- a sound filmstrip?
- a radiovision programme?
- tape-text?
- tape-model?
- tape-realia?
- some other materials?

combined audio and moving visual
- a sound cine film?
- a tape-film programme?
- a broadcast TV programme?
- video material on videotape?
- video material on videodisc?
- computer-generated graphics?
- interactive video?

Figure 1.6 (continued) **Choosing materials for individualized instruction**

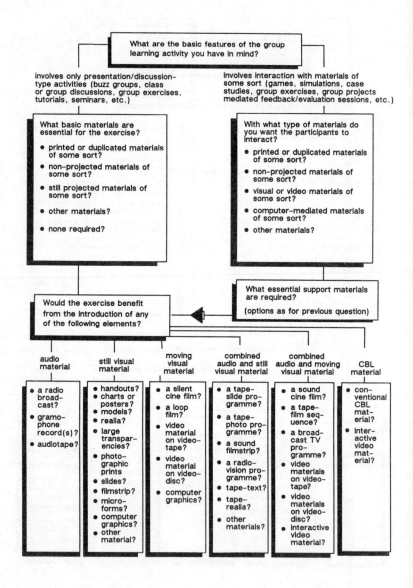

Figure 1.6 (continued) **Choosing materials for group learning**

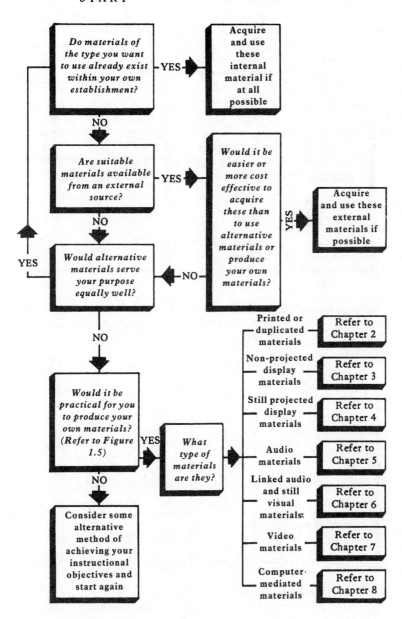

Figure 1.7 **Algorithm for deciding whether to produce your own instructional materials**

DECIDING WHETHER TO PRODUCE YOUR OWN MATERIALS

Once a decision has been reached as to which materials will be needed to implement a chosen instructional scheme, it is obviously necessary to set about acquiring such materials or, if they are not readily available, determining whether it would be possible to produce them yourself. If the materials are *not* available from other sources, and it is *not* practicable to produce them yourself, then it will clearly be necessary to carry out a radical re-think regarding the method by which you are to achieve the particular set of instructional objectives that it was hoped they would help overtake. If you decide that you do want to try to produce the materials yourself, on the other hand, you should find detailed guidance on how to set about this task in one of the remaining seven chapters of this book. The algorithm in Figure 1.7 has been designed to help you decide which course of action to adopt in any particular set of circumstances; this should be completely self-explanatory.

BIBLIOGRAPHY

Anderson, R H (1976) *Selecting and Developing Media for Instruction*. Van Nostrand Reinhold, Cincinnati.

Barker, J and Tucker, R N (1990) *The Interactive Learning Revolution*. Kogan Page, London.

Bretz, R (1971) *A Taxonomy of Communications Media*. Educational Technology Publications, Englewood Cliffs, New Jersey.

Elton, L R B (1977) Educational technology — today and tomorrow. In Hills, P and Gilbert, J (eds) *Aspects of Educational Technology XI*. Kogan Page, London.

Gibbs, G and Jenkins, A (eds) (1992) *Teaching Large Classes in Higher Education*. Kogan Page, London.

Hawkridge, D (1982) *New Information Technology in Education*. Croom Helm, London.

Kemp, J E (1980) *Planning and Producing Audiovisual Materials*. Harper and Row, Publishers Inc, New York.

Kemp, J E (1971) Which medium? *Audiovisual Instruction*, 16 (December), pp.32-6.

Levie, W H and Dickie, K E (1973) The analysis and application of media. In *Second Handbook of Research on Teaching*. Rand McNally, Chicago, pp 858-82.

Newble, D and Cannon, R (1991) *A Handbook for Teachers in Universities and Colleges*. Kogan Page, London.

Percival, F and Ellington, H I (1988) *A Handbook of Educational Technology*. Kogan Page, London/Nichols Publishing Company, New York.

Romiszowski, A J (1988) *The Selection and Use of Instructional Media*. Kogan Page, London.

Stephenson, J and Weil, S (1992) *Quality in Learning*. Kogan Page, London.

Stimson, N (1991) *How to Write and Prepare Training Materials*. Kogan Page, London.

Wittich, W A and Schuller, C F (1979) *Instructional Technology: Its Nature and Use*. Harper and Row, New York.

Chapter Two

How to Produce Printed and Duplicated Materials

INTRODUCTION

As we saw in Chapter 1, the various materials that can be prepared 'in-house' and run off in large numbers on a duplicator or printing machine constitute one of the most useful and versatile tools at the disposal of today's teachers and trainers. It is therefore appropriate that we should begin by discussing the preparation of such materials, despite the fact that they are, for some reason, often overlooked in texts on instructional media and audio-visual aids.

As in all subsequent chapters, we will start by taking a general look at how the materials can be used within the context of the different instructional strategies that were identified in Chapter 1. Next, we will carry out a detailed examination of how one should set about the task of planning and designing printed and duplicated materials, looking first at the basic principles that should underlie such design and then at the design of specific types of materials — handouts, worksheets, individualized learning materials, and so on. Finally, we will turn our attention to the various processes by which the materials can be mass produced, identifying the advantages and disadvantages of each process and offering guidance on which method to use in any particular situation.

HOW PRINTED AND DUPLICATED MATERIALS CAN BE USED IN DIFFERENT TEACHING/LEARNING SITUATIONS

In Chapter 1, we saw that there are three basic types of teaching/learning situations — mass instruction, individualized instruction and group learning — and that printed and duplicated materials can play a key, albeit different, role in each.

Mass Instruction

In the case of mass instruction, the role of printed and duplicated materials is essentially a supportive one, namely, providing the teacher, instructor or trainer who is carrying out the instruction with tools that help him to achieve specific objectives or sub-sets thereof. Among the most important of these tools are all the various forms of information-providing handouts that can be given to the members of a class — sets of notes, tables of data, copies of important diagrams, maps, and so on. Appropriate use of such handouts can not only improve the effectiveness of the mass instruction process (by, for example, ensuring that every member of the class — and not just those that are accomplished note-takers or good graphic artists — ends the lesson with a decent set of notes or a clear copy of a key diagram) but can also greatly increase its efficiency (by, for example, reducing face-to-face contact time or enabling a greater proportion of such time to be devoted to educationally useful activities such as exercises and discussions). At The Robert Gordon University, for example, the School of Electronic and Electrical Engineering made a policy decision in the early 1970s to cut down on formal class contact time by using handout notes to provide basic information wherever possible. This certainly did not reduce the effectiveness of its teaching (as measured by the examination marks and classes of degree obtained by its students before and after the change), but enabled it to make much more efficient use of its teaching staff (as measured by the unit costs associated with the students on its various courses, which fell significantly below those for other departments teaching comparable subjects). The change to handout notes also proved extremely popular with students, who not only obtained better sets of notes than before but also found that they had more time for private study because of their shorter timetables. Most of Robert Gordon University's other Schools have now adopted similar policies.

The other main class of printed and duplicated materials that can be used in mass instruction are assignment sheets of one form and another — problem sheets, worksheets, lab sheets, and so on. As in the case of handouts, appropriate use of such materials can greatly increase the effectiveness of mass instruction of all types. Use of a well-designed worksheet at an appropriate point in a taught lesson, for example, can introduce a welcome participative element into what may otherwise be a completely passive experience for the students, thus helping to maintain their concentration and interest. Research carried out in Glasgow University (see the paper by Johnstone and Percival listed in the Bibliography) has shown that the length of time for which a student can give full attention to the task of listening or taking notes (the so-called attention span) falls from roughly 12-15 minutes at the start of a taught lesson or lecture to around 3-5 minutes at the end, being interrupted by periodic attention breaks (micro-sleeps) lasting for about 2 minutes. The occurrence of such attention breaks can, however, be partly prevented by introducing variety into the lesson, one of the most effective ways of doing this being to get the students actively involved in a task of some sort. Clearly, assignment sheets of various types are ideal for this purpose.

Individualized Instruction

As we have already seen, the role of instructional materials in individualized instruction is much more crucial to the learning process that is the case in mass instruction, since it is these materials that have to constitute the actual vehicle whereby the instruction process is carried out. In other words, self-instructional materials not only have to convey information to the learner, they also have to structure and control the process by which this information is presented to and assimilated by the learner. Such materials therefore need to be much more carefully designed than materials that are simply to be used to support mass instruction. Indeed, experience has shown that they can take up to ten times longer to produce.

Printed and duplicated materials can play three basic roles in individualized instruction. First, they can be used as the actual medium of instruction, eg in the form of structured notes, worksheets or programmed texts. If they are well-designed, such materials can enable pupils, students or trainees to master the basic facts and principles of a subject or topic at their own pace. Also, there is a considerable amount of evidence to suggest that the resulting degree of mastery is generally greater than that attained in the course of a conventional expository lesson, where the pace is dictated by the instructor.

Second, printed and duplicated materials can be used as a vehicle for structuring and controlling the process by which learners acquire information rather than as a means of conveying the information itself. Good examples of such materials are the various forms of study guide, which can be used to direct learners to relevant chapters (or parts thereof) in textbooks or instruct them on how to make optimum use of other individualized learning media such as tape-slide programmes, multimedia packages and home experiment kits.

Third, printed and duplicated materials can be used to support other individualized learning media. They can, for example, provide worksheets or diagnostic instruments for use in conjunction with audiovisual programmes or computer-based learning systems, provide illustrative or extension material, or give learners their own personal copies of key material for subsequent study or revision.

Group Learning

Unlike mass and individualized instruction, group learning is essentially a process-centred activity with the emphasis being on the interactions that take place between the people taking part rather than on the teaching or learning of facts, principles, etc. Thus, the role of any instructional materials that may be used in conjunction with a particular group-learning exercise is usually mainly supportive, although, as we have seen, such materials can play a key part in making the exercise function smoothly.

Of the various media that can be used to support group-learning exercises, printed and duplicated materials are almost certainly the most versatile and important. They can, for example, be used to provide the basic resource materials on which the exercise is centred, provide the participants with instructions or guidance on how to carry out the exercise, and provide ancillary or illustrative material of various types. In most exercises that involve simulation or role play, for example, printed or duplicated materials are used to establish the basic scenario and brief the participants on their respective roles. They can also be used to provide things like worksheets, data sheets and background reading material, all of which are commonly used in group-learning exercises.

HOW TO PLAN AND DESIGN THE MATERIALS

Now that we have seen how printed and duplicated materials can be used in different types of teaching/learning situation, let us turn our attention to the way in which such materials should be planned and designed for specific purposes. We will begin by looking at some of the general principles that should underlie all such work of this type, then at how to tackle the design of particular types of printed and duplicated materials, looking in turn at handouts, worksheets, individualized study materials and resource materials for group learning exercises.

Basic Principles Underlying the Design of Printed and Duplicated Materials

Although printed and duplicated teaching materials come in a wide range of types and vary greatly in format, layout, level and so on, we have found that it is possible to adopt a standard basic approach to their planning and design. This has the following three stages:

- Identifying the specific instructional role that you want the materials to play.

- Formulating a basic plan for the materials.

- Writing and designing the materials.

The full production process has, of course, a rather crucial fourth stage — producing the materials in whatever form and quantity are needed — but this will be considered separately later in the chapter. Let us now look at the three planning and design stages in greater detail.

Identifying the Instructional Role

This is, of course, the starting point in the planning and design of all teaching or training materials. It involves taking a detailed look at the learning objectives that you are trying to achieve, and identifying the specific areas where printed or duplicated material could help you do this within the overall context of the basic instructional strategy that you have decided to use.

Formulating a Basic Plan for the Materials

Identification of the role that you want the materials to play should be of considerable assistance in the next stage of the design process — formulating a basic plan for the materials. Indeed, in many cases, you will find that the process is virtually automatic, with the basic design parameters for the materials (their format, content and structure) following logically from this role. It is best to consider these three design parameters in turn, beginning by deciding what sort of materials you want to use (a handout? a worksheet? a set of role sheets? and so on), then deciding on the basic content, and finally drawing up an outline structure. At each stage, it is useful to sketch your ideas out on scrap paper, a process that is helpful in clarifying your thinking, and eventually coming up with a workable scheme. Needless to say, we ourselves find that this may well take several attempts.

Writing the Materials

With some types of printed and duplicated materials, most of the creative work is done at the basic design stage, with the actual writing of the materials merely involving filling out these ideas and finalizing the layout. With others, the writing stage is where the hard work starts, involving many hours, days or even weeks of concentrated effort. This is especially so in the case of lengthy materials such as linked series of handout notes, suites of individualized instruction documents or integrated sets of resource materials for exercises of the game/simulation/participative case study type. Obviously, it is vitally important to adopt a systematic, disciplined approach to such work and readers should find the following guidelines helpful in achieving this.

Matching the content to the design objectives and target population: This is one of the most obvious things that a writer of instructional materials has to get right if the materials are to achieve their design objectives properly. Thus it is worthwhile spending some time thinking about detailed content before embarking on the writing task. One way of doing this is to ask yourselves the following three questions:

(a) What *must* the readers know after using the material?

(b) What, over and above (a), *should* the readers know after using the material?

(c) What, over and above (a) and (b), would it be useful if the readers knew after using the material?

Clearly, it is absolutely essential to include everything contained in category (a), highly desirable to include everything in category (b) and desirable to include as much of (c) as possible. Conversely, there is absolutely no point in including anything that falls into none of the three categories, unless it fulfils some other essential function.

Using an appropriate writing style: Adopting a writing style that is appropriate both to the type of materials and to the ability of the users is one of the most difficult tasks facing every author. If one is only used to writing formal reports or research papers for learned journals, for example, it is never easy to change to the radically different style that is required for educational writing, particularly if the material is to be used with younger or less able learners. A number of authors offer hints on how this can be done, however, among the most useful of which are the 'Twelve hints for effective writing' given by Derek Rowntree in his book *Basically Branching* (see Bibliography):

1. Write as you talk.
2. Use the first person.
3. Use contractions.
4. Talk directly to the reader.
5. Write about people, things and facts.
6. Use active verbs and personal subjects.
7. Use verbs rather than nouns and adjectives.
8. Use short sentences.
9. Use short paragraphs.
10. Use rhetorical questions.
11. Dramatize whenever possible.
12. Use illustrations, examples, case studies.

There are also a number of useful tests — both subjective and objective — that you can use to see whether your style needs to be improved in any way. The first, which is described in detail in *How to Write Self-Study Materials* by Roger Lewis (see Bibliography) involves reading something that you have written recently and asking yourself the following questions:

- Is my style pompous? formal? friendly? slapdash?

- Do I use too many clichés?

- Do I use more words than I need?

- Do I have favourite words and phrases that I over-use?

- Do I make frequent use of passive constructions? impersonal constructions? negatives?

- Are my sentences generally long or short?

- Do I use too many long words? abstract words? technical words?

If this self-evaluation process highlights any obvious faults in your writing style, you should make a deliberate effort to eliminate or mitigate them. If, for example, you find that you make too much use of the passive, check each paragraph that you write for a while and eliminate every passive verb; you will soon find that you make much less frequent use of such verbs.

A rather more objective test that can be used to determine whether the style of written educational material is suitable for the people who are to use it is the *Cloze Test*. This involves selecting a typical passage roughly 250 words long and, after a 35-word run-in, blanking out the next word and every tenth word thereafter until you have blanked out a total of 20. This blanking should be done by covering the words in question with suitable opaque material (eg plastic tape) that makes it impossible to read them. Once this has been done, select one (or, preferably, several) of the people in your target population and ask them to read the material. If they fail to provide the *correct* word or a *totally acceptable alternative* in at least 13 cases out of the 20, then the text is too difficult. If this is the case, modify the passage by simplifying the language and shortening the sentences.

Another objective method of determining whether the style of a text is appropriate to the people for whom it is intended is to calculate its *Modified Fog Index*, which gives a direct measure of the reading age of the material (ie the lowest age group by which the material is likely to be fully understood). This can be calculated as follows:

1. Choose a typical sample of the text, and work through a particular section, counting the words and sentences as you do so; stop at the end of the first sentence that takes you past 100 words. Calculate the average sentence length (asl) by dividing the total number of words by the number of sentences.

2. Work through the same sample again, counting the number of words with three or more syllables. Do not count words that are (a) capitalized, (b) combinations of short, easy words (like 'over-worked' or 'underground') or (c) verbs that have three syllables only because of endings like '-ed' and 'es' (eg 'deflated' and 'dismisses'). Calculate the percentage of hard words (%hw) in the passage by dividing the number of remaining words of three or more syllables by the total number of words and multiplying by 100.

3. Calculate the reading age of the passage using the formula:
    Modified Fog Index = reading age (in years) = 0.4 (asl + %hw) + 5

If the average reading age of several typical passages in a given text turns out to be significantly greater than the age of the group for which it is intended, it again obviously requires modification by simplifying the language and shortening the sentences. Indeed, the reading level of educational material should, ideally, be well below the maximum level of difficulty with which the group can cope if they are not to find that the struggle simply to read the material inhibits mastery of the content. For this reason, any instructional material with a Modified Fog Index of over 20 is probably too difficult for any group — even highly literate university students — to cope with easily.

Two further points should be made regarding the Cloze Test and Modified Fog Index. First, both tests can only be used on passages of continuous prose, and are therefore unsuitable for checking the level of instructional material that consists of short sections (eg programmed texts) or is broken up with equations, tables, etc. Second, both tests tend to give an over-high indication of the reading age of material that contains a high percentage of scientific, technical or other specialized terms, and due allowance should therefore be made for this if necessary. Despite these limitations, however, the two tests constitute a reasonably accurate and useful method of checking the appropriateness of the level of textual material.

Adopting an efficient method of composing text: At this point, it would probably be useful to mention some of the different methods of working that it is possible for writers to adopt and, in particular, to make readers aware of the way in which recent developments in micro-electronics have made the task of composing textual materials very much easier than in the past.

There are four basic ways in which it is possible to compose textual material, three of which have been in use for many years. The first of these traditional methods is to write the material out in longhand — a slow and laborious method, but still the one that some authors prefer. The second is to dictate the material, either to a secretary capable of making a verbatim shorthand record of what is being said or into a tape recorder of some sort. This is a very efficient method indeed if you have the ability to 'think in paragraphs' and if the material that you are developing lends itself to this type of composition. The third is to work directly at a typewriter — a method that has traditionally been used by many professional authors, since it is considerably quicker than the longhand method if you possess the necessary typing skills.

During the 1980s, however, a totally new method of composing text became generally available, namely, use of an electronic word processor. Such a device enables text to be created on the screen of a computer video display unit using a keyboard terminal and subsequently stored in the computer's memory system, from where it can be recalled or printed out in hard-copy form at any time. The main advantage of such a system over a conventional typewriter is that corrections and changes can be made to the text being worked on virtually instantaneously, thus enabling an author to produce perfect final copy as he works, without the need to type the same page over and over again if changes are required. Furthermore, the development of progressively cheaper word-processing equipment and software packages that enable inexpensive microcomputers to be converted into word processors has meant that more and more people have found that they have access to such systems. Indeed, some commentators believe that virtually all instructional writing will be done on word processors within a few years. Such machines are already much more common in schools, colleges and training establishments than typewriters were in the past, and, now that teachers and trainers have found out how easy and convenient they are to use, they are starting to use word processors in ever-increasing numbers. Let us therefore take a brief look at how to set about choosing a word processor capable of meeting your specific needs.

Choosing a suitable word processor: Word processors are now quite endemic. Indeed, students themselves are increasingly using them to produce reports, essays and dissertations. The sort of word processor you need depends on several factors, including:

- The sort of materials you intend to produce – ie whether mainly textual, or considerably illustrated with tables, diagrams and figures;

- whether you will produce the final master copies yourself, or hand over to an experienced 'finisher' to produce the finished version;

- your experience and preferences regarding different types of computers and software packages;

- the availability of other people experienced in particular word processors, as well as the availability of machines;

- the opportunity to compose both at work and at home (and possibly 'on the move' as well, using a portable system). This does not necessarily mean that you need to have identical systems in each location. It is often possible to translate computer disks from one word processing language into another (for example, software can be purchased to translate files in 'Wordwise +' used on elderly BBC Microcomputers to 'MacWrite' used on Apple Macintosh machines; and there are numerous translators which can convert programmes in common use on modern machines).

Figure 2.1 (a)
Henry Ellington's secretary, Doreen, at her word processor

Figure 2.1 (b)
A typical desktop publishing system (Macintosh)

Figure 2.1 (c)
A professional desktop publishing workstation (Macintosh)

Learning to use a word processor is largely learning-by-doing. You can spend hours reading manuals and still be quite unable to put what you have read into practice. Some word processing packages (for example, MacWrite and MacWrite II on Apple Macintosh machines) are highly 'visual' and 'instinctive', and many people have remarked that they have rarely if ever referred to the manuals – they simply get on and learn by doing. However, even with such systems, you can save yourself a great deal of time if you have access to someone who is already skilled at using the package. Such people can alert you to short-cuts and 'wrinkles' which it would take you a long time to discover for yourself.

All word processing packages offer you functions such as:

- the facility to save your work to computer disk;

- the ability to move words, phrases, paragraphs, and even several pages from one part of a document to another;

- the ability to edit your work on-screen.

Most word processing packages now provide features such as 'spellchecks' which alert you to any words which are misspelled (or are not already in the computer's dictionary), and allow you to add new words to the dictionary as and when you require.

The importance of layout: Whatever type of material you are producing, the layout can be just as important as the content in determining whether it does its job effectively. Thus it is essential that you give a considerable amount of thought to how this content is to be presented to the reader. In the case of lengthy textual materials, for example, it is always an advantage to divide the content into clearly defined sections, and to use a systematic and logical labelling system to tell the reader what these sections are, indicate material of different types or degrees of importance, and so on. Appropriate use of things like different sizes, types and weights of print, underlining, boxing in of certain material, blank spaces and illustrations can also help to produce a clear, visually attractive and interesting layout. The next section, on desktop publishing, provides further guidance on how to produce well-presented textual materials.

Desktop publishing: In many respects, this is similar to word processing, except that the term 'desktop publishing' is normally used for a system which produces the final master copy which can be used for reproduction. A desktop publishing system will normally comprise:

- a word processor

- a printer

- software to enable a range of fonts and print-styles to be used

- software to allow diagrams, graphs, tables and illustrations to be included.

There are several different types of printer. 'Dot matrix' printers are the least expensive, and can print both words and graphics when coupled to compatible word processor systems. Inexpensive dot matrix printers don't quite manage to print 'letter quality' text, and as the ribbons become exhausted, the print colour fades somewhat, making the copy unsuitable for reproduction on offset lithograph or photocopiers. 'Daisy wheel' and 'golf ball' printers resemble traditional typewriters in that only particular characters are available, and graphics cannot be printed. They produce 'letter quality' copy however. 'Ink jet' printers can produce high-quality images of both text and graphics. All the printers mentioned so far are usually fairly noisy. 'Laser Printers' are increasingly used as part of desktop publishing systems. These are quiet and can be relatively quick, and can do graphics and text together, but the cost per copy is rather more than for the simpler systems.

One of the main advantages of desktop publishing systems is the availability of a range of different choices of font, size and style of print. This can allow you to have full control of the size and density of headings, text and footnotes, and you can use bold print or italics (or both) to help make particular words or phrases stand out. Choice of font is a matter for your own taste, but fonts such as 'Helvetica' give text a 'modern' appearance, while 'Times' gives a more traditional look to your handouts (see Figures 4.9 and 4.10 for examples).

Scanners: These have been the most dramatic advance in the field of desktop publishing. A scanner works in a similar way to a photocopier, except that the image to be captured is memorized in a computer file, and can thereafter be reproduced at will and incorporated into other files. For example, if it is wished to quote a text extract, a photograph, a diagram, a table, or any other part of an existing publication, it can be scanned and then slotted in to a new piece of writing. Scanned images can be adjusted in size to whatever is wished in the new piece of writing. Extracts can be scanned from textbooks, journals, newspapers, memoranda — virtually anything. The final print quality of the final copy necessarily depends on the quality of the original extract. For example, if something is to be scanned that is originally very small or close-printed, and it is then required to enlarge the extract, there will be some loss of definition if the original is not of high clarity.

Even more useful, for text extracts, is the possibility of not only scanning an original source extract, but converting it to an existing word processing format. This means that text extracts can now be 'read in' to new documents, and edited on-screen, with any kind of adjustments being made in the process. For documents to be scanned in this way requires the ability of the software to recognize each letter, and some fonts are easier to deal with than others. Perhaps one day it will be possible to scan handwritten documents in this way, but for the present handwriting is rather too variable for this to be accomplished safely. The process of scanning is far faster (and requires less skills) than keying in the original extract. Naturally, there are serious concerns about the issue of copyright, as it is now very easy indeed to absorb extracts of original books and journals, reword them, and reprint them (often in a style that looks quite different from the original).

The new generation of authoring tools has caused a revolution in publishing in general. Publishers of textbooks and journals usually welcome new materials supplied directly on computer disk. It is possible for publishers to process such disks directly, avoiding the expensive and time-consuming task of keying in new manuscripts. For authors, this means a considerable saving on the task of proof-checking, as when work has been processed electronically rather than manually, the possibility of new errors (misspellings, words or lines missed out, and so on) is dramatically reduced. Additionally, authors now can have control of things such as page layout, for example avoiding new headings starting uncomfortably near the foot of a page. The term 'camera ready copy' is now often used in publishing. This can mean two things: originals which are visually in a form ready for photo reproduction, or originals which can be electronically processed to produce the final version.

How to Design Specific Types of Materials

Having dealt with some of the basic principles that should underlie the design of all types of printed and duplicated materials, let us now turn our attention to specific types of material and look at some typical examples.

Handouts

These can be used for a wide range of purposes, and the detailed design of any particular handout will, of course, depend to a large extent on the exact role that it is to be required to play. Some commonly used types are listed below.

- Complete sets of notes on specific areas or topics, designed to be given to learners to save them from having to take notes themselves during lectures, training sessions, etc.

- Skeleton sets of notes, containing blank spaces that learners have to fill in themselves during a lesson of some sort. These can have educational advantages over complete notes in some situations, since they involve some participation on the part of the learner.

- Shorter documents (often only a single sheet) that are given out during a lesson to save the students from having to copy a complicated diagram, map, set of data, etc or to illustrate some specific point(s).

- Miniature flexible learning modules, containing information, tasks and activities, discussions or responses to tasks. During the session, lecturers or trainers can expand on the information and give feedback to learners on their work on the tasks and activities.

- Checklists of assessment criteria, for learners to apply to work they have already done, using self-assessment or peer-assessment processes.

- Printed 'question and answer' sheets. When large groups of learners are being encouraged to submit questions to their lecturers in writing, the lecturers can issue such sheets periodically, giving responses to the most frequent (or most important) of the questions.

- Bibliography update sheets, referring learners to recently published books and journal articles, and linking them to the content of the course.

- 'Help' sheets, giving clarification of more difficult concepts or processes. Such sheets can provide worked examples, case study illustrations, and step-by-step discussions.

Figure 2.2 is typical of the sort of single-sheet handout that can easily be prepared by any teacher, instructor or trainer for use within the context of a taught lesson. It is in fact one prepared back in 1983 (before the advent of desktop publishing) for use in a second-year undergraduate course on atomic physics. The main purpose of this particular handout was to save the students from having to copy a rather complicated diagram into their notes, something that would not only take a considerable amount of time but which they would almost certainly get wrong in some way (the relative positions of the various horizontal lines, which represent electronic energy levels corresponding to different quantum numbers, are rather important).

We would like readers to note three things about this handout (do not worry about the content, which could be completely meaningless to non-scientists). First, it took less than half an hour to produce and required no professional graphic or secretarial support; nevertheless, it was just as effective as a highly polished, professionally-produced equivalent in achieving its educational objectives. (Nowadays, of course, it would probably be possible to produce such a 'highly polished' version just as quickly using desktop publishing!) Second, note that this particular handout would not be of much use in an individualized learning situation, because it contains very little in the way of explanation of the physics involved; this is supplied by 'talking round' the handout in the course of a lecture. Finally, note that lower-case printing rather than ordinary handwriting or upper-case printing is used for the bulk of the textual content, since research has shown that this is by far the easiest form of text to read. Thus, anyone who is planning to produce hand-written instructional materials of any type should try to develop a clear lower-case printing style; given a little practice, this can be produced almost as quickly as ordinary writing, and, in almost all cases, is much more legible.

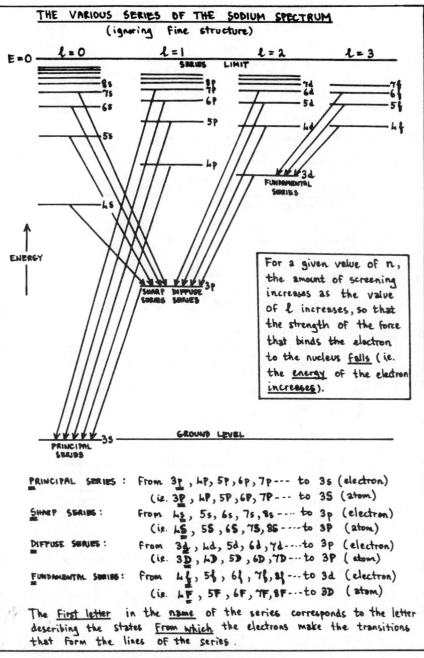

Figure 2.2 **A single-sheet handout designed for use during an undergraduate lecture on atomic physics**

4.   PEAT-FIRED POWER STATION

Examination of technical feasibility of building a peat-fired station
Elaskay is fortunate in having a source of peat in the easily accessible Moor of Bogle 3 km south of Portian (see map). You may assume that a detailed survey has shown that the recoverable reserves of dried high-grade peat are of the order of 800 000 tonnes.

Let us now examine the feasibility of building peat-fired stations of the various sizes shown in row 1 of the Work Sheet opposite. The number of units of electricity that each would be expected to produce in a year is given in row 2, and the amounts of energy (MJ) that these figures represent are given in row 3. (1 kWh = 3.6 MJ).

But a peat-fired power station has an overall efficiency of 25%. So the amount of energy that each station would have to get from its peat supply each year is given in row 4. Since every tonne of peat contains roughly 9500 MJ of energy, we can calculate the number of tonnes of peat that each station would consume every year (row 5).

Use the figures for the annual fuel consumptions of the various stations to calculate the length of time for which Elaskay's recoverable reserves of 800 000 tonnes of peat would last if stations of different sizes were built (row 6).

Now assess the feasibility of building stations of different sizes, bearing in mind that a peat-fired station has an effective operational life of 25 years and it can only be justified economically if there is sufficient peat to keep it running throughout this period (row 7).

Examination of economic viability of building a peat-fired station
In this project, we will assume that it is the cost of the electricity produced which will largely decide which type of power station will be built. In order to calculate this figure for a peat-fired station, it is first necessary to know the costs of the station. These can be found as follows.

First, use the figures for capital cost per installed kW of generating capacity that are given in row 8 of your Work Sheet to calculate the capital cost of each station. (Note that the cost per installed kW falls as the size of the station increases; this is true for nearly all types of power station, and is one of the main reasons why Generating Boards generally build a few really big stations rather than a large number of small ones). Write down your answers to row 9.

A loan would have to be taken out to pay the full cost of building the station. Calculate the annual repayments on that loan, assuming that a low-interest loan is available such that the loan is repaid and the interest is covered by annual payments of £7.82 throughout the 25 year life of the station for every £100 borrowed (row 10).

Next, calculate the total annual cost of extracting, transporting and processing the peat needed to fuel the stations, assuming that every tonne used would cost £6 (row 11).

Finally, calculate the total annual costs (row 13) of the different stations by adding the annual repayments on capital cost (row 10), the annual extracting and processing costs (row 11) and the annual running and maintenance costs (row 12).

The cost per unit of electricity produced by the different stations (row 14) can now be obtained by dividing the total annual costs (row 13) by the annual electrical output (row 2).

6

Figure 2.3

Case study on peat power from Alternative Energy Project (text)

WORK SHEET FOR PEAT POWER				
1.	Size of station (MW)	5	10	15	20
2.	Annual electrical out-put (million kWh units)	10	20	30	40
3.	Amount of energy this represents (million MJ)	36	72	108	144
4.	Amount of energy that has to be produced from combustion of fuel (million MJ)	144	288	432	576
5.	Annual fuel consump-tion (tonnes)	15 100	30 300	45 400	60 600
6.	Times for which fuel reserves would last (years)				
7.	Feasibility of building station with operational life of 25 years (yes/marginal/no)				
8.	Capital cost per installed kW (£)	600	550	525	500
9.	Capital cost of building station (£ million)				
10.	Annual repayments on capital cost (£)				
11.	Annual cost of extracting, trans-porting and drying peat (£)				
12.	Annual running and maintenance costs of station (£)	50 000	70 000	85 000	95 000
13.	Total annual opera-ting costs of station (£)				
14.	Cost per unit of electricity generated (p)				

7

Figure 2.3
**Case study on peat power from Alternative Energy Project
(worksheet)**

Worksheets

These come in almost as many forms as handouts, and can be used in just as wide a range of instructional situations. Again the detailed design will depend to a great extent on the purpose for which the worksheet is intended. We can, however, distinguish between at least two basic types:

- Highly structured, 'convergent' worksheets, where the answers or other material that the learner has to fill in are largely (or completely) predetermined by the writer.

- More open-ended worksheets, where the responses are not nearly so circumscribed and allow the learner scope for divergent thinking or the exercise of creativity.

Both types can be used in all three of our basic classes of instructional situation (mass instruction, individualized instruction and group learning), although the former is probably the one that is best suited for individualized instruction, where the learning experience generally needs to be fairly tightly structured.

Typical examples of the two types of worksheet are given in Figures 2.3 and 2.4. The first (an example of a 'convergent' worksheet) is one of a set of five similar worksheets that are included in an interactive case study known as the *Alternative Energy Project* (published by the Association for Science Education). This involves five small groups in carrying out independent feasibility studies into the possibility of generating electricity on the hypothetical Western Scottish island of 'Elaskay' by exploiting different alternative energy resources, after which the groups pool their findings and draw up a 50-year rolling programme for meeting Elaskay's future electricity needs. The worksheet is used in conjunction with the text on the facing page, with the two components (the text and the worksheet) together constituting a highly structured mini-case study into the feasibility of building peat-fired power stations of different sizes on the island. (The case study would, incidentally, be just as suitable for use in an individualized learning situation as in the small-group learning situation for which it was written.)

The second example (a typical 'divergent' worksheet) is one that is used in another group learning exercise known as *Which Material?*. This was developed in RGIT during the early 1980s for use in the new 'Foundation and General level Science' courses that were then being introduced into Scottish schools. The exercise is basically a very simple one, involving small groups trying to decide what would be the most suitable materials with which to manufacture different articles. Each group is allocated a different article (the frame of a chair, the casing of an electric plug, a power transmission cable, and so on) and has to try to think of four possible materials from which it could be made. The group then tries to identify the advantages and disadvantages of each material, and, on the basis of these, decides which material would be best. The solutions that the various groups come up with are then used as the basis of a class discussion.

WHICH MATERIAL? Pupil Worksheet		
Item to be manufactured [ ]		
Possible material	Advantages	Disadvantages
Recommended material [ ]		

Figure 2.4
The pupil's worksheet from Which Material?

As can be seen by comparing Figures 2.3 and 2.4, the two worksheets are completely different in character, and are designed to give the users totally different types of learning experience. Examples of other types of worksheet can be found in *Worksheets and School Learning* (see Bibliography), an inexpensive booklet that is highly recommended to any schoolteacher who is interested in producing such items.

Individualized Learning Materials: Open and Flexible Learning

As we said earlier, materials that are designed for use in an individualized way have to be much more carefully designed than most other types of instructional materials, because they need to control or manage the actual process of learning as well as supply the content to be learned. We also saw that printed or duplicated materials can play three basic roles in self-instructional systems:

- providing the entire vehicle through which learning takes place; or

- structuring or managing the learning process, with the main content to be learned being found in other resources (such as books, videos, manuals and so on); or

- providing supplemental support to other learning media and processes.

This section is based on ideas from *The Open Learning Handbook* (see Bibliography) and aims to help teachers develop flexible learning materials from the resources they already use with their students. It suggests how to make an 'additionality' approach at least as effective as employing off-the-shelf flexible learning resource materials.

Flexible, Open or Distance Learning?

Each of these terms is used in connection with individualized learning materials, and has been defined in different ways by different writers. Perhaps the simplest way to explain the similarities, differences and overlaps between them is to describe how the respective types of learning usually happen.

Distance learning: Learners are separated by distance from providers for some, most, or even all of the time. Examples include the Open University (UK), various correspondence learning agencies, and some in-company training schemes where trainees are studying at their own base rather than in a training centre. Usually (but not always) distance learning is done by people working on their own.

Open learning: This term is broader, and includes all the examples of distance learning given above. Open learning usually means that learners have some control over three primary factors: time, place and pace, or in other words –

- where they learn,
- when they learn,
- how they learn.

'Open learning' can sometimes also be taken to mean 'open to all comers'. For example, the Open University takes people without the formal entry qualifications required by many traditional institutions of higher education. However, in practice, most open learning programmes need learners to have already reached particular levels of competence or experience, as laid down in the 'prerequisite knowledge and skills' listed in the materials.

Flexible learning: This term is even broader, and includes all forms of open and distance learning, but also includes other learning situations which at first sight appear more traditional. For example, 200 people in a lecture theatre can be 'learning flexibly', if (for example) they are spending five minutes where everyone is working through a handout and trying to answer some questions. In other words, flexible learning involves people taking some control regarding how they learn. Flexible learning should be considered as part of a toolkit of ways of developing successful learning outcomes and demonstrable competences in our students. Essentially, developing flexible learning processes from traditional teaching processes is largely a matter of putting into print not only the content of the syllabus, but particularly the *support* which would be offered to the students by teachers. Since it is recognized that most learning occurs by *doing*, the key aspect of the development of flexible learning resource materials is the *interaction* between learners and materials – in particular how well the materials respond to learners' attempts to answer self-assessment questions.

   Important aspects of the support and interaction which can be built into flexible learning resources are:

- the *tasks and exercises* whereby learners gain competence;
- the *feedback* learners receive on their progress;
- the *guidance* learners are given regarding use of textbooks and resources; and
- details of the *assessment criteria* which will be indicative of successful outcomes.

By far the best situation in which to develop flexible learning resource materials is by being involved face-to-face with 'traditional students'. The ultimate aim may be to produce resources which can promote learning without the presence of a tutor, but the handover of control is best done one step at a time, with thorough monitoring of each move towards learner autonomy. A longer-term aim may be to establish distance-learning pathways, built initially from those flexible learning resources which prove their worth with conventional students.

Adopt, adapt, or start from scratch?

Does something suitable exist already?: If the 'perfect' open learning materials (perfect for your learners' needs) exist already, the most logical thing would seem to be to *adopt* them. This may mean negotiating with whoever owns the materials to get quantity discounts. If (as is often the case) there are materials which *nearly* meet your learners' needs, you may well be able to 'make up' any deficiencies with tutorial support, or with things you add-on to the materials. There are various catalogues and databases which can be valuable in helping to identify and locate materials which already exist. However, there is no substitute for getting your hands on existing materials, before deciding whether they can be used as they are, or whether they lend themselves to adaptation for your students. You may need to use all the tricks you can think of to get a good look at such materials. Better still, it's worth trying a small-scale pilot before committing yourself to the purchase of large quantities of materials.

Another way of tracking down potentially relevant learning materials is through informal contacts with colleagues from other institutions. Coffee breaks at conferences can be very profitable if used to help find people with whom you can exchange resources and information! A good checklist should be useful in helping you decide which materials may be good enough to *adopt*. You could use the checklist on pages 71-4 as a starting point, and refine it to tune-in to the needs of your learners.

Have you time to start from scratch?: Writing open learning materials from scratch takes time – a lot of time! Open learning writing has often been paid for on the basis of ten hours to write up the equivalent of one hour's learning. In practice, it may take more like 100 hours to write up one hour of learning, when preparation, piloting, editing, adjusting and so on are taken into account. If something fairly close to what is needed already exists, it can be more economical to adapt rather than start from scratch. However, you'll learn many valuable things from having a go at writing your own materials. If you really *want* to create new materials, the time issue seems to take care of itself.

Could the 'not invented here syndrome' affect you?: Most teachers and trainers feel a little uncomfortable working with materials written by others. We tend to prefer to work with materials where we have a sense of 'ownership'. Even if alternative materials are better than our own, our instinct is to prefer our own, and it's only too easy for us to see all sorts of weaknesses in other people's materials. This can be a reason for starting from scratch and writing new flexible learning resource materials. However, the *real* reason should be based on the needs of our learners. If these needs are best served by writing new materials specially for them, starting from scratch is indeed justified.

What are the advantages of adapting?

Adapting existing resource materials can have many advantages, including the following.

- It can save time and expense.

- You probably already own materials which can be adapted.

- You can adapt materials a bit at a time.

- You may be able to try out the adapted bits face-to-face with conventional classes, to gain feedback and enable improvements.

- You may be able to use small pieces of published material without copyright problems or payments – but seek expert help and advice. Librarians often know a lot about copyright rules and regulations.

- You'll still feel 'ownership' for the materials if you've done all the fine-tuning yourself (ie avoiding the 'not invented here' feeling).

- It can be much less expensive than having to purchase complete packages for each of your learners.

- Adapting can be excellent practice towards writing some materials from scratch in due course.

Learning by doing – the heart of flexible learning

Most learning happens when we actually try to *do* something. Learning doesn't happen efficiently when we merely read about something or listen to someone talk about it. The measure of a good open learning package is *what the students do* as they work through it. Therefore, preparing to put together an open learning package (or adapting something which exists already) is *not* so much a matter of collecting together all the things students need to read – it's about collecting together a set of things for students to *do*.

When you already teach a subject face to face, you are likely to have a considerable collection of tasks and activities you give your students – in other words you are already well on your way to having one of the most important ingredients of your open learning packages.

What may I have already, that can be used or adapted?

- Your experience of teaching.

- Your knowledge of students' problems.

- Your ability to help students to find solutions to their problems.

- Syllabus objectives or competences you work with already.

- Your own handout materials: usually no copyright problems and often already containing central material.

- Existing resource materials: class exercises; case study details – usually already the basis for learner activity and the essential part of flexible learning.

- Your own lecture notes – these may cover most of the content your learners need, already in concise form.

- Textbook extracts – it may be possible to obtain clearance to include small extracts without charge or it may be possible to get learners to refer to books (bought or borrowed from libraries).

- Manuals – usually are already some way towards being interactive material. It may be possible to use extracts without copyright difficulties or to refer learners to 'available' manuals directly, or it may be easy to recompose extracts to avoid copyright difficulties.

- Worksheets and assignments you already give your students.

- Problems and projects you design for your students.

What may need to be added for flexible-learning usage?
Some or all of the principal features of the best open learning materials can be added to transform your existing materials into flexible learning resources.

- *User-friendly objectives:*
  - warming up things like 'the expected learning outcome is that the student will….' to 'by the end of … you'll be able to …'.
  - making objectives more directly relevant to learners' needs.
  - making them appropriate to the assessment criteria involved.

- *Responses to questions, tasks and activities:*
  - not just model answers, but *responses* to what learners do when they have a go at the questions/tasks/activities.
  - discussion of anticipated errors/difficulties.
  - positive encouraging comments for learners who have succeeded.
  - reassuring and encouraging comments for learners who did not succeed.

- *Additional questions, tasks and activities:*
  - in self-assessment format, with responses as above.

- *Written study-skills help:*
  - the sort of help and support you'd give face-to-face learners informally.

- *Assessment criteria:*
  - to link with objectives and performance standards.
  - to give learners a good frame of reference regarding standards they're aiming at.

- to alert learners to what counts and what could lose them credit.
- to build learners' confidence, allowing them insight into 'the rules of the game'.

■ *Summaries/reviews/checklists:*
- provide 'repeats' of crucial points, allowing learners to see what is most important.
- provide useful revision aids.

■ *Feedback questionnaires should:*
- be short, structured, easy-to-complete in format, but with additional space for comments from learners, who *want* to expand on the basic questions.
- help find out which parts learners can handle easily on their own, and which parts learners need more support with.

■ *Audiotape commentaries and discussions:*
- relatively cheap and simple to produce.
- can make it less lonely for learners working on their own.
- can be useful for talking learners through things like textbook extracts, derivations, complex diagrams and so on.
- can also be used to help learners self-assess more complex tasks they may have done as part of their work – ie talking them through good answers and common mistakes (can be more friendly than a long printed response).

■ *Briefings:* for use of external resources such as textbooks, manuals, audiotapes, video, or practical kits.

How can a package be put together efficiently?

Turning your existing resources into an open learning package can be done more easily than you might have imagined. It's best to get the various separate components of your package into good working order, trying them out with groups of your students whenever you can. Then gradually build the components together into a draft package and see how your students cope with it.

At first, the task of putting together an open learning package may seem a formidable task – especially if you want to equal the best published packages. However, Rome wasn't built in a day, and the best open learning materials were created gradually, step by step, with a great deal of piloting at each stage. Most of these steps are simple extensions of things you do in your day-to-day work with your students. For detailed advice regarding composing self-assessment questions and responses, you are advised to refer to *The Open Learning Handbook* or *53 Interesting Ways to Write Open Learning Materials* (see Bibliography). The following sequence can save much time and trouble.

1. Design *self-assessment questions* and *activities* for your open learners, based on the class-work exercises you presently use, and the assign-

ments and projects you set your existing students, linking these to the syllabus *objectives* or *competences* in the same way as you already do. Adjust the working of all these components as you go, so they become as straightforward and clear as possible, so that learners don't need you to explain what the words mean.

2. Write *responses* to each self-assessment question and activity. Base these responses on the way you deal with your live students. Write in the explanations you give them when they make mistakes. Keep striving to make the questions and responses as self-explanatory as you can so that you don't need to be present in person. Try out each draft with your live students and observe any difficulties, and adjust questions and responses as necessary.

3. Start turning your notes and handouts into short sections of text. Make these sections bridge the gaps between the *response* to one question and the next question. Each chunk of text therefore has a distinct function – to lead up to the next student activity.

4. When there are questions or activities which really do need a human response rather than a pre-prepared one, turn the questions into *tutor marked assignments,* and build these in to your package.

5. Go through the bits and pieces of your package, adding *summaries* or *reviews* at key points. Make such additions every time your students may need reinforcement of principal ideas and concepts.

6. Now that your package is nearing a 'working' form, go through it again adding *short introductions* or *'lead-in'* paragraphs, preparing your students for what is to come in each part. It's far easier to write well-tuned introductions when you've already written the parts you're leading up to.

As you can see from the above sequence, writing an open learning package is not done in the same way as writing a textbook. It's not a matter of starting by writing page 1 and working through in a linear sequence. Open learning packages are designed around the *learning* that students will gain from them. This takes the emphasis away from the text itself – and means you don't need to try to write everything you know about the subject — only writing the things your students *need* to gain. It's often advisable to start working on the middle of your package, then work outwards in both directions. Writing the very beginning is one of the most crucial tasks. This is much easier to do if you've already written later parts of the package – you know then exactly what you're introducing.

Responses — not just answers
The responses you write for self-assessment questions and activities are by far the most important ingredient of your open learning package, and therefore you should given them careful attention. (It's sadly all too easy

to tell that questions and responses have been added to many open learning packages at the last minute – almost as an afterthought.) If you think about the best quality face-to-face teaching, some of the most important skills include:

- explaining to students what to do when they can't yet answer a question;

- helping students to feel a glow when they do something correctly; and

- helping students find out exactly what went wrong when they make mistakes.

Writing open learning materials gives you the chance to package up these valuable skills, so that your help is extended to students even when you're not there in person. The response to a good self-assessment question should enable each student to find out two things: *'was I right?'* and *'if not, why not?'*

When open learning materials are scrutinised by professional open learning writers, the first items that they turn to are the responses to self-assessment questions and activities. If these responses are working well, the package is a good one.

Structured questions are easier to respond to! Responding to open-ended questions is possible but usually difficult. A good response needs to cover every answer that learners may reasonably have given, and more. Structured questions involve learners making a decision such as:

- which is the correct option?

- which is the most sensible course of action?

- which is the best order in a sequence?

With such questions, you can respond directly to learners who choose a 'wrong' or 'less-good' option, explaining exactly why their choice is not the best one.

Some Guidelines for briefings

Many open learning materials avoid the chore of duplicating large amounts of content by referring out to existing resources such as textbooks and other documentation. The Open University, for example, adopts a wide range of textbooks as 'readers' for most of its courses, and open learning materials are designed to support the usage of these resources. 'Briefings' represent one area of support and advice that is normally handled quite informally in face-to-face sessions. Students at such sessions have the extra advantages of tone of voice and facial expression, helping them find out more about exactly what they are intended to do with the textbooks and literature references they are given. The same level of support needs to be put into print, if students studying by flexible learning pathways are to derive the same amount of

Self Assessment Question

Look at the list of things you may do in lectures. In each case enter a tick in the appropriate column, depending on whether you think it is something which is 'active' or 'passive' as far as learning is concerned.

	Active	Passive
(a) copying down what you see on the blackboard or screen		
(b) writing down things that the lecturer says		
(c) writing down your own thoughts and ideas		
(d) asking the lecturer questions		
(e) asking *yourself* questions – jotting them down so you can research the answers later		
(f) answering questions posed by the lecturer		
(g) doing calculations, solving problems, and so on		
(h) yawning, shuffling, fidgeting, staring out of the window (if there is one), watching fellow students, chattering to them, muttering to yourself, and so on!		
(i) thinking about what you will be doing that evening		
(j) looking at the lecturer, the blackboard or the screen		
(k) discussing things with students near to you, when directed to do so by the lecturer		

Figure 2.5 **Example of a self assessment question, designed to help students think about how best to handle large-group learning experiences such as lectures**

'Active' versus 'passive' in lectures

	Active	Passive
(a) copying down what you see on the blackboard or screen		✓
(b) writing down things that the lecturer says		✓
(c) writing down your own thoughts and ideas	✓	
(d) asking the lecturer questions	✓	
(e) asking *yourself* questions – jotting them down so you can research the answers later	✓	
(f) answering questions posed by the lecturer	✓	
(g) doing calculations, solving problems, and so on	✓	
(h) yawning, shuffling, fidgeting, staring out of the window (if there is one), watching fellow students, chattering to them, muttering to yourself, and so on!		✓
(i) thinking about what you will be doing that evening		✓
(j) looking at the lecturer, the blackboard or the screen		✓
(k) discussing things with students near to you, when directed to do so by the lecturer	✓	

Figure 2.6 **The above would only begin to serve as a response to the self-assessment question. This is because it does not yet give any explanation regarding *why* particular actions are designated as 'active' or 'passive'**

Next, let's go through each of the things in turn, and see if you agree with the reasons that I made my decisions about 'active' versus 'passive' above.

(a) copying down what you see on the blackboard or screen
You may have thought this would be 'active' – yet I chose 'passive'. Your pen may be active if you're busily copying things down, but it's all too easy for your mind to go into limbo while you do it! You can get into the mode of a human photocopier – or a shorthand typist. You may indeed be making faithful records of what's going on, but without much of it really going through your mind. If someone were to stop you, when in this 'copying' mode, and asked you 'explain to me what you were writing about ten minutes ago?' would you be able to do it? If it's not going through your mind, your notes will not have the benefit of any real attempt to structure them and make them as useful as possible.

(b) writing down things that the lecturer says
I put this as 'passive' too! Of course, there will be times when you need to write down things the lecturer says, word for word – but only occasionally (for example when a definition or a memorable quotation is given). My advice is to make notes about things the lecturer says – which is a different matter altogether from just writing it all down. Making notes is about making decisions. You can decide what is important enough to make notes of, and what just to listen to without writing anything. It takes a bit of practice (and courage) not to write everything down at first, but it will pay dividends.

(c) writing down your own thoughts and ideas
'When will I get time for this?' you may ask. It's worth making time for it. I ticked it as an 'active' process – and it can have a very high learning payoff in the long run. If you've got a lot of lectures, your own ideas and thoughts in today's lecture will soon fade and be swamped by other information – but not if you've written your thoughts down. Don't let your thoughts and ideas go to waste, store them so you can exploit them later. Besides, writing down your own thoughts and ideas can help alleviate the boredom of some lectures!

(d) asking the lecturer questions
This is of course active, and useful. If you ask a question, you are automatically awake and thinking. However, as we've already seen, you may not feel like putting yourself under the spotlight. Some lecturers don't welcome interruptions. You may be afraid that you'll be ridiculed for asking the question (and therefore for not knowing the answer). However, almost every time someone asks a question in a lecture, there are several other students who also did not know the answer, and who are glad that someone asked the question. There are also several other students who did not realize that they should have been able to answer the question – in other words they didn't even think of the question till someone asked it. However, if you still don't feel like asking questions (and who can blame you in some lectures!), there's always (e) below.

(e) asking yourself questions – jotting them down so you can research the answers later
This too is 'active' of course. If you don't write your questions down, two hours later you may not even be able to remember what the questions were – let alone research the answers. Writing down your questions doesn't take a lot of time – it takes less than a second to draw a large red ? next to something that you can't understand. It may be worth a few extra seconds to add a word or two to remind you of exactly what it is that you don't yet understand. If you know what the questions are, there's every chance you can find out the answers – for example:

Figure 2.7 **This is the sort of extra discussion which is needed for a true *response* to the self-assessment question – explaining the reasoning why particular choices are to be regarded as 'active' or 'passive'.**

- ask friends
- look up books
- approach a tutor later
- work it out for yourself.

(f) answering questions posed by the lecturer
Naturally, this is 'active' – at least for you when you're picked on to give an answer. However, when you're picked on, (or when you volunteer to answer) there's every chance that everyone else in the room will mentally switch-off for a few moments, while you get on with it. If you've got lecturers who ask a lot of questions, make sure that you benefit from them by trying to answer them all (privately) by jotting down a word of two of the question, and a short answer.

(g) doing calculations, solving problems, and so on
These are 'active' processes, and are useful practice for things you may be leading up to in exams. In the large-group situation, at least you have the chance to ask for help if you get stuck – you can't do that in exams!

(h) yawning, shuffling, fidgeting, staring out of the window (if there is one), watching fellow students, chattering to them, muttering to yourself, and so on!
Obviously, you're not doing much real learning if you're inextricably engaged in these processes! You may be achieving one useful outcome – letting the lecturer see that you're bored. However, it is usually better to engage in active learning strategies of your own (for example making sense of last week's lecture – or even looking back at a completely different subject, if the present lecture is totally useless).

(i) thinking about what you will be doing that evening
You're not alone! After all, you may have several lectures in a week, and each particular lecture can't be the highlight of your life. When one has problems outside college, it's quite natural that they will creep into your mind whenever there's not much else going on. If you're excited about the prospect of something you've been looking forward to, it's natural that your thoughts will stray (even during quite splendid lectures). The only real way to get your thoughts back to the subject of the lecture is to give yourself something quite definite to do – for example, concentrate on making particularly well-structured notes (maybe in a pattern, or a table of questions, or a diagram showing how one thing relates to others).

(j) looking at the lecturer, the blackboard or the screen
Almost everyone does these things during lectures – but the learning payoff can be small. It's possible to look at something or someone, without actually thinking much about what you see. In lectures, most students manage to look 'with it' – even when they're totally 'without it'! So don't imagine because you're busy looking at things, that these things are automatically getting filed and sorted out in your mind.

(k) discussing things with students near to you, when directed to do so by the lecturer
This can be a very useful way to get the most out of large-group sessions. Sadly, some lecturers seem to feel that they should be the ones doing the talking and discussing, and that 'other discussions' are a challenge to their authority. Enlightened lecturers realise that when everyone is involved in a vigorous discussion (even if only for a minute or two at a time), everyone is thinking.

Figure 2.7 continued

benefit from briefings to resource materials. The following suggestions give some ways of ensuring that printed briefings serve learners effectively.

- *Keep them short and specific*: it is better to have briefings to *short extracts* than to whole books or chapters, eg 'Now work through Sections 2.3 and 2.5' is better than 'Now read Chapter 2'.

- *Make briefings active*: ie don't just ask learners to 'read' things, but give them things to do while they read them – or even before reading things (not just after they have read them).

- *Include 'commentary' elements in briefings*: eg 'Chapter 3 gives a good overview of ..., watch out particularly for the way ... is discussed. Don't worry about ... at this stage, you don't need to know the sort of detail that you'll see in Section 3.5!'

- *Include 'signposting' in briefings*: eg 'In Section 4.8 we've already seen why ... happens. In Section 4.9 you'll find out what happens when ..., which is useful when you need to work out how to ...'.

- *plant questions in learners' minds*: When learners have already got some questions in mind before reading something, they have a subconscious 'thirst' for the answers to the questions. This means that when they come across the 'answers' as they read, those parts are more memorable to them. This makes reading far more efficient.
  Eg 'As you study Section 6 try to find answers to the following three questions:
  Why does ...?
  How could ...?
  When might you find ...?'

- *Include 'steering in briefings:* eg 'You don't need to spend much time on Section 7 unless you want to'; 'The heart of the matter is explained very well near the end of Section 5.7'; 'Aim to spend about half an hour simply getting the feel of Chapter 4 before having a go at the next set of self-assessment questions'.

A checklist for Flexible Learning Resources

Objectives

- Is there a clear indication of any prerequisite knowledge or skills?

- Are the objectives stated clearly and unambiguously?

- Are the objectives presented in a friendly way? (ie *not* 'the expected learning outcomes of this module are that the student will...'!).

- Do the objectives avoid 'jargon' which may not be known to learners before starting the material?

Structure and layout

- Is the material visually attractive?

- Is there sufficient white space? (for learners to write notes, answer questions, do calculations, and so on).

- Is it easy for learners to find their way backwards and forwards?

Self-assessment questions and activities

- Are there plenty of them?

- Are the tasks set by the questions clear and unconfusing?

- Are the questions and tasks inviting? (Is it clear to learners that it's valuable for them to have a go rather than skip?)

- Is there enough space for learners to write their answers?

- Collectively, do the SAQs and activities test the learners' achievement of the objectives?

Responses to self-assessment questions and activities

- Are they really *responses to what the learner has done*? (ie not just answers to the questions).

- Do the responses meet the learners' need to find out: *'Was I right?' 'If not, why not?'*

- Do the responses include encouragement or praise (without patronizing) for learners who got them right?

- Do the responses include something that will help learners who got it wrong *not* to feel like complete idiots?

Introductions, summaries or reviews

- Is each part introduced in an interesting, stimulating way?

- Do the introductions alert learners to the way the materials are designed to work?

- Is there a clear and useful summary/review?

- Does it provide a useful way to revise the material quickly?

The text itself

- Is it readable and unambiguous?

- Is it relevant? (eg does it keep to the objectives as stated?)

- Is it 'involving' where possible? (ie plenty of use of 'you' for the learner, 'I' for the author, 'we' for the learner and author together.)

Diagrams, charts, tables, etc.

■ Is each as self-explanatory as possible?

■ Does the learner know what to do with each? (ie *to learn it, or to note it in passing, or to pick out the trend, or even nothing at all*.)

■ 'A sketch can be more useful than 1000 words': is the material sufficiently illustrated?

Some general points to look for

■ Is the material broken into manageable chunks?

■ Does the material avoid any sudden jumps in level?

■ Does the material ensure that the average learner will achieve the objectives?

■ Will the average learner *enjoy* using the material?

Conclusions

If you are already working face to face with students, you have several advantages when it comes to gradually turning parts of what you do into individualized learning materials or flexible learning resources.

■ You *know* your students, ie one of your target audiences.

■ You can *try things* and get quick feedback on whether they work or not.

■ You can turn *existing class exercises and homework questions* into self-assessment questions and activities.

■ You can turn the *feedback* you would give orally or in comments on marked work into printed responses to self-assessment questions and activities.

■ You can transform *your own notes* into the textual parts of flexible learning materials.

■ You can continue to use *face-to-face* sessions for the things that are difficult to wrap up in print.

Increased use of flexible learning within conventional programmes of study allows learners more opportunity to learn in 'high-quality' ways:

■ Learning by doing, rather than by being taught;

■ Learning at their own pace, rather than at yours;

■ Learning in their own style, rather than in the way you happen to teach; and

■ Learning again and again from their materials where necessary, rather than once as you teach.

Group Learning Materials

As in the case of mass instruction and individualized instruction, printed and duplicated materials are capable of playing a wide variety of roles in group learning situations. Again, the detailed design of the materials depends to a large extent on the exact nature of this role. Some of the most commonly used types are listed below:

- Materials providing instructions or guidance on how to carry out or run an exercise (instruction sheets for participants, organizer's guides, and so on).

- Basic resource materials for use in the exercise (role sheets, background information documents, data sheets, worksheets, and so on).

- Ancillary, illustrative and extension materials of various types.

When designing the resource materials for a group-learning exercise, it is important to ensure that each item is capable of fulfilling its own specific function, fits into the general context of the exercise and is consistent with all the other materials in the package. This will almost certainly require a certain amount of 'tuning', ie revising or amending particular items as the work progresses in order to produce a self-consistent, balanced package. Readers who are interested in making use of group-learning techniques in their work, and who wish to receive further guidance on how to design the necessary resource materials, are referred to *A Handbook of Game Design* and *Case Studies in Game Design* (see Bibliography). These cover the design of virtually all the different types of printed and duplicated materials that can be used in group-learning exercises, with the latter containing large numbers of illustrative examples of such materials.

A typical example of a resource document designed for use in a group-learning exercise — in this case, a structured debate on the safety and social acceptability of nuclear power — is given in Figure 2.8. This particular exercise forms the last of three projects in an educational package entitled *The Nuclear Debate* that was published by the Scottish Council for Educational Technology in 1984. The document shown is one of the 16 briefing sheets that are supplied to participants in the debate, and illustrates the three basic functions that such sheets should fulfil: (i) introducing the scenario of the exercise, (ii) telling the participant what this role will be, and (iii) providing any information specific to the role.

HOW TO PRODUCE MULTIPLE COPIES OF THE MATERIALS

Having dealt at some length with the planning and design of printed and duplicated instructional materials, let us now turn our attention to the various ways in which it is possible to produce multiple copies of such materials for use by a class, group or set of individual learners. Basically, there are five practical methods by which this can be done within

The Nuclear Debate   Briefing Sheet 3.1

Introduction
The object of Project 3 of *The Nuclear Debate* is to examine the question of whether nuclear power is socially and environmentally acceptable in an open society such as Britain. This will involve trying to answer the following questions:

(i) Are workers in the nuclear power industry subjected to unacceptably high accident and/or health risks?

(ii) Does the nuclear power industry constitute an unacceptable hazard to the health and safety of the general public?

(iii) Does nuclear power constitute an unacceptable genetic hazard to the human race?

(iv) Does nuclear power constitute an unacceptable political hazard because it is likely to lead to a reduction in personal freedom and to the spread of nuclear weapons?

The exercise will take the form of a structured debate in which each of the above issues will be discussed in turn.

Your role in the exercise
You have been given the task of speaking **against** nuclear power in stage (i) of the debate (discussion of the danger to workers in the nuclear power industry). To help you do so, you have been provided with information about the radiation safety limits that are currently in operation. Use this to prepare as strong a case as possible. An overhead projector and screen will be available during the debate, and it is strongly recommended that you make use of the blank acetate sheets and felt pens with which you have been provided to prepare visual materials to support your arguments (eg tables).

Your information
1. It has long been recognized that ionizing radiation is dangerous, and potentially lethal. Many of the early scientific workers on radioactivity, X-rays, etc subsequently died of various forms of cancer such as leukaemia that were directly attributed to the radiation to which they had been exposed (Madame Curie, for example). Also, radioactive materials may be ingested or inhaled, thus giving rise to continuous long-term exposure to radiation.

2. Since 1910, as evidence increasingly linked cancer to exposure to radiation, the permissible exposure limits have been progressively lowered. In the 1930s, medical reports showed that workers in the uranium mining industry were subjected to well above average cancer risks. Later, during the 1950s, it was shown that *even small* doses of radiation cause damage to the basic genetic materials shared by animals and men. Small doses of X-rays given to children while in their mother's womb, for example, were found to increase greatly the risk that they would subsequently develop leukaemia. Also, the effects of exposure to radiation never disappear. In Japan, for example, over 100 people still die *every year* because of the radiation that they were exposed to as a result of the atom bombs dropped on Hiroshima and Nagasaki. All the evidence suggests that there is *no such thing as a 'safe' dose of radiation*. Any dose, however small, is potentially harmful. (See Introductory

Figure 2.8 **One of the briefing sheets for participants in Project 3 of 'The Nuclear Debate'**

Booklet for further information about the harmful effects of ionizing radiation.)

3. Despite all this evidence, radiation safety levels are still set at an unacceptably high level, namely 5 rems per year for workers in the nuclear power industry, and 0.5 rems per year for members of the general public (see the Introductory Booklet for the definition of the rem). Thus, workers in the nuclear power industry are liable to be subjected to *over 30 times the dose that they receive from natural sources* (roughly 140-180 millirems per annum, depending on where they live).

4. As an illustration of the unacceptably high nature of these limits, consider the situation at Windscale, where the workforce is subjected to a total of roughly 10,000 man rems of radiation *every year*.* It has been estimated that this will result in at least one cancer death per decade for every year of exposure at this level. Thus a large number of Windscale workers have already been condemned to premature death due to cancer.

* The total dose sustained by the workforce at Windscale was 12,000 man rems in 1976 and 8,000 man rems in 1979.

Figure 2.8 (continued)

a school, college or training establishment — direct production using a laser printer, photocopying, hectographic duplication, stencil duplicating and small offset lithographic printing. We will therefore look at each of these in turn, explaining how they work and identifying their main strengths and weaknesses, after which we will discuss how to set about choosing which method to use in a particular situation.

Direct Production Using a Laser Printer

In practice, laser printing is not primarily used for preparing large numbers of copies of documents or handouts, but is highly useful for preparing single 'master' copies of high quality, which are then used for photocopying or offset lithography. Also, laser printers almost always operate from 'electronic' originals rather than physical documents – in other words, the original documents are normally transferred to the laser printer directly from a word processor or desktop publishing system. Laser printers are considerably more expensive than dot-matrix or ink-jet printers, but prices are falling. In 1992, typical prices for a relatively sophisticated laser printer ran between £2000 and £4000, but 'personal' laser printers are now available for less than £1000.

The main advantage of laser printers is the very high print resolution which can be achieved. In particular, the colour of text is very black indeed compared with dot-matrix printers, making the copies very suitable for photocopying. Essentially, they are dot-matrix printers, where the 'dot' is a computer controlled laser beam, and such printers can deliver a wide range of fonts, print styles, print sizes. When coupled to suitable desktop publishing software, they can also deliver graphics of high quality, including tables, charts, pictures and so on. Laser printers are increasingly being used to provide publishers with 'camera-ready copy'. This means that authors can retain control over the exact layout and design of pages, tables, and illustrations, and can have their work published without any of the usual problems which seem to arise at the publication stage (such as important new headings occurring near the foot of a page). However, it is increasingly becoming even easier for publishers to accept authors' work on computer disks directly, in which case the authors' layout may be retained or adapted as the publisher sees fit.

Laser printers are almost silent, unlike dot-matrix or daisy-wheel printers. They normally print a whole page at a time, irrespective of whether it contains text, illustrations or tables.

A new generation of colour laser printers is rapidly sweeping into colleges and training centres at the time of writing (1992), and these can deliver very attractive multicoloured copies – particularly useful when coloured diagrams and graphics are being used to reinforce learning points. However, as with any new advance of technology, it will be some time before coloured laser printers are at the direct 'beck and call' of practitioners in education and training – in other words, for the present you'll normally have to liaise with an expert to have your masterpiece reproduced in glorious, precise colour.

Photocopying

The generic term 'photocopying' covers a wide range of different processes, but they all make use of light of some sort to produce a copy (or multiple copies) of an original document. Possibly the greatest advantage of this method is that the original requires no special preparation since virtually any type of document (a typed or handwritten sheet, a sheet carrying graphic information, a page in a magazine or book, or even a photograph) can be copied on most modern machines.

The principle on which the photocopiers that are most useful for making multiple copies operate involves making use of electrostatic forces to transfer pigmented powder of some sort to the parts of the copy paper on which an image is to be produced and then using heat to fuse this powder to the surface of the paper in order to make the image permanent. Two main processes are used: direct electrostatic (where the pigment is deposited directly on to the surface of the copy paper) and transfer electrostatic (where the pigment is first deposited on the photosensitive surface of a rotating drum and then transferred on to the copy paper). Transfer electrostatic photocopiers have two considerable advantages over direct electrostatic machines. First, they use ordinary paper as copy paper, as opposed to the special (and more expensive) zinc oxide-coated paper that is needed for direct electrostatic machines. Second, they can be made to operate much faster than direct machines, a considerable advantage when it comes to producing multiple copies. For these reasons, most multiple photocopying is now done on transfer electrostatic machines, which are becoming increasingly versatile and

Figure 2.9 (a) **A small office photocopier**

(b) **A large photocopier (Xerox 5090)**

sophisticated every year.

A typical small office photocopier is shown in Figure 2.9(a). Such machines are extensively used by academic staff to run off limited numbers of copies of handouts and other teaching materials. They are now to be found in most college departments and training centres, and are available for public use – at a cost – in High Street shops and public libraries. A much larger, faster and more sophisticated machine of similar type is shown in Figure 2.9(b). Machines of this type are generally housed in a college's central reprographic unit, which handles all the large jobs and long print runs. There is, of course, no limit on the number of copies that can be produced from a given original.

One slight disadvantage of the use of photocopiers to run off copies of hand-prepared materials is that certain colours of ink – blue, for example – do not copy well (or at all) on some machines. Thus, when preparing the masters of such materials, care should be taken to employ colours that will reproduce on the machines to be used.

Hectographic Duplicating

This method, which is also known as *spirit duplicating* or *Banda* (from the trade name of one of the leading manufacturers), is one of the simplest non-photographic methods of producing multiple copies of single-sheet material. It is also by far the easiest method of producing multi-colour copies. It was once a very common method, but has now largely been superseded by photocopiers and laser printers. However, there are sufficient remaining hectographic machines to make it worthwhile exploring how best to use them.

Preparing the Master

Unlike photocopying, hectographic duplication involves preparing a special master copy (known as a hectograph master) of the material to be duplicated. This is done by typing, writing or drawing on a special sheet of plain glossy paper which is in contact with the dye side of the hectograph transfer sheet of the required colour. This is coated with a special type of aniline dye, some of which is transferred on to the underside of the master, where a reversed image of the original materials is produced. Multi-colour masters can be produced by using different coloured master sheets, one after the other.

Hints on hectograph master preparation: If the master is being typed:

- Use a standard-sized typewriter rather than a light, portable machine.

- Set the typewriter to *stencil* or remove the ribbon.

- Use the special backing sheet supplied in the box of transfer sheets.

If the master is being prepared by hand:

- Lightly sketch out the material on the matt side of the master sheet before inserting the master sheet.

- Place the master sheet and transfer sheet on a sheet of glass or similar hard, smooth surface during the actual preparation; use a fine ball point pen or stylus to write or draw on the material.

- Fill in any blocks of colour required by rubbing hard with a soft (B) pencil.

In both cases, leave a margin of at least 1cm all round. To correct mistakes, first cover with special paint or eraser, *or* cover the mistake with a small piece of clean master paper, *or* carefully scrape off the dye with a scalpel or razor blade. Then insert the correction using a fresh corner of transfer sheet.

Running Off Multiple Copies

This is done using a machine of the type shown in Figure 2.10.

The completed master is fixed to the master drum of the duplicating machine, dye side outwards. A carefully aligned stack of copy paper is placed in the input tray, and sheets are then pulled through the machine one by one by turning the handle (or, in the case of some machines, switching on the motor). As it passes through the machine, each sheet is first lightly moistened with spirit by means of a felt pad (hence the name spirit duplication), and is then pressed against the rotating master drum by a pressure roller. As the paper is pressed against the master, the

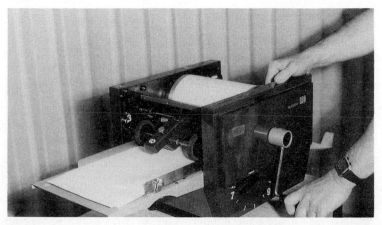

Figure 2.10 **A hectograph duplicator**

moistened paper picks up a small amount of dye, thus producing a permanent image on its surface.

Since some of the dye on the master is used up every time a copy is made, each master can only be used to produce a limited number of copies — possibly as many as 200 when the purple dye is used and considerably fewer (perhaps only 100) with another colour. Also, the method does not give high-quality, high-definition copies (since the nature of the dye transfer process gives rise to some spreading and smudging) and can be messy for the user. Nevertheless, it is a quick, cheap and handy method that will probably remain in use for some time yet.

Stencil Duplication

Like hectograph duplication, stencil duplication is also commonly referred to by the names of leading equipment manufacturers. Thus, in the UK, the name *roneo* is used, while in the USA, the corresponding name is *mimeograph*.

Preparing the Master

Again, as in the case of hectograph duplication, stencil duplication involves preparing a special master — the stencil from which the process gets its name. This is made from a thin sheet of special porous paper coated with a waxy substance that is impervious to ink, the stencil being prepared by typing or otherwise breaking through the coating (eg by drawing or writing) in order to produce the required image.

Hints on stencil preparation: If the stencil is being typed (the easiest and most effective method):

- Use a standard-sized typewriter rather than a light portable machine.

- Set the typewriter to *stencil* or remove the ribbon.

- Insert a sheet of carbon paper between the stencil paper and the backing sheet in order to make the image clearly legible.

If the stencil is being prepared by hand:

- Lay the stencil (with backing sheet still attached) on a suitable hard surface — preferably a special stencil preparation board.

- Carefully write or draw on the material using a suitable stylus (or, if not available, a fine ball point pen), taking great care not to tear the stencil.

In both cases, keep within the guidelines shown on the stencil that correspond to the size of copy paper that is to be used.

Electronic stencil cutters, which make stencils from original documents in the form of single sheets, are also available but these are both slow and expensive to use.

To correct mistakes, cover the error with a thin layer of stencil correction fluid and, once this has dried, carefully re-type , re-write or re-draw the relevant material, making sure that the layer of dried correction fluid has been penetrated.

Running Off Multiple Copies

Stencil duplication involves squeezing ink through the holes in the impervious, waxy coating of the stencil on to porous copy paper, where it is absorbed into the surface to produce a permanent image once the ink has been allowed to dry. This is done using a machine of the type shown in Figure 2.11 — a machine that is in many ways similar to a hectograph duplicator.

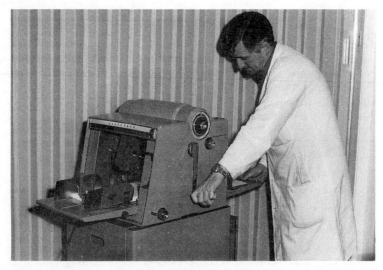

Figure 2.11 **A stencil duplicator**

To run off copies using a particular stencil, the thick paper backing sheet is removed and the stencil attached to the ink-drum, which is made of porous metal that allows the ink to ooze through from the inside to the outer surface, on to which the stencil is stuck (literally). Copies are then run off by turning the handle (or switching on the motor in the case of an electrically powered machine). This pulls sheets of copy paper through the machine one at a time, the sheets again being pressed against the rotating drum by means of a pressure roller. Since the ink on the completed copies may take a little time to dry, it is advisable to stack them in a dry, warm place for some time before use (a few hours is usually sufficient).

Stencil duplication has two advantages over hectorgraph duplication. First, it can be used to produce many more copies — several thousand, if the stencil is carefully handled and is cleaned and properly stored between print runs. (Special stencil storage boxes, in which the stencils are hung vertically by the cardboard tops to which they are attached, are used for this purpose.) Second, they can, if well prepared, produce a much sharper, better-quality image. Stencils are messy to use, however, and the ink is difficult to remove from hands and clothing. For this reason, stencil duplicators have now been replaced by more modern systems, such as fast photocopiers or laser printers, in many educational and training establishments, although they are still widely used in primary and secondary schools – and will probably continue to be used for some time.

Small Offset Litho Printing

The term 'small offset' is used to describe the small-scale offset lithographic machines that are now becoming increasingly widely used in situations where large numbers of high-quality copies of documents have to be made. Such machines are available in a wide range of types, sizes and prices, ranging from basic table-top machines that cost little more than a stencil duplicator to highly sophisticated presses that are comparable to those found in commercial printing firms.

Preparing the Master

Like the previous two duplication processes described, small offset printing requires the preparation of a suitable master. These come in a wide range of types, catering for a variety of purposes — and budgets. The cheapest paper plates can cost less than the stencils used in stencil duplication, and can be used to produce similar numbers of copies — up to several thousand. More expensive metal plates produce better quality prints, and can be used to produce much larger numbers of copies — tens of thousands if need be. Both types of plate can be given their image either directly or via some plate-making process. Direct methods include typing (using a special greasy lithographic ribbon in the typewriter), writing or drawing with a special ballpoint pen, or painting. Provided that greasy finger marks are kept off the surface, such direct preparation can be almost as easy and trouble-free as the preparation of hectograph masters. At the other end of the scale, plates for the highest quality work — including full four-colour printing — can be made using conventional photo-litho methods similar to those used by commercial printing organisations. Basically this involves first making a film negative of the material to be printed, and transferring the image to a light-sensitive lithographic plate which is then developed. It is a slow and expensive process however, and unless exceptionally high quality is essential, a number of quicker and cheaper photocopy methods can be used.

Printing the Copies

Small offset lithographic printing is based on the same principle as ordinary offset lithographic printing, and is carried out using machines like the one shown in Figure 2.12.

Figure 2.12 **A typical modern offset litho printing machine in the Central Printing Services Department at The Robert Gordon University**

The lithographic process involves producing a master plate on which the image area is greasy (so that it repels water but attracts ink) whereas the remainder is kept clear of grease (so that it attracts water). Thus if the plate is first coated with water and then with ink, the water will adhere to the non-image areas only, preventing the ink from adhering to these areas when it is applied; the ink will thus only adhere to the image area. In the offset lithographic process, the ink that adheres to the image area of the master is first transferred to a rubber offset cylinder and hence to the copy paper, so that the paper and master never actually come in direct contact. This prevents the surface of the plate from being damaged by the hard, rough paper. The process is shown schematically in Figure 2.13.

Advantages of small offset litho include its great versatility (it can reproduce images of virtually all types — including photographic images), the high quality of the material produced, and its low running costs, which can make it economical for print runs as low as 30 copies in some cases. The main disadvantages of this system are its high capital cost (for all but the most basic machines) and the fact that it normally has to be run by specialist staff. Thus most organizations who install small offset litho have to centralize the service via a central reprographic unit

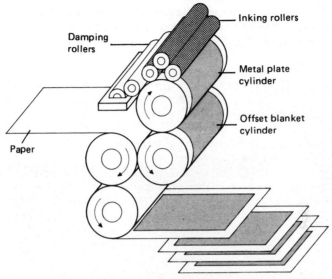

Figure 2.13 **The offset lithographic process**

or similar set-up. This inevitably causes delays when staff require materials, since, unlike (say) a local photocopier or hectograph duplicator, the system is not directly available to them.

Choosing which Method to Use

In some cases a teacher, instructor or trainee who wants to produce multiple copies of handouts or similar materials will have very little choice as to how this can be done, being restricted to whatever reprographic system happens to be available in the institution. In other cases, a variety of systems may well be available, and then it will be necessary to decide which system is most suitable for the particular job he has in mind. Obviously, this choice will depend on a number of factors, including such things as the nature of the material to be copied, the number of copies required, the quality required, whether colour is needed, the urgency with which the material is required, cost constraints, and so on. Thus anyone who wanted to produce (say) 30 copies of a single-sheet handout for use in a lesson due to take place later in the same morning or afternoon would probably have to use a laser printer, a photocopier or a hectograph duplicator, with the final choice depending on availability, personal preference and whether more than one colour was required. Someone wanting to produce 300 copies of a 50-page set of lecture notes for distribution to students at the start of the following term, on the other hand, would probably either have the material typed on stencils and have the sets run off by a technician or member of the clerical staff, or make use of the high-speed photocopying or small offset litho facilities available in a central reprographic unit. He would not, in this case, try to do the job himself on (say) a small local photocopier, because this would not only be highly expensive, but would take an inordinately long time and maybe burn out the machine in the process.

A summary of the respective advantages and disadvantages of the four main reprographic methods available to teachers, instructors and trainers is given in Figure 2.14 and it is hoped that this will be of help to readers faced with making such decisions.

Note on Copyright Restrictions Regarding Multiple Copying of Documents

In Figure 2.14 it is, of course, assumed that the person carrying out or instigating the production of multiple copies has the legal right to do so. If you produced the original material yourself there is generally no problem, since the author of a document automatically holds copyright in respect thereof unless this copyright is vested in or shared with some other person or body under the terms of a contractual or other agreement (eg if the author was paid to write the material for someone else). If you did *not* produce the material yourself, on the other hand, the law of copyright strictly forbids you from making multiple copies — even for educational purposes — without the prior consent of the copyright holder (normally the author or his agent, but sometimes the organiza-tion for which he works). Anyone who breaches this law, by (say) making multiple copies of a chapter of a book for use as a handout to students without being authorized to do so, runs the risk of facing legal action and punitive damages — as does the organization for which he works. Thus before making multiple copies of any material, you should establish whether you are legally entitled to do so. This can be done using the algorithm shown in figure 2.15.

Method	Advantages	Disadvantages
Laser printers	☐ Produces 'camera-ready copy'. ☐ Machines almost silent. ☐ Can be programmed to produce high-quality print in a wide range of fonts, styles, densities and print-sizes. ☐ Makes good masters for subsequent photocopying or offset lithograph printing. ☐ Can produce copy from computer disks. ☐ Machines relatively easy to use. ☐ Expensive machines are relatively quick. ☐ New-generation machines can produce high-quality multicoloured copies.	☐ Fast machines expensive. ☐ Less-expensive machines can be very slow. ☐ Unit costs can be high. ☐ For high quality, printers need to be loaded with software relating to fonts, styles, print densities and print sizes. ☐ Machines need expert servicing and careful handling. ☐ Best limited to the production of final masters for later larger-scale reproduction.
Photocopying	☐ Simple and convenient to use. ☐ Generally directly available to staff. ☐ No special master required — can copy any material. ☐ Produces high-quality copies. ☐ No restrictions on print run. ☐ Collation facilities often available.	☐ Machines expensive ☐ Machines require careful handling and regular maintenance if they are not to break down or produce inferior copies. ☐ Unit costs can be relatively high. ☐ Certain colours do not reproduce on some machines.
Hectograph duplication	☐ Simple and convenient to use. ☐ Generally directly available to staff. ☐ Machines and materials relatively inexpensive. ☐ Can produce multi-colour copies.	☐ Special master required. ☐ Quality of copies comparatively poor. ☐ Limited to small print runs (not more than 200 or so). ☐ Can be messy.
Stencil duplication	☐ Can produce fairly high-quality copies. ☐ Can produce large numbers of copies — up to several thousand. ☐ Stencils can be stored for subsequent re-use. ☐ Low unit cost per copy.	☐ Special master required. ☐ Only suitable for certain types of material. ☐ Extremely messy to use. ☐ Time may be needed for copies to dry after printing.
Small offset litho	☐ Extremely versatile – can produce virtually all types of material. ☐ Can produce extremely high quality copies. ☐ Can produce large numbers of copies (tens of thousands, if necessary) at low unit cost.	☐ Special master required. ☐ Equipment expensive, and normally involves centralized operation.

Figure 2.14
Advantages and disadvantages of different reprographic methods

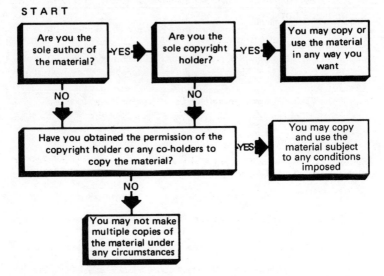

Figure 2.15 **Algorithm for establishing entitlement to make multiple copies of material**

BIBLIOGRAPHY

Anderson, R H (1976) *Selecting and Developing Media for instruction.* Van Nostrand Reinhold, Cincinnati (Chapter 8).

Beavis, R and Weatherley, C (1980) *Worksheets and School Learning.* Scottish Council for Educational Technology, Glasgow.

Bosworth, D P (1991) *Open Learning.* Cassell, London.

Ellington, H I (1987) *How to Design Programmed Learning Materials.* CICED Publications, RGIT, Aberdeen.

Ellington, H I, Addinall, E and Percival, F (1981) *A Handbook of Game Design.* Kogan Page, London/Nichols Publishing Company, New York.

Ellington H I, Addinall, E and Percival, F (1984) *Case Studies in Game Design.* Kogan Page, London/Nichols Publishing Company, New York.

Harrison, N (1991) *How to Design Effective Text-Based Open Learning.* McGraw Hill, London.

Hartley, J (1985) *Designing Instructional Text* (2nd edn), Kogan Page, London/Nichols Publishing Company, New York.

Jeffries, C *et al* (1990) *The A-Z of Open Learning.* National Extension College, Cambridge.

Johnstone, A H and Percival, F (1981) Attention breaks in lectures. *Education in Chemistry,* **13,** 3, pp. 49-50.

Kirkland, G (1978) *Reprography: a Basic Guide.* Jordanhill College of Education, Glasgow.

Lewis, R (1981) *How to Write Self-Study materials.* Council for Educational Technology, London.

Megarry, J (1978) *Programmed Learning: Writing a Programme.* Jordanhill College of Education, Glasgow.

New, P G (1975) *Reprography for Librarians,* Clive Bingley Ltd, London.

Paul, R H (1990) *Open Learning and Open Management.* Kogan Page, London.

Race, P (1989) *The Open Learning Handbook.* Kogan Page, London.

Race, P (1992) *53 Interesting Ways to Write Open Learning Materials.* TES, Bristol.

Rowntree, D (1966) *Basically Branching.* Macdonald, London.

Rowntree, D and Conners, B (eds) (1980) *How to Develop Self-Instructional Teaching. A Self-Instructional Guide to the Writing of Self-Instructional Materials.*

Published Packages from which Specimen Material is Included in Chapter

Alternative Energy Project. Written by H I Ellington and E Addinall. Published by Association for Science Education, Hatfield (1980).

The Nuclear Debate. Written by H I Ellington and E Addinall. Published by Scottish Council for Educational Technology, Glasgow (1984)

Which Material? Written by H I Ellington and E Addinall. Published by Scottish Curriculum Development Service, Dundee Centre (1984).

Teaching and Learning in Higher Education, Series 3, 'Lectures'. Written by P Race. Published by CICED, Aberdeen (1989).

Chapter Three

How to Produce Non-projected Display Materials

INTRODUCTION

In Chapter 1 we saw that the various non-documentary materials that can be displayed to or studied by learners without the need for an optical or electronic projector constitute some of the most basic — and most useful — of all teaching and learning aids. In this chapter, we will carry out a detailed examination of such materials, starting by taking a general look at how they can be used in different instructional situations. After this we will examine the main types of non-projected materials in turn, looking first at chalkboard and markerboard displays, then at 'adhesive' displays (feltboards, hook-and-loop boards and magnetic boards), then at charts, posters and other flat display materials and finally at three-dimensional display materials (mobiles, models, and so on). In each case, we will identify the main uses of the materials and show how they can be produced 'in-house' by teachers, instructors and trainers.

HOW NON-PROJECTED DISPLAY MATERIALS CAN BE USED IN DIFFERENT TEACHING/LEARNING SITUATIONS

Like printed and duplicated materials, non-projected display materials can be used in a wide range of instructional situations, covering all three of the basic classes identified in Chapter 1. Let us now examine their potential role in each.

Mass Instruction

This is probably where non-projected display materials are capable of making their most important contribution. Indeed, many of the materials that fall into the category are specifically designed for use as visual aids during expository teaching of one form or another. In such teaching their role is, of course, entirely supportive. It must be added, however, that with mass instruction now being extended to group sizes of several hundred, even large non-projected display resources have relatively limited usefulness.

Individualized Instruction

Although some types of non-projected display materials are of little or no use in individualized instruction, others are capable of playing an extremely useful role. Models, for example, can be used in a wide range of self-instructional situations, as can various types of realia (eg geological and biological specimens). In most cases, such materials play a key role in the instruction process by providing the actual objects of study.

Group Learning

Many non-projected display materials can also play a useful supportive role in group-learning situations, eg by providing visual aids during presentation/discussion-type activities such as seminars and tutorials or providing the subject matter for small-group exercises.

All these various uses of non-projected display materials will be discussed in greater detail in the sections that deal with specific types of materials.

CHALKBOARD AND MARKERBOARD DISPLAYS

The first group of non-projected display media that we will consider are the various dark-coloured surfaces on which displays can be written or drawn using chalk (*chalkboards*) and the various light-coloured surfaces on which similar displays can be produced using suitable markers, pens or crayons (*markerboards*). Let us now look at these in turn.

Chalkboards

The chalkboard (or blackboard as it was called until it was realized that such boards were very seldom black any longer) is so much a part of classrooms that it has become a symbol for education itself. Indeed, until the development of the overhead projector during the 1940s and its more recent spread into virtually every classroom and lecture theatre, the chalkboard was probably the most important of all instructional aids (apart from the printed page). Even today such boards are still a standard fixture in virtually all teaching and training environments, although their use is by no means as automatic and universal as was the case in the past.

The Different Types of Chalkboard

Until the 1950s, practically all chalkboards were still black, consisting of large sheets of wood covered with matt black paint. Since then, most such boards have been replaced by other types of surface, such as cloth, various forms of plastic and other synthetic materials. In addition, most chalkboards are now coloured, the most common colour being green and other widely used colours being blue and brown. This is because coloured boards have been found to produce less glare and reflection, are less prone to 'ghosting' (marks left when the chalk is rubbed out), and, in general, provide greater legibility than the traditional 'blackboard'.

Another comparatively recent development in the evolution of the chalkboard has been the appearance of the *magnetic chalkboard* — a surface made of ferro-magnetic material covered with a thin layer of dark-coloured vitreous particles. This can be used in the same ways as magnetic markerboards, and will be discussed later in the chapter.

How Chalkboard Should (And Should Not) Be Used

Traditionally, the chalkboard was used in virtually every situation where textual, mathematical or graphical material had to be displayed to a class or small group — and, in some establishments, is still so used. Certainly it is a versatile, inexpensive and useful teaching aid, and, if a teacher, instructor or trainer so wishes, can be used for such straightforward expository purposes as:

- The systematic display of virtually the entire subject matter of a lecture or taught lesson to a class.

- The display of a 'skeleton guide' to such a lecture or lesson, eg in the form of a set of section and sub-section headings.

- The display of specific items (maps, diagrams, tables, etc) during such a lecture or lesson.

We would, however, seriously suggest that all these functions can be fulfilled just as effectively — and a great deal more conveniently — by use of the overhead projector. What, for example, is the point of laboriously copying a lengthy mathematical proof, scientific derivation or complicated map or diagram on to a chalkboard, only to have to rub it out after it has been used once? Would it not be much more sensible to produce a permanent copy of the material in overhead transparency form, so that it can be used again and again?

It is now generally acknowledged that the most appropriate — and most effective — way of using the chalkboard in the modern classroom is as a means of displaying impromptu material (words, equations, diagrams, etc that have become necessary due to an unexpected turn in a lesson) and material which is developed in the course of the lesson by interaction with the class (ideas produced by buzz groups, experimental results, solutions to tutorial exercises, and so on). Thus, it is still strongly advisable that teachers, instructors and trainers should take the trouble to become reasonably proficient in the use of the chalkboard so that they can cope effectively with such 'off-the-cuff' requirements.

How to Develop Basic Chalkboard Skills

Despite its long tradition of use, many teachers and trainers find the chalkboard a difficult medium to handle — often simply because they have never taken the trouble to master the necessary basic techniques. Many people, for example, hold the chalk the wrong way — holding it like a pen or pencil rather than in the correct way shown in Figure 3.1 below. As can be seen, the chalk should be held between the fingers and thumb, with the non-writing end pointing in towards the palm of the hand, and should be presented to the board at a fairly low angle.

Also, many people make the mistake of trying to use the fingers to write with the chalk, as they would with a pen or pencil. The correct technique is to use the fingers and thumb simply as a chuck to hold the chalk, and to use the entire hand to make the writing stroke, executing the stroke by movements of the shoulder joint and (to a lesser extent) by wrist, elbow and body movements. Some other useful points of technique are given below.

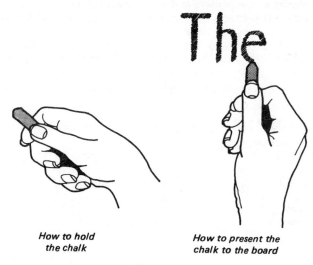

**How to hold
the chalk**

**How to present the
chalk to the board**

Figure 3.1

- Rotate the chalk slightly as you make each stroke, and change to a new facet of the chalk face for each new stroke or word (this helps to keep the lines of uniform thickness).

- Always try to place the chalk length in line with the stroke being drawn, so that the chalk is pulled across the board (note that this may necessitate the wrist being placed in an awkward position).

- Stand in such a position that you can reach the board easily with the elbow of your writing arm only slightly bent.

- Use body sway and bending of the knees to reach different parts of the board during a stroke, keeping a balanced stance throughout.

- Try to develop a clear writing or printing style that can be read without difficulty from the back of the classroom in which you are working; check this by going to the back of the room yourself.

- Leave generous spaces between words — this greatly increases legibility.

- Always try to achieve a neat, systematic lay-out, with level, uniformly spaced lines of writing; if necessary, draw light guidelines on the board using a chalkboard ruler or T-square.

The subject of basic chalkboard technique is dealt with in much greater length in the book by Pringle that is listed in the Bibliography, and interested readers are referred to this. The book by Mugglestone also provides useful information on how to use the chalkboard effectively.

Some Useful Methods of Producing Graphic Displays

For the benefit of those who still like to use the chalkboard to display graphic material such as maps and diagrams, let us now examine some of the 'tricks of the trade' that can be used to produce such displays. Some people, of course, have no need to resort to such methods, since they possess the artistic and graphic skills to produce all such material freehand, but most of us need all the help we can get.

The grid method: This is one of the simplest methods of producing an enlarged version of graphic material, whether on a chalkboard, markerboard, or any other medium. It involves covering the material to be copied with a pattern of square grid lines, either by drawing the lines on the material itself or by covering it with a transparent sheet on which the grid has been drawn. (We recommend the latter method since the grid, once prepared, is available for future use.) If a similar grid, scaled up by whatever factor is required, is now lightly drawn on to the surface on which the enlarged copy is to be made (or, even better, projected on to the surface using an opaque or overhead projector), the resulting grid lines will probably enable even the least talented of artists to produce a reasonable copy of the original material.

The projection method: This is another standard technique that can be used to produce enlarged versions of graphic or photographic materials on surfaces of all types. It involves projecting a suitably enlarged image outline and whatever other detail one wishes to reproduce. Note that the method can be used with both transparent and opaque originals by using the appropriate type of projector — a slide projector for photographic slides, a filmstrip projector for filmstrip frames, an overhead projector for large transparencies and an art-aid or opaque projector for photographic prints and other opaque items. Also note that an ordinary overhead projector can be used as a makeshift opaque projector by placing the material to be copied on the platen, image side upwards, and illuminating the material from above using a portable lamp of some sort (see Figure 3.3).

The template method: Another technique that can be used to draw outline figures on both chalkboards and marker boards is the template method. This is particularly useful in cases where standard shapes (eg maps, scientific apparatus, geometrical figures or dress patterns) have to be drawn repeatedly with some accuracy. It involves preparing a suitable template of the shape using some suitable stiff, lightweight material such as thin sheet metal, thick card, plywood or rigid plastic, a template that can then be placed on the board and traced round whenever the shape has to be drawn. Templates can be produced from smaller originals by drawing them on a sheet of the chosen material using the projection method described above. It is, incidentally, a good idea to fit such templates with a handle of some sort to make it easier to hold them against the board while in use.

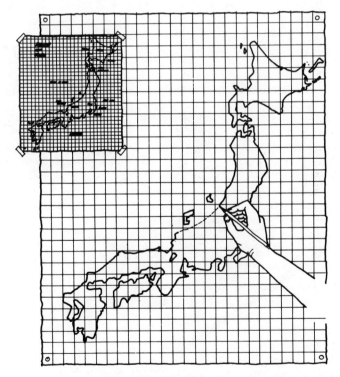

Figure 3.2 **The grid method of producing enlarged copies of graphic material**

The pounce pattern method: This is another method that can be used to reproduce standard shapes which have to be drawn repeatedly and with accuracy. It involves first producing a line drawing of the required shape on a large sheet of paper or thin card, and then punching small holes along the lines at regular intervals (between ¼ inch and 1 inch apart, depending on the detail required). With paper, this can be done using a special tool fitted with a spiked wheel, which is run along the lines when the paper is placed on a suitable surface (eg a sheet of soft wood). With card, the holes can be punched out using a leather worker's punch or similar device. If the completed pounce pattern is now placed flat against the surface of the chalkboard, held in position using strips of adhesive tape, and the lines to be drawn lightly tapped with the face of a dusty chalkboard eraser, the outline of the shape will be transferred on to the board in the form of lines of dots. These can then be joined up to produce the required figure. By preparing such pounce patterns before lessons, it is possible to impress classes considerably by the ease and skill with which you apparently draw complicated diagrams freehand.

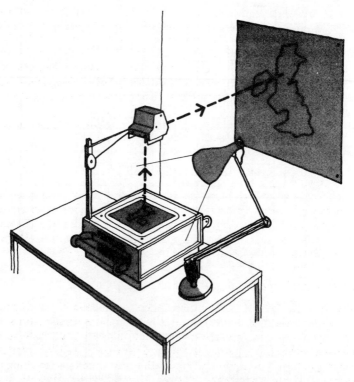

Figure 3.3 **Using an overhead projector and desk lamp to produce an enlarged projection of an image on an opaque medium**

The above techniques are described in more detail in the books by Wittich and Schuller and by Minor and Frye listed in the Bibliography.

Markerboards

These boards, which are also known as *whiteboards*, are sometimes fitted in teaching rooms instead of conventional chalkboards. They consist of large sheets of white or light-coloured plastic material with a surface texture suitable for writing or drawing on using felt pens, markers or crayons, and can be used in much the same way as chalkboards. They have, however, a number of advantages over the latter. There is, first of all, none of the mess that always results when chalk — even the 'dust-less' variety — is used. Second, a much wider range of colours and tone strengths can be used, and the resulting display is invariably sharper, better defined and clearer than is possible using chalk. Third, a marker-board — unlike a chalkboard — can double up as a projection screen if required.

There is, however, one possible problem that can arise with marker-boards: difficulty in cleaning the surface properly so that 'ghost' marks are not left behind. For this reason, it is strongly advisable to use only the types of marker pens or crayons that are recommended by the manufac-turer of the particular board you are using, and to make sure that you know how the board should be cleaned. In some cases this can be done simply by wiping with a dry or damp cloth, while in others a special cleaning fluid or solvent is required. If this is the case, always make sure that a supply is readily available — together with a suitable cloth or eraser.

The techniques for producing displays on markerboards are basically the same as those just described for chalkboards.

ADHESIVE DISPLAYS

The second major class of non-projected display materials that we will look at are those where the display is stuck to the display surface in some way (other than by drawing pins or glue). The most important members of the class are *feltboard* displays, *hook-and-loop board* displays and *magnetic board* displays, which will now be examined in turn.

Feltboard Displays

The *feltboard* (which is also known as the *flannel-board* or *flannel-graph*) relies on the fact that shapes cut out of felt, flannel or similar fabrics will adhere to display surfaces covered with like material. Such systems can be used both to create permanent or semi-permanent wall-mounted dis-plays, but their most important application is in situations requiring the movement or rearrangement of pieces. They are, for example, ideal for displaying things like table settings, demonstrating changes in plant layouts or corporate structures, showing how words can be joined to-gether to form phrases and sentences, and illustrating basic arithmetical and geometrical concepts. One such application (demonstration that the area of a triangle is equal to half the product of the length of its base and its height) is shown in Figure 3.4. As can be seen, it simply involves displaying a felt triangle that is composed of three pieces (Figure 3.4(a)) and then moving the two smaller pieces to the positions shown in Figure 3.4 (b).

Making Your Own Feltboard

Although ready-made feltboards can be bought from educational suppliers, it is a very simple matter to make your own. All you need is a large sheet of felt or flannel, which can either be pinned to a convenient wall or bulletin board or stuck to a suitably-sized sheet of plywood or hardboard, thus producing a portable display surface that can be set up on an easel wherever it is required.

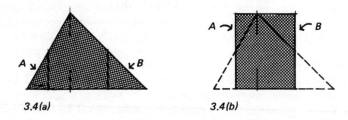

3.4(a)   *3.4(b)*

Figure 3.4 **Use of a feltboard to show that the area of a triangle** = ½ **base × height**

Producing Feltboard Display Materials

Feltboard materials, designed for use in a wide range of instructional situations, are available commercially but it is again a very simple matter to create your own. The required shapes (like the ones shown in Figure 3.4) can simply be cut from any convenient sheet of felt or flannel (of a different colour from the display surface) and can be made even more cheaply from felt-embossed wallpaper. If you are planning to make regular use of home-produced feltboard displays, purchase of a roll of this wallpaper will provide you with an almost unlimited supply of the necessary raw materials at very low cost – especially if you can get hold of an 'end-of-line' bargain roll. Use of embossed wallpaper for the preparation of feltboard display materials has the added advantage of providing a light surface on which words or letters can be written, images drawn, etc. If you want to produce more rigid display materials, these can be cut from thin card and then backed with felt or embossed wallpaper in order to make them stick to the feltboard.

Hook-And-Loop Board Displays

The *hook-and-loop-board* (which is also known as a *teazle board* or *teazle graph*) works on the same basic principle as the feltboard. In this case, however, the display materials are backed with special fabric (such as velcro) which incorporates large numbers of tiny hooks, while the display surface is covered with material incorporating tiny loops with which the hooks can engage. This creates a much stronger bond than that which is formed between two pieces of felt, thus allowing much heavier display materials to be attached to the surface of a hook-and-loop board. Such boards can be used for much the same purposes as feltboards, but only offer a real advantage over the latter in situations where the material being displayed is heavy — demonstrating the components of an actual piece of equipment, for example, or displaying items of realia as shown in Figure 3.5.

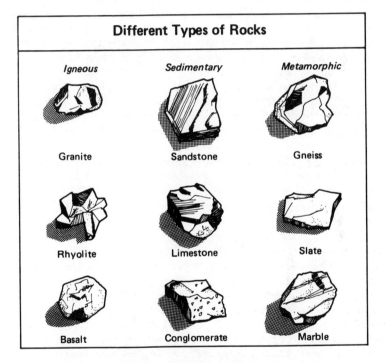

Figure 3.5 **Use of a hook-and-loop board to display rock samples which have had strips of hook tape cemented to flat surfaces filed or ground on their backs**

Making Your Own Display Board

Hook-and-loop display boards can be made in exactly the same way as feltboards, ie by getting hold of a suitable piece of fabric (available from educational supply companies) and either pinning this to a convenient wall or bulletin board or producing a portable board by sticking or pinning it to a piece of plywood or hardboard.

Producing Display Materials

Objects of virtually any type can be prepared for use in hook-and-loop displays by attaching suitable strips or pads of hook tape to their backs. Such tapes are available in a number of forms, including dry adhesive-backed, pressure-sensitive adhesive-backed, solvent-activated adhesive-backed, and non adhesive-backed.

Magnetic Boards

Even more useful and versatile than feltboards and hook-and-loop boards are the various forms of *magnetic board*. These come in two main forms — the *magnetic chalkboards* that were described on page 92 and *magnetic markerboards* (sheets of ferro-magnetic material with specially painted light surfaces on which material can be written or drawn using suitable markers or pens). Both types of board enable display items made of (or backed with) magnetic material to be stuck to and moved about on their surfaces, and both enable this movable display to be supplemented by writing or drawing on the board. Thus, magnetic boards can be used to produce highly sophisticated displays that enable movement and change in systems to be clearly demonstrated to a class or small group. They are, for example, the ideal medium for demonstrating military tactics or carrying out sports coaching. For coaching a basketball or football team, for example, the field of play can be painted permanently on the board, with the individual players being identified by clearly marked magnetic discs that can be rearranged and moved about as and when required and the various movements, run patterns, etc being shown by adding suitable arrows or lines using chalk or marker pen.

Figure 3.6 **Use of a magnetic board in sports coaching**

Making Your Own Magnetic Board

Both magnetic chalkboards and magnetic markerboards can be made using readily available materials and, although such boards will probably not prove as satisfactory as commercially purchased versions, they can be used to fulfil exactly the same basic functions. In both cases, the basic board should be made from a thin sheet of ferro-magnetic material such as mild steel, which should preferably be mounted on a thicker sheet of wood or chipboard in order to give it the required rigidity. To produce a magnetic chalkboard, the surface should be painted with a suitable dark-coloured matt paint, while to produce a magnetic marker board, a suitable light-coloured silk or gloss paint should be used.

Producing Magnetic Display Materials

There are two main ways of producing such materials. The first is to make them out of special magnetic rubber, which is available in sheet and strip form. The second is to make them out of non-magnetic material such as stiff card and then to stick strips of magnetic rubber or small magnets to their backs, so that they will adhere to the board. A wide range of ready-made materials such as magnetic letters and numbers that can be used to form displays is also available from educational suppliers.

CHARTS, POSTERS AND SIMILAR FLAT DISPLAY MATERIALS

The various forms of *chart*, *poster* and other flat pictorial display materials have always been among the most useful and versatile visual aids at the disposal of teachers and instructors of all types. Let us now look in turn at some of the more important varieties.

Flipcharts

These constitute a simple and, when used in an appropriate context, highly effective method of displaying information to a class or small group. Such charts consist of a number of large sheets of paper, fixed to a support bar, easel or display board by clamping or pinning them along their top edges so that they can be flipped backwards or forwards as required.

Such charts can be used in two basic ways. First, they can be used to display a succession of pre-prepared sheets, which can be shown in the required order either by flipping them into view from the back of the suspension system one by one or by revealing each successive sheet by flipping the previous one over the back of the suspension system out of the way. If the former method is to be used, the sheets should be clamped to the display system in reverse order of showing, ie with the one to be shown last uppermost; with the latter method, the sheets should be clamped to the display system in the correct order of showing, ie with the one to be shown first uppermost. When preparing such flipchart sequences, it is best to keep the message or information on each sheet fairly simple, since this increases their impact. Also, it is obviously essential to make sure that they can be read or seen clearly by all the members of the class or group; again you should check this by inspecting them from the back of the class or the furthest distance from which they have to be viewed.

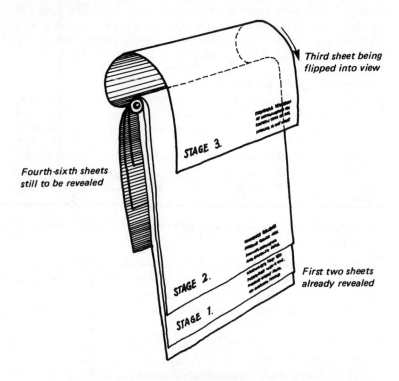

Figure 3.7 **Use of a set of pre-prepared flipcharts to show the various stages of a six-stage process by progressively building up the complete process**

The other main way in which flipcharts can be used is by providing an instantly renewable series of blank surfaces on which material can be jotted down on an impromptu basis in the course of a lesson, group discussion or other activity. They can, for example, be used to list replies from class members to questions or ideas generated by buzz groups.

When a series of flipcharts is produced arising from discussions and questions, it is often useful to arrange that they can continue to be visible. This can be done by using 'Blutack' or adhesive tape to stick completed charts onto doors, walls, window frames and other surfaces of the room. With flipchart pads, there are usually two holes punched

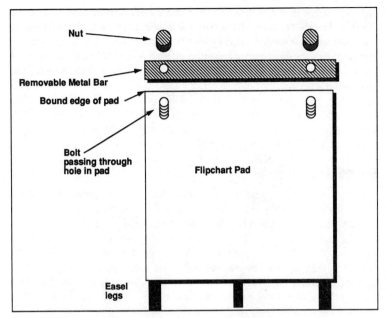

Figure 3.8 **Removing the metal bar, so that flipchart sheets can be
detached neatly as required**

Some Discussion Questions

- *Who participated most?*

- *Who participated least?*

- *Which actions helped your team to achieve
  its task?*

- *What actions hindered the team in
  accomplishing its task?*

- *What form(s) did leadership take in your
  team?*

- *What feelings did you experience as the task
  progressed?*

- *What suggestions would you make to
  improve team performance?*

- *How can you apply what you've learned
  from this activity?*

Figure 3.9 **Example of a prepared flipchart, to provide an agenda for
discussions after some group work**

near the top of the chart that are then placed over protruding bolts built into the flipchart easel. A bar is then screwed on, to retain the flipchart pad securely. However, when you intend to paste up flipchart sheets round the room, it is useful to remove the bar, so that you can tear off sheets neatly at the very top of each sheet, leaving the holes intact. This means that if you later wish to bring back a particular chart for detailed discussion, you can replace it over the bolts on the easel. (If the metal bar is left in place, and flipcharts are simply torn off, the holes will be lost, and a ragged edge will be obtained at the top of the charts, giving an impression of untidiness or unprofessionalism).

Electronic Flipcharts

A recent advance has been the introduction of 'electronic' flipcharts, which are similar to a 'roller' whiteboard, but which can give reduced-size photocopies of what has been written or drawn on them. Normal markerboard pens of various colours can be used on these (but make sure you do not use 'permanent' marker pens!). The contents of the electronic flipchart can be erased with a soft cloth. Normally, an electric motor drives the 'flipchart' surface, so that at the touch of a button you can continue to write at a comfortable height. The contents of the board can be extended till both sides are used. The 'new technology' aspect is that these flipcharts can be used to produce *reduced* paper copies of the contents. This is normally done when one or both sides of the chart are full, and the copy is then produced from a paper roll. The copies can then be photocopied with a normal photocopier so that everyone present can be given a copy of exactly what was on the flipchart. This can be far faster than expecting students to write down the contents of flipcharts. At present, electronic flipcharts are found mainly in conference centres and training institutions – it is unlikely that they will become commonplace in teaching rooms at large. If you are fortunate enough to have one available to you, you will find it a very useful device. We suggest, however, that before using an electronic flipchart for the first time, you practise with it for a while, so that you know exactly how to make best use of it – for example, you may find that some colours copy better than others, and that your writing needs to be of a reasonable size (and quality) for the copies to look good.

Charts and Wallcharts

The various forms of *chart* and *wallchart* have always been popular in all sectors of education and training because of their versatility and ease of use and, even with the spread of more sophisticated visual aids such as slides, films and videos, are still capable of playing an important role in such work. Although the distinction between charts and wallcharts is sometimes a bit blurred, the former term is generally taken to refer to displays on large sheets of paper or cloth that are designed to be shown to a class or group in the course of a lesson. The latter term is used to describe similar displays that are pinned to a wall or bulletin board and are mainly intended for casual study outside the context of a formal lesson.

Another distinction between the two groups is that the material on charts is usually larger and easier to see or read than that on wallcharts, since the former has to be clearly distinguishable or legible at a distance whereas the latter can be studied at close quarters. Apart from this, however, the principles that underlie the design of the two are basically the same.

One of the great advantages of both charts and wallcharts is that they can be made fairly large, and can thus contain far more complicated and more detailed displays than it would be possible to incorporate on (say) an overhead transparency or a 35mm slide. They can, for example, be used to show highly detailed maps (one of their most important and most universal uses) and detailed structural, taxonomic, and organizational diagrams of all types.

How to Produce Your Own Charts and Wallcharts

Although a wide range of charts and wallcharts is available commercially or as good-will 'giveaways' from industrial and other organizations, it is still often necessary to make one's own in order to cover a given topic in a specific way — particularly if the topic to be taught is of a specialized or unusual nature. Before embarking on the task of making up a chart or wallchart, however, it is always worthwhile investigating whether one that could be used for the job you have in mind is already available, either within your own organization or from an external source (from a central resources centre, an educational supplier, an industrial or other organization, and so on); if it is, you could save yourself a great deal of time and effort.

If you do decide to go ahead with the production of your chart, you should bear the following basic principles in mind:

■ Make the chart and all items on it big enough to be seen clearly by the entire class or group that you will be using it with or, in the case of a wallchart, in the context within which it is to be used.

■ Aim for maximum clarity, using a layout and printing technique that make the 'message' that you are trying to get across perfectly clear.

■ Do not make the chart unnecessarily complicated, especially with a chart designed for display to a class during a lesson; too much detail may well lead to loss of clarity and/or confusion.

■ Try to make the chart visually attractive, using colour if at all possible.

Some useful standard formats that can be used as the basis of charts are shown overleaf.

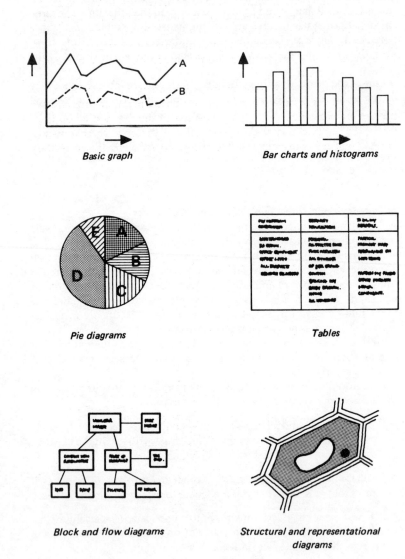

Basic graph

Bar charts and histograms

Pie diagrams

Tables

Block and flow diagrams

Structural and representational diagrams

Figure 3.10 **Some standard formats that can be used in charts**

Producing the Graphic Material

In many cases, the main graphic content of a chart or wallchart can be produced using simple drawing aids such as a ruler, T-square and compasses. In some cases, however, it may be necessary to reproduce a complicated drawing or schematic diagram, often from a smaller original contained in a book or magazine. In such cases, two of the techniques suggested earlier for producing similar drawings on chalkboards and markerboards — the grid method and the projection method (page 94) should prove useful.

If the original drawing is larger than the version that you want to produce, however, a variation of the projection method known as *reverse projection* may be employed. This makes use of the fact that all optical systems are reversible, so that a system such as the lens of an overhead projector which is normally used to throw an enlarged image of the

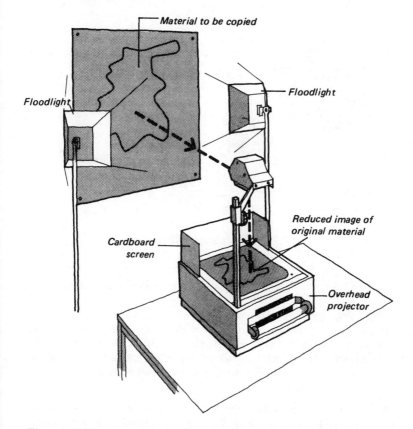

Figure 3.11 **The reverse projection technique for producing reduced images of graphic material**

material on its platen on to a screen, can also be used to produce a reduced image of a poster, chart, etc on the surface of the platen. This technique, which may have to be carried out in a partially darkened room, involves illuminating the material to be copied with floodlights and copying the resulting reduced image behind a suitable shield. The set-up is shown in Figure 3.11.

It is becoming increasingly attractive to use desktop publishing systems to produce graphic display materials. For example, with Macintosh computers, there is a range of graphic packages available, including MacDraw, and PowerPoint, and there are libraries of graphic materials in software such as HyperCard. With modern laser printers, it is possible to print out large copies of diagrams, charts, pictures and so on, after editing them on screen as desired. The copies can then be pasted onto large sheets for display. Figure 3.12 shows a simple illustration adapted from a HyperCard file, to use as part of a graphic display about a postgraduate certificate programme at the University of Glamorgan.

Figure 3.12 **Part of a computer-generated graphics display**

Producing Lettering on Charts

If you possess the necessary graphic skills, it is possible to produce perfectly clear and acceptable lettering on charts by freehand use of appropriate pens or markers. Most people find this difficult, however, and prefer to use one of the many lettering aids that are available. These include the following:

- *Instant lettering*, in the form of dry transfer letters on plastic sheets that can be transferred to the work by rubbing with a burnisher, rounded pencil point or ball point pen. This produces high-quality results if used properly, but is expensive and time-consuming.

- *Stencils*, usually in the form of transparent plastic strips carrying the complete alphabet in a given style and size. These can produce reasonably good results, but not of the quality of transfer lettering or some of the other methods described below.

- *Template lettering guides;* such systems (of which the best known is manufactured by Leroy) make use of a special pen fitted with a tracing pin that is moved round the shapes of the letters in the guide. They can produce better results than stencils, and are also quicker; they are, however, more expensive.

- *Lettering machines*, which operate on the 'Dymo' principle and can be used to print lines of lettering on special adhesive ribbon; the ribbon can then be cut into sections, and laid out in the required way. These can also produce very good results, but are again comparatively expensive to use.

- *Phototypesetting*: use of a word processor-like device to compose text, which is produced in the form of a photographic negative that can be used to produce a positive print of whatever size is required. This again gives excellent results, but the equipment is expensive.

- *Desktop publishing*: use of desktop publishing techniques to generate text in the required form, the final copy being produced using a laser printer.

Further information about the first five of these techniques can be found in *Techniques for Producing Visual Instructional Media* (see Bibliography).

Adding Colour to Charts
This can be done by a wide range of methods, some of the most useful of which are outlined below.

- Poster paint, applied with a brush: the standard method of producing bold colours on a poster or chart.

- Water colour paint: useful for more subtle colours, or for producing subdued washes of colour.

- Coloured adhesive paper: this is available in a wide range of colours; if cut to the shape required, it can produce a sharpness and finish that is difficult to achieve using paint; it is also relatively cheap.

- Coloured transfer films: these can be used in the same way as adhesive paper, but are much more expensive.

Using Ready-Made Material and Photographic Prints
In many cases, it is possible to make use of ready-made material such as photographs or diagrams from magazines in the preparation of charts and wallcharts. This can not only save a great deal of time, but can also produce excellent results. Specially prepared photographic prints can also prove useful on occasions, especially on wallcharts and other permanent or semi-permanent displays.

Posters

These are similar in many ways to charts, but are usually smaller, simpler and bolder in content and style. Their main uses in the classroom are as a means of providing decoration, atmosphere and motivation, although they can also be used to make or remind learners of key points.

Producing Your Own Posters

As with charts and wallcharts, ready-made posters are available from a large number of sources — very often free of charge. Nevertheless there are occasions when it is necessary to produce 'home-made' posters for specific purposes. When doing so, you should bear the following points in mind.

- To attract attention a poster should be dramatic, with any prominent or central feature(s) standing out sharply.

- Having caught the viewer's attention, the poster should get across its message clearly and quickly; this message should therefore be a simple one, capable of being taken in at a glance.

- A poster should also be visually attractive, even though its subject matter may be anything but pleasant (warnings about health hazards, the dangers of war, etc).

Apart from these points, the techniques for producing posters are basically the same as those described above for producing charts and wallcharts.

THREE-DIMENSIONAL DISPLAY MATERIALS

The final group of non-projected display materials that we will look at differ from those described so far in that they are all three-dimensional. The group includes four basic types of materials — *mobiles, models, dioramas* and *realia* — which will now be described in turn.

Mobiles

A *mobile* is, in essence, a three-dimensional wallchart in which the individual components can move about. Instead of displaying a related system of pictures, words, etc on the flat surface of a wall, they are drawn on card, cut out and hung independently from the roof or a suitable beam using fine threads. The resulting display, which turns and changes shape as it is affected by random air currents, acquires a vitality which can never be produced in a flat display of the same material. A typical mobile, displaying the useful products that are obtained from farm animals, is shown in Figure 3.14.

Figure 3.13 (a) **A display board being prepared for an exhibition on language teaching**

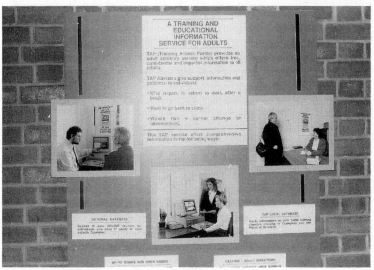

(b) **Part of a display board for a training exhibition**

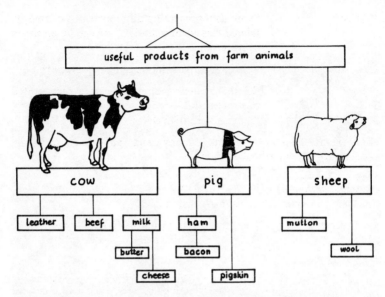

Figure 3.14 **A typical mobile, showing the products from farm animals**

Such mobiles can be suspended in a corner of a classroom, where they will not get in people's way, but will still be clearly visible to the pupils. They are particularly suitable for use with younger pupils, who are generally fascinated by the continuous movements that take place in such displays, which helps to fix the information that the mobiles carry in the children's minds.

Mobiles can be used in virtually any situation where pupils have to acquire and consolidate a set of related facts, and where a wallchart would normally be used to reinforce this material. Some specific subjects where they might prove useful include:

Basic vocabulary: Here, words can be grouped by sound, meaning, structure, etc, and mobiles constructed to illustrate whichever set of relationships is to be demonstrated. Word cards are, in fact, the simplest type of components from which mobiles can be created.

Geography: A country's exports can be arranged in related groups (minerals, agricultural products, industrial products, etc).

Biology: Related species, parts of the body, etc can be arranged in groups.

Chemistry: Related groups of elements and compounds can be displayed.

Physics:	Symbols representing different forms of energy, related classes of materials, etc can be arranged in patterns.
Home economics:	Related groups of foods can be displayed.
History:	Related sequences of events can be represented pictorially and arranged in the correct pattern, together with their dates.

No doubt most readers can think of many more applications, including some in their own particular fields.

How to Create a Mobile

Producing a mobile involves three basic stages:

1. *Conceptual design*: This involves choosing the basic theme for the mobile, deciding what items to include and establishing the patterns that you want to illustrate.

2. *Production of components*: This involves designing and producing the individual components, which may be simple word cards, cut-out models, symbols or even items of realia (which can make effective mobiles).

3. *Assembly and mounting*: This is the most difficult part, and is best done by first assembling the simplest groups of items, then combinations of such groups, and so on until a balanced, freely moving display is achieved. At each stage, the correct position for suspension should be determined by trial and error. The final display should be hung from a hook or drawing pin *firmly* fixed into the ceiling, or from a wooden rod fixed across a corner of the room at a suitable height (such a rod can be used as a permanent suspension system for mobiles).

Models

Models (ie recognisable three-dimensional representations of real things or abstract systems) can play a useful role in a wide range of instructional situations. They are, however, particularly useful in three specific roles, namely as visual support materials in mass instruction, as objects for study or manipulation in individualized learning, and as construction projects for individuals, small groups or even entire classes. When using models in the first of these roles, however, it should be remembered that even the best three-dimensional model invariably appears two-dimensional except to those who are very close, so it is usually worthwhile getting the learners to gather round the model when its salient features are being demonstrated; unless you do this, you could probably achieve the same objectives in most cases by using a two-dimensional representation such as a slide or OHP transparency.

Some specific applications of models are listed below:

- They can be used to reduce very large objects and enlarge very small objects to a size that can be conveniently observed and handled.

- They can be used to demonstrate the interior structures of objects or systems with a clarity that is often not possible with two-dimensional representations (eg the crystal models shown in Figure 3.15).

- They can be used to demonstrate movement – another feature that it is often difficult to show adequately using two-dimensional display systems.

- They can be used to represent a highly complex situation or process in a simplified way that can easily be understood by learners. This can be done by concentrating only on essential features, eliminating all the complex and often confusing details that are so often present in real-life systems.

Making Your Own Models

The range of methods available for making models for instructional purpose is enormous, but readers may find some of the following standard techniques useful.

- Use of commercially available kits of parts, such as the ball-and-spring systems that are used to make models of molecules and the various types of tube-and-spigot systems that can be used to make models of crystals (as shown in Figure 3.15).

- Use of construction systems such as Meccano and Fisher-Price to make working models.

- Use of inexpensive materials such as cardboard, hardboard, wood and wire to make up static models of all types (models of buildings, geometrical bodies and three-dimensional shapes, and so on).

- Use of materials like modelling clay and plasticine to produce realistic models of animals, anatomical demonstrations, and so on.

- Use of materials like plaster of Paris and papier mâché to produce model landscapes.

Dioramas

These are still display systems that combine a three-dimensional foreground of model buildings, figures, etc with a two-dimensional painted background, thus creating a highly realistic effect. They can be used in the teaching of a wide range of subjects, including:

- History, drama, religious studies (representations of historical or dramatic scenes, battles, etc).

- Geography and geology (representations of towns, landscapes, pre-historic landscapes and scenes, etc).

- Biology and natural history (representations of animals in their natural habitats).

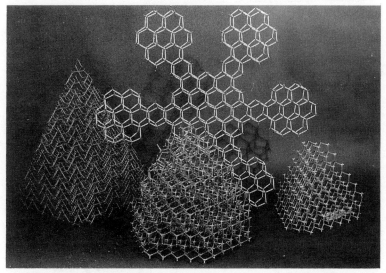

Figure 3.15 **Models of crystals made up from 'do-it-yourself' kits of parts**

Producing a Diorama

Although sophisticated dioramas of the type that are seen in museums can be expensive, time-consuming and difficult to make up, it is perfectly possible for anyone possessing even the most basic of graphic and artistic skills to produce highly effective displays of this type. This can be done as follows.

1. Make a semi-circular base of the required size out of chipboard, hardboard, thick card or some other suitable material.

2. Make up a strip of thin white card of suitable height that is capable of extending all the way round the curved side of the base, draw and/or paint the required background scene on this, and fix it to the base (eg with drawing pins).

3. Build up any landscape required in the foreground using plaster of Paris or papier mâché, and paint this in the required colour(s).

4. Produce or acquire any materials that are required for the foreground and set them in position; such materials can include

model figures (cardboard cut-outs, plasticine models, etc), model buildings, model trees, model ships, tanks or other vehicles, pieces of rock, and any other materials that you feel will enhance the realism of the scene being depicted.

The basic features of a typical diorama representing a religious scene are shown in Figure 3.16.

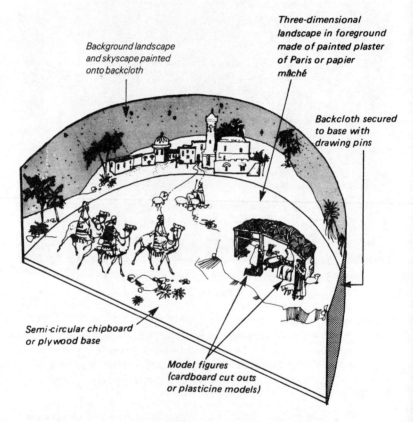

Figure 3.16 **A typical diorama depicting a religious scene**

Like the construction of models, construction of dioramas can provide excellent practical projects for individuals, small groups or even whole classes.

Realia

The supreme instructional 'model' is, in some cases, the article itself, since there are often considerable advantages to be gained from letting learners see or handle the 'real thing' as opposed to a mere representa-

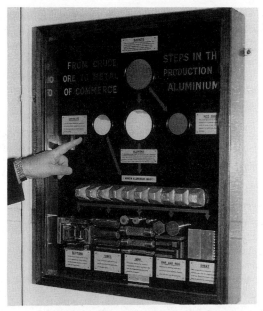

Figure 3.17 (a) **An exhibition of realia showing uses of aluminium and various stages in its manufacture**

(b) **An exhibition showing various types of turbine**

tion thereof. In many cases, of course, this will not be practicable on grounds of availability, accessibility, safety, expense, and so on, but there are many other cases where no such objections apply and, in such cases, serious consideration should be given to the use of realia. Such materials can be used both to support expository teaching and in individualized and group-learning situations, where they can provide learners with the sort of direct experience that can never be obtained through mediated learning, no matter how well contrived. When studying geology, for example, there is simply no satisfactory substitute for actually handling and examining real rock specimens, while the same is true of many aspects of the study of biology, physiology, and similar subjects.

Acquiring Items of Realia for Instructional Purposes

The way in which one sets about getting hold of items of realia for teaching or training purposes will, of course, depend on a number of factors including the nature of the item(s) required, the existence (or otherwise) of convenient local sources of supply, the financial resources one has at one's disposal, and so on. It is, however, often possible to acquire specific items or even whole collections of items at very little cost merely by exercising a little resourcefulness. For example, one of the authors built up a fairly comprehensive collection of geological specimens at practically no cost by a combination of visiting local sources armed with a large hammer and persuading colleagues, relatives and friends who were known to be visiting certain areas to bring back specific items. Other types of material can sometimes be obtained from industrial firms and other organisations, who are often only too pleased to help.

BIBLIOGRAPHY

Anderson, R H (1976) *Selecting and Developing Media for Instruction*. Van Nostrand Reinhold, Cincinnati (Chapter 9).

Cable R (1965) *Audio-Visual Handbook*. University of London Press (Chapter 1).

Dale, E (1969) *Audiovisual Methods in Teaching*. Holt, Rinehart and Winston, New York.

Kemp, J E (1980) *Planning and Producing Audiovisual Materials*. Harper and Row, Publishers Inc, New York.

Minor, E and Frye, H R (1970) *Techniques for Producing Visual Instructional Media*. McGraw Hill, New York.

Mugglestone, P (1980) *Planning and Using the Blackboard*. George Allen & Unwin Ltd, London.

Pringle, B (1966) *Chalk Illustration*. Pergamon Press, Oxford.

Romiszowski, A J (1988) *The Selection and Use of Instructional Media*. Kogan Page, London (Chapter 4).

Wittich, W A and Schuller, C F (1979) *Instructional Technology — Its Nature and Use*. Harper and Row, New York.

Chapter Four

How to Produce Still Projected Display Materials

INTRODUCTION

In this chapter, we will turn our attention to the third major group of still display materials: those that require some sort of optical projector or viewer to enable them to be shown to or studied by learners. This category includes two of the most important and most widely used of all visual aids: *overhead projector transparencies* and *slides*, both of which will be examined in detail.

As usual, we will begin the chapter by taking a general look at how still projected display materials can be used in the three main classes of instructional situations that were identified in Chapter 1. Next, we will look in turn at the two types of still projected materials mentioned above – OHP transparencies and photographic slides. In each case, we will again identify the main uses of the materials and offer guidance on how they may be produced.

HOW STILL PROJECTED DISPLAY MATERIALS CAN BE USED IN DIFFERENT TEACHING/LEARNING SITUATIONS

Like the other two classes of still materials, still projected materials can be used in virtually all types of teaching/learning situation, covering all three of the areas identified in Chapter 1 (mass instruction, individualized instruction and group learning). Let us now look briefly at the role that they are capable of playing in each.

Mass Instruction

This is where still projected materials are capable of making their greatest contribution to the instructional process and is, in fact, the area for which most such materials were specifically developed. Indeed, it is probably true to say that one of the media involved – the overhead projector – is the most useful single display aid available to anyone who wishes to carry out expository instruction of virtually any type. The role of still projected materials in such instruction is, of course, entirely supportive.

Individualized Instruction

Still projected materials – particularly slides and filmstrips – are also capable of playing a key role in individualized instruction, particularly when used in conjunction with audio materials. This role will be examined in greater detail in Chapter 6.

Group Learning

Many still projected display materials are also capable of playing a useful supportive role in many group-learning situations. The overhead projector, for example, is the ideal vehicle for learners to use to present visual material at seminars, group discussions, etc and also during group exercises such as games and simulations. Slides and filmstrips can also be used to provide illustrative material in such exercises.

OVERHEAD PROJECTOR TRANSPARENCIES AND SIMILAR MATERIALS

As has already been stated, the *overhead projector* (OHP) is probably the most versatile and useful visual aid that can be used to support mass-instruction methods. It has already largely replaced the chalkboard as the main teaching aid in many schools, colleges and training establishments, relegating the latter to a secondary role more suited to its characteristics (the display of impromptu material, etc).

The overhead projector has a number of definite advantages over other methods of presenting visual information. A teacher or trainer can, for example, use it in exactly the same way as a chalkboard or markerboard (for writing out notes, working through calculations and proofs, drawing graphic material, and so on) but with the great advantage of always facing the class, and thus being able to maintain eye contact with the learners. Such eye contact, which is, of course, impossible when a teacher or instructor is writing on a chalkboard or markerboard, can play a useful role in expository teaching, serving both as an outward non-verbal communication channel for the teacher and as a means of obtaining feedback from a class on how a lesson is going. Another important advantage over the chalkboard or markerboard is that the OHP can also be used to show pre-prepared material, thus enabling teachers and trainers to build up banks of notes, diagrams, tables, etc that can be used over and over again. In this way teachers can gradually build up a systematic collection of 'instant lectures', covering virtually all the areas that they are called upon to teach. When well planned and designed, such sets of overhead transparencies can also provide all the cues and *aides-mémoire* that are needed during a lesson, so that no conventional teaching notes are required. Other advantages of the overhead projector are that it is clean, quiet, and 'user friendly', requiring no technical skill or knowledge on the part of the operator apart from the ability to change the occasional lamp. Finally, unlike most other projected visuals aids, it

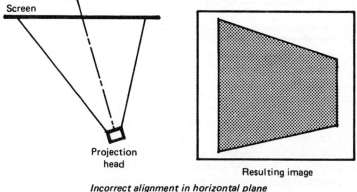

Incorrect alignment in horizontal plane

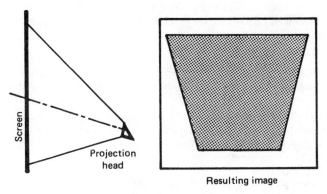

Incorrect alignment in vertical plane

Figure 4.1 **The two causes of keystoning on OHP displays**

requires little or no room darkening, so that students can take notes throughout the lesson.

Some Basic Guidelines on How to Use the OHP Effectively

Despite its near universal use, many teachers, instructors and trainers fail to get the best out of the overhead projector for various reasons. Many of these relate to the use of the machine itself, since even experienced teachers sometimes fail to observe all the following basic rules:

■ Position the projector and screen so that the latter can be seen clearly by *all* the members of the class or group with whom you will be using the machine. In many cases it is best to place the screen in one of the front corners of the room, especially if locating it in a central position would deprive you of access to a fixed chalkboard or markerboard, which you might well find that you want to use in the course of the lesson.

■ Arrange the projector and screen in such a way as to eliminate or minimize the two forms of keystoning shown in Figure 4.1. The first type arises when the axis of projection is not at right angles to the screen in the horizontal plane, and can be eliminated by placing the projector opposite the centre of the screen. The second type arises in cases when the axis of projection is not at right angles to the screen in the vertical plane, usually because the projection head is too low. It can usually be eliminated or made acceptable by tilting the screen forward (if this is possible). In the case of a fixed vertical screen, the only way to solve the problem may well be to raise the level of the overhead projector itself, provided that this can be done without blocking the learners' view of the screen.

■ Adjust the distance from the projector to the screen so that the image fills the full area of the latter when properly in focus; failure to use the entire area of the screen can make it difficult for people at the back of the room to make out details.

■ Make sure that the platen and head lens surfaces are clean and free from dust; dirty or dusty surfaces can reduce image brightness and detract from the clarity and quality of the display. Seasoned users of overhead projectors have been known to carry around a small container of methylated or surgical spirit and a soft cloth for on-the-spot cleaning of the lens and platen.

Sizes and shapes of overhead projectors

Some years ago, nearly all overhead projectors were of the sort described in the section above, with an approximately 'square' platen area. It mattered little whether you were using acetates in a 'landscape' (horizontal) mode, or a 'portrait' (vertical) mode as they all fitted comfortably onto the squarish platen. Nowadays, however, you will often find acetate sheets of A4 size, matching the standard used for paper sheets in printers and photocopiers. Indeed, since many acetates are now produced by such machines, the proportion of A4 acetates has increased dramatically.

If you place an A4 acetate on a traditional 'square platen' projector, it can be distracting to have the vertical edges of the acetate showing on the screen. A simple way of avoiding this is to design a cardboard mask as shown in Figure 4.3. This can also help you not to use the extreme top or bottom of the acetate, which would not both be projected at the same time on such a machine.

Since so many modern acetates are A4 in shape, it is not surprising that a new generation of A4 projectors has appeared. Some of these projectors have rotating heads, so the A4 shape can be presented to the screen either in vertical ('portrait') or horizontal ('landscape') format. To

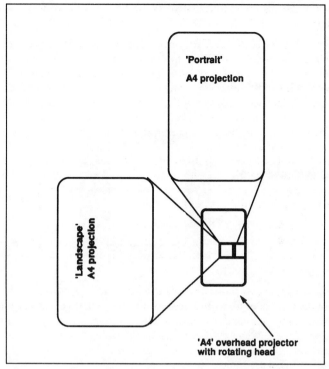

Figure 4.2 **Some overhead projectors are 'A4' in shape, and may have a rotating head, so that either portrait or landscape images can be projected. (The head and projector are both turned through 90° to project the respective images onto the same screen)**

move from one to the other, you need to turn the projector itself through 90° as well as rotating the head (unless you are positioned in a corner of a room, exactly equidistant from two screens – a rare luxury!). Figure 4.2 shows how the images would be formed by turning the projector head alone.

The two formats have their respective advantages: it is usually best to show lists of points in vertical format, while it is often useful to use horizontal format for flowcharts and diagrams. If you find yourself using different projectors in different rooms, and never know which sort of projector you will be using next, you can see how the cardboard mask shown in Figure 4.3 can help you keep to the 'safe' area of acetate shown in Figure 4.4 as you design and produce your acetates. Armed with a mask, and the knowledge that your acetates are compatible with either type of machine, you can be confident that whatever OHP you happen to be provided with, it will appear that all your acetates have been made specially for the projector you are using – adding to the feeling of professionalism of your presentation.

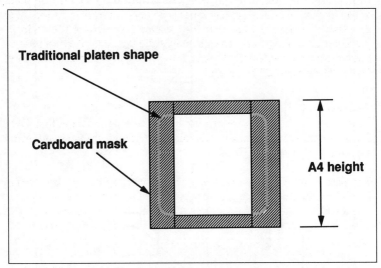

Figure 4.3 **Design of a cardboard mask to ensure that your A4 acetates can be projected neatly on a traditional 'square platen' projector**

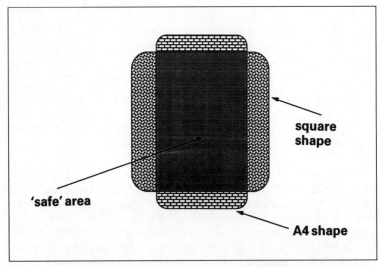

Figure 4.4 **Overhead projectors – and acetate sheets – come in two main sizes. To use either size of sheet with either size of projector necessitates keeping to the 'safe area' as shown above**

How to Design and Produce OHP Software

Even if they succeed in getting everything right from a hardware point of view, many overhead projector users do not give sufficient thought to the design of the software that they use or take sufficient care in its preparation to make sure that it achieves the desired objectives. Let us therefore take a systematic look at how the design and production of OHP software should be tackled.

The Two Basic Forms of OHP Software

First of all, let us take a brief look at the two basic forms that OHP software can take – the continuous roll and the single transparency – and examine their respective uses.

The continuous roll: Some overhead projectors are fitted with a system whereby a long roll of acetate film can be wound across the platen from one spool to another. This enables a virtually endless supply of blank film to be used in the course of a lesson, either for writing out a continuous set of notes or for providing a succession of blank surfaces for the display of specific items of material.

Continuous rolls of this type are best suited to the requirements of those who prefer to create their supportive display material during the actual course of a lesson rather than produce it beforehand. They are, for example, the standard display method that is now used by many mathematics lecturers. When we were students, such lecturers had to write all their materials on a chalkboard, which not only entailed their having to rub old material out at regular intervals in order to make room for new materials, but also covered their hands and clothes with chalk dust. Now, however, thanks to the advent of the overhead projector with its virtually endless roll of acetate film, they can work their way through an entire lecture without having to rub anything out and, furthermore, can do so sitting down without any messy dust. It must be added, however, that many modern overhead projectors, particularly the portable varieties, no longer cater for continuous film rolls.

The single transparency: The predominant form that OHP software can take is the single transparency, whether mounted or unmounted. Some years ago, most OHP acetate sheets were rather thin, and were usually mounted in large cardboard or plastic frames in order to make them easier to handle and prevent them from curling up during use. Now, however, sheets are thicker and less prone to curling up during projection, so that there is no longer the same need to mount them, although some users still prefer to do so. Others simply use them as they are – unmounted – since this makes them much easier to store and carry round, the boxes in which blank sheets are supplied being ideally suited for both purposes.

Although single OHP transparencies can again be used for the creation of display material during the actual course of a lesson, their principal use is in the production of pre-prepared materials. It is with the design and production of such single OHP transparencies that most of the remainder of this section will be concerned.

Designing OHP Transparencies – Basic Principles

Although OHP transparencies can be produced in a wide range of forms, there are two basic principles that should underlie the design of all such materials.

First, *do not try to put too much information on a single transparency.* This is one of the most common mistakes that are made when preparing overhead projector materials. Ideally, you should restrict the content of each transparency to the presentation of a single concept or limited subject area, using a series of such simple transparencies to cover a complicated topic rather than trying to include everything in a single frame. Remember that including too much detail will not only make the material difficult for the viewers (especially those at the back of the room) to see, but will probably also cause conceptual confusion.

Second, *use a clear, systematic layout.* As with all still visual display materials, the way in which the information is presented is often just as important as the intrinsic content in determining whether the material is effective from an instructional point of view. Thus, the material should be laid out clearly and systematically, with any key words or items highlighted in some way (eg by making use of contrasting colours).

Producing the Transparencies

Overhead projector transparencies can be produced by a variety of methods but, whichever method is used, there is one basic rule that overrides all others:

Make sure that all the material will be seen when the transparency is projected. Because most of the blank acetate sheets that are supplied for use with the overhead projector are larger than the effective size of the platen, there is a danger of 'running off the edges' – either vertically or horizontally – unless due care is taken. Also, most overhead projectors 'cut the corners' off the image, so any material in the extreme corners of the transparency may well also fail to be seen. Fortunately, there is a simple and foolproof way of avoiding all such problems. This involves cutting out a square of thick white card of suitable size (roughly 12 inches square) and marking on it the effective limits of the OHP platen using a black marker pen with a reasonably wide point. This should then be used as a work surface and guide during the preparation of all OHP transparencies to be used with the machine in question or machines with the same platen size and shape. The usefulness of such a guide can be further increased by ruling a system of guidelines on its surface using a fine-tipped marker pen. The best system is a grid of ¼ inch squares, produced by ruling horizontal and vertical lines ¼ inch apart. It is helpful to stick two small piece of Blu-tack or similar 'rubber adhesive' to the top

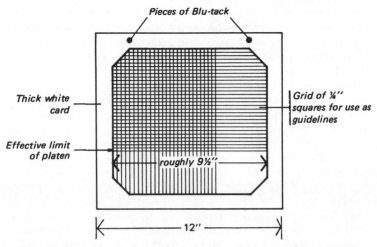

Figure 4.6 **A home-made work surface for the preparation of OHP transparencies**

edge of the card, as shown in Figure 4.6; this enables the acetate sheet to be held firmly in place while you are working on it.

Producing transparencies by hand: By far the quickest means of producing your own OHP transparencies is to prepare them by hand, using suitable marker pens. Either water-soluble or permanent pens can be used for this purpose, but we strongly recommend the latter, since water-soluble material tends to smudge when touched. We find medium-tipped pens best for OHP work, and tend to work with four basic colours – black, red, blue and green; these are sufficient for most purposes. If large areas of colour are required, these can be added using transfer film, which should be cut to the exact shape required using a scalpel *after* it has been applied to the transparency.

When putting verbal information on OHP transparencies by hand, it is important to use a writing or printing style that all members of the viewing group will be able to read without difficulty. We strongly recommend that you try to develop a clear lower-case printing style for this purpose, since this is generally far easier to decipher than either upper-case printing or ordinary handwriting (see page 54). Also, it is absolutely essential to make the letters big enough to be seen by those furthest from the screen. The recommended sizes for different forms of printing and writing are as follows:

- Lower-case printing: just over ⅛ of an inch (excluding ascenders and descenders).

- Upper-case printing: roughly ¼ of an inch.

- Handwriting: as for lower-case printing.

It is also advisable to leave a gap of roughly ¼ of an inch between lines and to leave generous spaces between words, since this greatly increases legibility. Thus, use of guidelines ¼ of an inch apart (as recommended in the previous section) can be of considerable help in getting both the size of the lettering and the spacing of the lines right.

It is, of course, also possible to use some form of stencil or template system to add verbal information to OHP transparencies, or even to use instant lettering or machine-generated lettering of some sort if a particularly high-quality finished product is required. For most purposes, however, hand-produced lettering is perfectly adequate and much quicker (though in practised hands, desktop publishing systems can produce highly professional-looking overheads very quickly).

Typing OHP material: Another popular – albeit much abused – method of producing OHP transparencies is to type the material. This can be done either by typing directly on to the acetate sheet using a special ribbon or carbon sheet or by first typing the material on to paper and then making a transparency from this (eg using a thermal copier or a photocopier that can copy onto acetate). It must, however, be stressed that a standard office typewriter should *never* be used for such work since the letters that it produces will always be far too small to be seen clearly when displayed using an overhead projector. A special typewriter (known as a *bulletin* or *primary typewriter*) which produces letters roughly twice as large as an ordinary machine can be used for OHP work.

Producing OHP transparencies from opaque originals: Another standard method of producing OHP transparencies is to use a thermal copier or similar machine to prepare a transparency from an opaque original – eg a page of text. This can produce perfectly acceptable results *provided that the original material is suitable for OHP projection.* As we have seen, ordinary typed material is useless for this purpose, and the same is true of most printed materials, since these are normally intended for individual study at close quarters rather than long-range viewing by a group. Thus producing an OHP transparency from (say) a diagram in a book or journal is nearly always worse than useless, since the resulting material will almost invariably be far too small and/or too highly detailed to be seen clearly when projected, especially by the people at the back of the room. Such materials can, however, often be made suitable for overhead projection by enlarging them using a photocopier that possesses a 'zoom' facility.

Producing computer-generated OHP transparencies: In the same way as word processors and desktop publishing systems can be used to produce handouts of high quality, similar results can be obtained with overhead projection acetates. Many laser printers can print directly on to suitable acetate sheets – but be careful! If you put the wrong kind of acetate into a laser printer (or into a photocopier), the acetate will melt, causing

```
Some tools for the learners' task

•   clear useful objectives

•   unambiguous text

•   unambiguous visuals

•   lots of activity: learning by doing

•   plenty of practice and variety

•   feedback to allow progress to be
    measured

•   helpful support with errors

•   help on study skills

•   good signposting
```

Figure 4.7 **The sort of transparency that would be produced by a typewriter: monotonous and uninspiring**

SOME TOOLS FOR THE LEARNERS' TASK

- **CLEAR USEFUL OBJECTIVES**
- **UNAMBIGUOUS TEXT**
- **UNAMBIGUOUS VISUALS**
- **LOTS OF ACTIVITY: LEARNING BY DOING**
- **PLENTY OF PRACTICE AND VARIETY**
- **FEEDBACK TO ALLOW PROGRESS TO BE MEASURED**
- **HELPFUL SUPPORT WITH ERRORS**
- **HELP ON STUDY SKILLS**
- **GOOD SIGNPOSTING**

Figure 4.8 **This would be clear enough as a transparency, but is relatively dull and tiring on the eyes, because of monotonous use of upper case letters**

SOME TOOLS FOR THE LEARNERS' TASK

- **CLEAR USEFUL OBJECTIVES**
- **UNAMBIGUOUS TEXT**
- **UNAMBIGUOUS VISUALS**
- **LOTS OF ACTIVITY: LEARNING BY DOING**
- **PLENTY OF PRACTICE AND VARIETY**
- **FEEDBACK TO ALLOW PROGRESS TO BE MEASURED**
- **HELPFUL SUPPORT WITH ERRORS**
- **HELP ON STUDY SKILLS**
- **GOOD SIGNPOSTING**

Figure 4.9 **This would be clear enough as a transparency, but is somewhat irritating, being completely in 'Times' which although a good font for small print can be overpowering when there is too much of it in large letters on a screen, particularly in upper case**

Some tools for the learners' task

- clear useful objectives
- unambiguous text
- unambiguous visuals
- lots of activity: learning by doing
- plenty of practice and variety
- feedback to allow progress to be measured
- helpful support with errors
- help on study skills
- good signposting

Figure 4.10 **A much more attractive version for a transparency. The heading is clear and prominent, and the remainder of the wording is clear and 'unfussy' in Helvetica font**

Some tools for the learners' task

- clear useful objectives
- unambiguous text
- unambiguous visuals
- lots of activity: learning by doing
- plenty of practice and variety
- feedback to allow progress to be measured
- helpful support with errors
- help on study skills
- good signposting

Figure 4.11 **An alternative, using Avant Garde font, which is easily read, but makes a change from Helvetica**

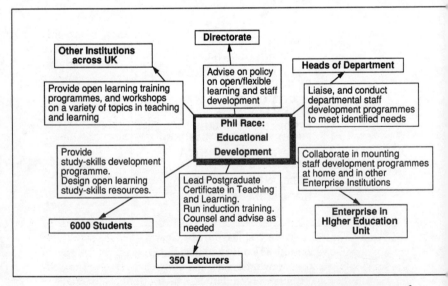

Figure 4.12 **A 'tongue-in-cheek' landscape-style computer-generated acetate, created by one of the authors of this book, daydreaming about the importance of educational development at his college!**

severe damage to the equipment. (One only does this once!). Acetate sheets designed for laser printers or photocopiers are made of a kind of acetate which withstands a considerable amount of heat. However, it is quite difficult to tell one kind from another, so refer to the original packaging in which the acetate was delivered – and if in any doubt, don't use it.

It can be worth experimenting with producing your master copy on paper, then photocopying on to acetate sheets, rather than printing directly on to acetate with a laser printer. Sometimes, the carbon film deposited by a laser printer does not adhere very well to the acetate sheet, and it's been known for lettering to 'slide off' acetates as they are being displayed. The photocopying process seems to give a more stable coating. In any case, it is useful to have a paper master for each acetate – for example in case other people wish to have photocopies of your acetates.

When photocopying high-quality computer-generated masters onto acetate, it is useful to vary your colours. Acetate (the thermal variety) is available in at least four colours (red, blue, green and yellow), and can provide an inexpensive and attractive way of adding some colour to your presentations. This is particularly welcome if you're using a fair number of computer-generated acetates in succession, as the print itself will normally be black (of course with hand-drawn acetates you have control of the print colour too).

The new generation of colour laser printers can print your acetates in a wide range of colours, but the chances are that if you have access to this sort of printer, it will be in a specialized central reprographics unit, and there will be someone there responsible for the preparation of the materials, and you'll have the luxury of someone preparing your highly professional-looking acetates for you. The series of illustrations shown above (Figures 4.7 – 4.12) gives some idea of ways of making computer-generated transparencies attractive, and also you may see some things to avoid.

The various manual methods of producing OHP transparencies are described in detail in the books by Kemp and by Minor and Frye that are listed in the Bibliography, and interested readers are referred to these.

Some Useful Display Techniques
Let us now look at some of the standard techniques that can be used to increase the effectiveness of OHP displays.

Progressive disclosure: This is one of the basic techniques that can be used in overhead projector displays, and one of the most useful from an instructional point of view. It involves covering up all or part of the material on a given transparency, and progressively revealing the material as the presentation proceeds. This has the double advantage of concentrating the mind of the learner on whatever item or section is being discussed at the time and maintaining interest by keeping him in suspense over what is going to be revealed next (a good psychological ploy).

Progressive disclosure can be achieved in a number of ways, the easiest of which is simply to cover the material to be hidden with a sheet of paper, card or other opaque material and then to move it out of the way as and when required. This can be quite effective when used with a simple list of headings or key points, which can be revealed and discussed one by one. There is, however, a tendency for the mask to fall off the projector before the material at the bottom of the transparency is reached, something that can be prevented by weighing it down with a suitable heavy object (eg a bunch of keys or a ruler). Alternatively, a special mask consisting of a sheet of paper with a strip of thin metal, wood or plastic stuck along its top edge can be used. A short plastic ruler is ideal. It is useful to carry such a masking device in one's briefcase ready for use whenever required.

A more sophisticated and more versatile way of achieving progressive disclosure is to cover the various items or sections with individual masks of the required shape and attach these to one or more of the edges of the transparency by means of suitable hinges (eg pieces of Sellotape). The masks can then be pulled back one by one in order to reveal the different items or sections. This technique is particularly useful with graphic displays such as block and flow diagrams, since it enables the various sections of such a diagram to be revealed one by one, thus showing how the complete system is built up. The use of such hinged masks is illustrated in Figure 4.13.

It should be added, however, that members of an audience can become irritated by too much progressive disclosure. It can feel to them as if they are being visually controlled too much. Therefore, we advise you to use progressive disclosure only when it really is necessary, and to give your audience 'full' disclosure sometimes.

Use of overlays: Another standard technique that can be used to build up

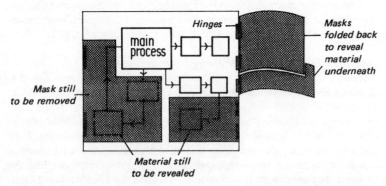

Figure 4.13 **Use of a system of hinged masks to allow progressive disclosure of the various sections of a block diagram**

the information content of an overhead projector display is the use of *overlays*. This differs from progressive disclosure in that the whole of the area of the transparency is revealed from the start, with additional information being added to the original display by superimposing further transparencies on the original. This can be used to guide learners through the development of a complicated display stage by stage, thus avoiding the confusion and/or distraction that might well arise if the entire display were shown right from the start.

There are two basic ways in which material can be overlaid on an OHP display. The first is simply to lay further transparencies, carrying the new information, on top of the first. This may give rise to problems of registration, however, particularly if the display is a complicated one or if exact positioning of the new information is crucial. The second method is to make use of hinged overlays attached to some or all of the edges of the original transparency, overlays that can then be flipped into position as and when required. Use of this system clearly enables the registration problems mentioned above to be avoided, the secret of achieving perfect registration being to add the information to each successive overlay *after* it has been attached to the original transparency and moved into a display position. The way in which a progressively more detailed display can be built up by adding a series of hinged overlays is illustrated in Figure 4.14. Clearly, appropriate use of colours can add greatly to the effectiveness of such a display.

Use of animation: Although the overhead projector is classed as a 'still visual display' system, it is in fact possible to add an element of animation to certain types of OHP display. This can be used to show such things as a flow of fluids along pipes and the direction of flow in flow diagrams. Two basic methods are used to produce such apparent movement. The first is to incorporate special polarizing materials in the display and to add a polarizing spinner to the optical system of the projector, between the platen and the projection head. The second is to make use of moirée fringes to create an illusion of movement in parts of the display. The materials and ancillary equipment needed to produce both types of animation can be obtained from specialist educational suppliers.

Producing Transparencies for Individualized Study
Although by far the most important use of large transparencies of the type described above is in conjunction with the overhead projector, it is also possible to study them at close quarters using a light box of some sort. Thus, such transparencies can be used in individualized study situations as well as in expository and group learning. Transparencies that are primarily intended for such close study rather than for display to a class or group can be produced in exactly the same way as ordinary OHP transparencies. They can, however, be made to incorporate rather more detail, and can also have smaller lettering because of the different conditions under which they are designed to be used.

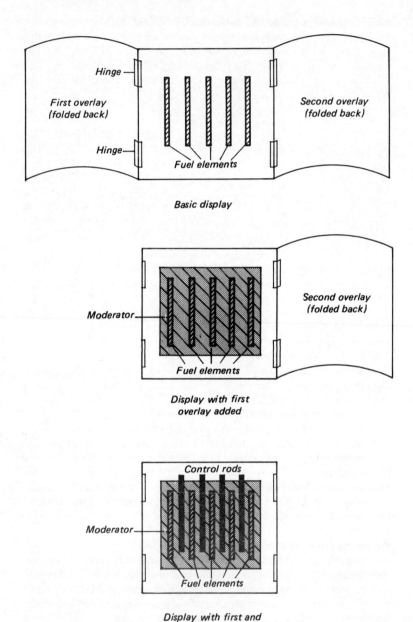

Figure 4.14 **Use of a series of overlays to build up a progressively more detailed schematic diagram of the core of a nuclear reactor**

PHOTOGRAPHIC SLIDES AND SLIDE SEQUENCES

Ever since the days of the 'magic lantern', *slides* have been one of the simplest and most popular methods of introducing supportive visual materials into a lecture or taught lesson. The original 'lantern slides' (which were roughly 3¼ inches square) are very rarely used today, however, having been almost entirely superseded by the newer 'compact' (2 inch × 2 inch) slides. These consist of single frames of 35mm or similar film mounted in cardboard, metal or plastic binders, often between twin sheets of glass for added protection, and are considerably easier to make, handle, use and store than their more cumbersome predecessors – as well as being much cheaper. Such slides can be of considerable assistance to teachers, instructors and trainers of all types in providing visual reinforcement of what is being said, and are particularly useful for showing photographs, diagrams and other graphic material. The main disadvantage is that they require the room to be darkened, so that students normally cannot take notes while slides are being shown.

Apart from their use as a visual aid in mass instructional and group-learning situations, slides constitute a useful medium for individualized instruction, usually combined with an audiotape to form a *tape-slide* (or, more correctly, a *slide-tape*) *programme*. This role of slides will be discussed in detail in Chapter 6.

Producing Your Own Slides

There are two main ways in which compact slides can be produced for instructional purposes:

1. Taking photographs of actual scenes, systems, objects, etc.

2. Taking photographs of material carried on other media.

Let us now look at what each of these involves.

Photographing Actual Scenes, Objects, etc
To do this, you will need a basic 35 mm camera plus any ancillary equipment that is required for particular types of work (indoor work, close-up work, etc).

The basic camera: Most 35 mm cameras are similar in appearance to the one shown in Figure 4.15, consisting of a camera body to which different types of lens systems can be attached. They generally come fitted with a standard 50 mm lens (ie a lens that brings light from a remote object to a focus in a plane 50 mm behind it).

If you are serious about producing your own instructional slides, you would probably be best advised to purchase a general-purpose camera of semi-professional quality, otherwise the camera will almost certainly lack some of the facilities that you will require.

Figure 4.15 **A 35mm camera fitted with a standard 50mm lens**

Additional lenses that you will probably need: Although the standard 50mm lens that is fitted to your basic camera may well enable you to take the great majority of the shots that you require, you will probably find it useful to have a number of alternative lenses available for specific shots. For most purposes, the following should be sufficient.

■ A *wide-angle lens*, for increasing the field of view obtainable from a given position.

■ A *zoom* or *telephoto lens*, to enable you to photograph a specific part of a scene in detail or magnify remote objects.

If you have to carry out close-up photography of really small objects, however, you will probably find that you also require a set of *lens extension tubes*. These enable the standard 50mm lens to be converted into close-up lenses suitable for work at different fixed distances. Indeed, if you have to carry out a lot of work of this type, you may well find it advisable to purchase a *close-up bellows* and *bellow lens system*, which will enable you to work at any distance simply by adjusting the bellows (see Figure 4.16).

Other equipment required: Although the camera can be hand-held for most shots, there will undoubtedly be occasions when you will find it advisable to mount it on a *tripod* – especially for close-up work.

If you intend working indoors, you will also require some form of artificial lighting. The simplest way to provide such light is to use an *electronic flash* system, but there may well also be situations where you will find that it is necessary to use *floodlights*. A reasonably good pair of tungsten lamps, with stands, will probably be sufficient for most purposes.

Armed with the above equipment and a supply of suitable film, you should find that it is possible to produce satisfactory photographic slides of virtually any scene, system or object – outdoors or indoors. Further guidance can be obtained from any basic text on photography (eg the one by Langford listed in the Bibliography).

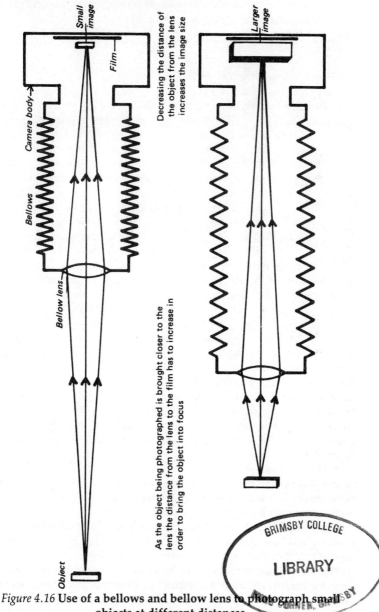

Figure 4.16 **Use of a bellows and bellow lens to photograph small objects at different distances**

Taking photographs through a microscope: If you want to produce slides of really small objects, this can be done with the aid of an ordinary microscope. Simply focus the microscope on the object visually and then remove the eyepiece, placing the camera (focused for infinite distance) as close to the open top of the tube as possible, pointing down the tube. Even better results can be obtained by using a *microscope adaptor*, which enables a 35mm camera (minus lens) to be screwed directly on to the end of the microscope draw tube.

Producing Slides from Other Media

It is probably true to say that the great majority of the slides that are used for instructional purposes are not original photographs of real scenes or objects but 'second-hand' photographs of material in other media – photographs and diagrams from books, specially prepared text or artwork, and so on. It is probably also true to say that most of the slides so prepared are made illegally, since the laws of copyright expressly forbid copies being made of other people's material (other than in certain special cases) without the prior permission of the copyright holder.

Thus, before make slides of material from a book or other publication, you should always seek the permission of the copyright holder if you wish to remain within the law. In most cases, this permission will be readily given provided that you are making the slides for genuine educational purposes and not for commercial gain. If you are using material that you have produced yourself, of course, no such problem arises. Thus one way of getting round the copyright law in respect of making a slide of a diagram in a book (say) is to produce your own version of the diagram (which is perfectly legal) and then photograph this. You may well find that this is a good idea in any case, because much of the graphic material that is published in books, journals etc is totally unsuitable for use in making slides in its original form because it contains too much detail, has too small lettering, and so on.

Preparing material for slide-making: When preparing original material for slide-making, whether it is textual or graphical in nature, the same basic rules as were stated earlier for OHP transparencies (see p 126) apply – only more so. Thus you should *never* try to put too much information on a single slide, and should always aim to produce a clear, simple layout that will enable all the information on the slide to be distinguishable by the viewer. This is particularly important if the slide is to be shown to a large group of people, or projected in a large room. If you are in any doubt about the clarity or legibility of a slide once you have produced it, go to the back of the room in which it is to be shown and see whether you have any difficulty in deciphering it.

When preparing the artwork for slides that are to carry verbal information, a good rule of thumb is to restrict yourself to a maximum of six lines of print if the slide is to be screened horizontally and eight if it is to be screened vertically. (Vertical format slides are not recommended, however, because most screens are designed to show horizontal slides; thus, if the projector is arranged so as to fill the screen with such slides, any vertical format slides shown will be 'topped and tailed' – much to the annoyance of viewers.) The easiest way to produce the artwork for such textual slides is to type or print it in a rectangle roughly 8cm × 6cm. This will produce artwork with the correct aspect ratio (ratio of horizontal to vertical size) and will also produce lettering of a suitable size for distant viewing. Use of a modern electric typewriter to produce the artwork generally produces satisfactory results; this should be set at double the normal spacing in order to increase the clarity of the text. Alternatively, a word processor linked to a suitable printer can be used.

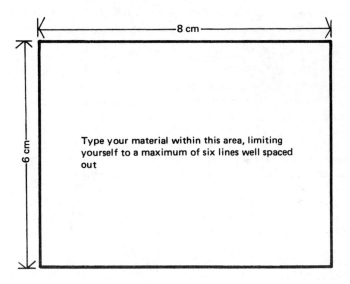

Figure 4.17 **The frame within which textual material for 35mm slides should be typed**

Photographing the material: In order to make photographic slides from opaque originals, it is essential to use some sort of rigid mounting system for the camera; holding the camera by hand simply does not produce satisfactory results.

There are two basic techniques that can be used for such copy work. The first – and simplest – is to place the material to be copied on a support stand of some sort and to mount the camera on a tripod – preferably one with a pan/tilt head in order to allow it to be angled downwards. If the artwork is then illuminated using a pair of suitable lamps, as shown in Figure 4.18, it is possible to produce satisfactory slides by this method.

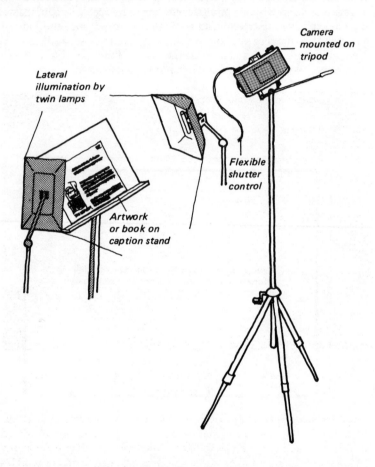

Figure 4.18 **Use of a caption stand and tripod-mounted camera for making slides**

Although the caption stand and tripod method is perfectly satisfactory for occasional use, anyone who intends to make large numbers of slides from opaque material would probably be advised to buy or make some sort of *copy stand*, since the use of such a system makes the work much easier. If you have the necessary funds, it is possible to buy a complete copy stand system of whatever sophistication you require, but such systems tend to be rather expensive, so that their purchase can probably only be justified if you have a very large throughput indeed. It is, however, a relatively simple matter to construct a rudimentary copy stand that is satisfactory for most purposes. Basically, all that is needed is a vertical column of some sort to which the camera can be fixed so that it can be moved up and down directly above the material to be copied and a system of lamps whereby the latter can be illuminated without producing reflected glare (lamps angled at 45° to the vertical are best). Such a set-up is shown in Figure 4.19.

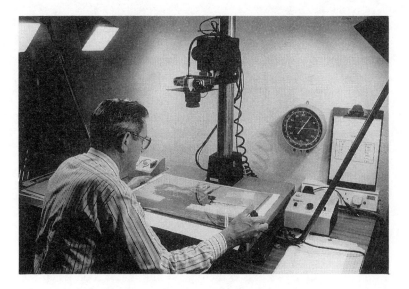

Figure 4.19 **Slides being made from flat copy using a modern copy stand**

Producing slides from computer-generated material: As we saw earlier, it is now possible to use a computer to design and produce overhead projector transparencies (see p 128). Software is available for many desktop publishing systems to enable direct production of 35mm slides using the same electronic information used to produce overhead projection transparency masters. However, despite the increased ease of producing highly professional slides, most usage of computer generation facilities seems to be to produce OHP transparencies. Probably one of the most significant reasons for this is that there is (on average) far less that can go wrong with overhead projection than slide projection. For example, if an OHP breaks down, it is usually possible to procure another within minutes; if a slide projector fails, there may not be another available at all in a given building. Also, it is easy to 'shuffle' your pile of OHP transparencies to respond directly to the questions coming from your audience; with a pre-loaded carousel of slides, your order is 'fixed', and it can be quite annoying to an audience to have several slides 'flicked past' without comment as you try to reach the one you want to talk about.

Figure 4.20 **Graphic slides being generated by computer**

The Different Types of 35mm Film and their Main Applications

There are four main types of 35mm film, all of which have different applications.

1. *Colour negative film:* this is the type of film that is used when the final product is to take the form of colour prints, the prints being produced in whatever size is required using a suitable enlarger; such film is not normally used for making slides.

2. *Colour reversal film:* the main type of film used for making colour slides, with the film that is used to take the photograph being reversed from a negative to a positive during processing.

3. *Panchromatic monochrome film:* monochrome film that is sensitive to the entire visible spectrum. Its main use is in preparing negatives for eventual conversion into monochrome prints, but it can also be processed through to the positive stage in order to produce positive monochrome slides.

4. *Line film:* special monochrome film that is used for photographing line originals which possess no half tones. Slides produced using such film have the image in white against a black background, but the lines can be coloured using special photographic dye if required.

Line negatives are also used in the production of *diazo* slides, which are made from such negatives by a secondary process (involving ammonia fumes) in which the image is transferred to diazo film. The resulting slides have a white image on a coloured background (usually blue).

There are in fact several processes by which photographic slides can be produced, but discussion of these is beyond the scope of an introductory book of this nature. Information on such processes can be found in specialized books on photography (see, for example, the book on *Basic Photography* listed in the Bibliography).

Preparing Slides for Use

Once a roll of 35mm film has been exposed, it is obviously necessary to process the film before it can be used. The easiest way to do this is to pay to have the film processed in a commercial laboratory, although this can cause a considerable time lag between taking the pictures and being able to use them. If you have the necessary skills and facilities, or have access to a photographic processing service 'in-house', such delays can obviously be avoided, although the final cost of the slides may in fact turn out to be higher than if you had them processed externally once you have taken labour and cost of materials into account.

If you have slides processed by a commercial organization, they will almost invariably be returned to you in cardboard mounts, without glass. If the slides are to be subjected to heavy use, however, it will probably pay you in the long run to remove the transparencies from these mounts (by slitting the latter open with a scalpel or razor blade) and re-mount them in plastic or metal mounts, preferably between glass. This will not only protect them from damage, but will also prevent them from popping or buckling during projection. If you are processing the slides yourself or having them processed 'in-house', they should be mounted in this way right from the start.

The final thing that has to be done before the slides are ready for use is *spotting* and *labelling*. In order to ensure that a slide is always inserted into a projector or viewer the right way round and right way up, a spot should be stuck or marked on the bottom left-hand corner of the front of the slide (ie the side from which the image appears right way round when the slide is held up to the light). When the slide is subsequently loaded into a projector, this spot should always appear at the top right-hand corner when viewed from behind the projector (since the image on a slide is inverted and laterally reversed during projection, the slide has to be turned through 180° about an axis perpendicular to its surface before being loaded if it is to appear right way up when projected). When the slide is loaded into a 'straight through' magnifying viewer, on the other hand, the spot should be on the bottom left-hand corner.

Labelling of slides (essential if confusion is to be avoided during subsequent storage and use) is best carried out by sticking a self-adhesive slide label along the bottom or top edge and writing on this. Such labels often incorporate a spot at one end, so, by sticking them on the bottom edge, separate spotting is made unnecessary.

Duplicating Slides

If more than one copy of a slide is needed, and this is known before the original photographic work is carried out, it is obviously a good idea to shoot as many copies of the slide as are required right at the outset. This will ensure that all the copies are of the same high standard. Should additional copies become necessary after the photography has been completed, however, these can be produced either by having duplicate slides made by a commercial laboratory or by carrying out the duplication yourself. Such duplication can be carried out in two ways.

1. *The projection method:* This involves projecting the slide on to a screen and photographing the resulting image using a camera mounted as close to the axis of projection as possible; some loss of colour and increase in contrast is inevitable during the process, however.

2. *The transmission method:* This involves mounting the slide in front of a suitable source of light and making a direct copy using a camera fitted with a suitable lens extension tube or bellows so that 1 : 1 size focusing can be obtained. This generally produces much more satisfactory results than the projection method, especially if a custom-designed slide duplication unit is used. Indeed, modern slide duplicators generally produce copies that are virtually indistinguishable from the original.

Storing Slides

Although slides can, at a pinch, be stored in the small boxes in which they are received from the processing laboratory or in empty slide mount boxes, a more convenient and systematic method is advisable if large numbers are involved. Possible alternatives include the following:

■   Use of custom-designed slide cabinets, in which the slides are held in individual slots or between movable partitions in drawers. This is a reasonably inexpensive method, but one that requires an individual slide to be removed from the storage system before it can be inspected.

■   Use of transparent hanging files fitted with slide pockets, another inexpensive method that enables the slides to be stored in a standard filing cabinet and also enables an entire sheet of slides to be viewed at the same time (by holding it up to the light or placing it on a light box).

■   Use of a storage display cabinet, in which the slides are stored on open vertical or horizontal racks which can be slid out in front of an

Figure 4.21 **A slide storage display cabinet being used for slide sorting**

in-built light source for inspection. This is by far the best method, if you can afford the relatively high price of such a cabinet; the one shown in Figure 4.21 can hold up to 3000 slides, arranged in racks of 100, and can be used both for storage and for sorting slides into sequence.

Planning and Using Slide Sequences

Although individual slides can be of considerable use in providing visual back-up material during a lecture or taught lesson, it is generally more effective to employ them in carefully planned linked sequences. When planning and using such sequences, we have always found the following general guidelines useful.

- Plan your sequence of slides in such a way that it gives a logical structure to your presentation, using title slides at the start of each major section and subsection; these will not only serve as useful 'signposts and links' for your audience, but will also help to cue you into each section.

- Within each section, use the slides to illustrate and reinforce the points that you want to make, preferably using a fresh slide for each new point covered.

- Make sure that the slide that is on display at any given time is relevant to what is being said – if it is not, it may well distract the listeners; if necessary, make use of blank slides (ie slides with dark fields) to cover any sections where no suitable slides are available.

■ Prepare your sequence of slides for use by laying them out, in order of showing, on a light box or in a rack of a slide storage display cabinet. Transfer them into the slide projector magazine in complete sections.

■ If at all possible, use a magazine with sufficient capacity to hold all the slides in your presentation; if there are too many for one magazine, change magazines at the end of a major section – *not* right in the middle of a continuous sequence.

■ Use a projector with a remote change facility, and make sure that the cable to the hand control is long enough to enable you to give your presentation from the front of the group that you are talking to, and also to enable you to move about if necessary.

■ Remember that your audience will not be able to take notes during your presentation; thus, if you want them to have a permanent record of what is covered, prepare a suitable handout to support your lecture or lesson.

The use of slide sequences in individualized instruction will be discussed in Chapter 6.

Figure 4.22 **Two of the most commonly used types of slide projector ('carousel' and 'linear magazine' types)**

BIBLIOGRAPHY

Anderson, R H (1976) *Selecting and Developing Media for Instruction.* Van Nostrand Reinhold, Cincinnati (Chapters 4 and 5).

Kemp, J E (1980) *Planning and Producing Audiovisual Materials.* Harper and Row Publishers Inc, New York.

Langford, M J (1973) *Basic Photography.* Focal Press, London and New York.

Langford, M J (1973) *Visual Aids and Photography in Education.* Focal Press, London and New York.

Minor, E and Frye, H R (1970) *Techniques for Producing Visual Instructional Media.* McGraw Hill, New York.

Romiszowski, A J (1988) *The Selection and Use of Instructional Media.* Kogan Page, London (Chapter 4).

Rowatt, R W (1980) *A Guide to the Use of the Overhead Projector.* Scottish Council for Educational Technology, Glasgow.

Vincent, A (1970) *The Overhead Projector.* Educational Foundation for Visual Aids, London.

Wittich, W A and Schuller, C F (1979) *Instructional Technology – Its Nature and Use.* Harper and Row, New York.

Chapter Five

How to Produce Audio Materials

INTRODUCTION

Having completed our examination of the three main classes of still visual display materials that can be used by teachers and trainers, we will now take a look at a completely different type of medium – audio materials. In their own way, these have had just as great an impact on instructional methodology as any of the visual media discussed so far and, as we shall see in Chapter 6, are also a key component of some of the most important linked audio and visual systems developed to date.

Following our established pattern, we will begin by taking a general look at how audio materials in general, and audiotapes in particular, can be used in different types of instructional situation. Next we will take a fairly detailed look at the basic guidance on how to design audio materials for specific instructional purposes, including audiotapes for individual and class use and materials for language laboratories.

HOW AUDIO MATERIALS CAN BE USED IN DIFFERENT TEACHING/LEARNING SITUATIONS

As in the case of still display materials, audio materials can be used in virtually all types of teaching/learning situations, covering all three of the basic classes identified earlier. Let us therefore see what basic roles they are capable of playing in each.

Mass Instruction

Here, we can identify at least three highly important roles for audio materials. The first is as a source of supportive and illustrative material for use in expository teaching – recorded music, poems and plays, recorded extracts from talks and speeches, foreign languages spoken by native speakers, and so on. Such materials can be used in all situations where an audio input of some sort would increase the effectiveness of the instructional process – or simply help to maintain student interest and concentration by varying the method of presentation.

The second way in which audio materials can be used is as the actual vehicle by which the mass instruction is carried out. Examples of such mediated instruction include the various types of educational radio broadcast, either used 'off-air' or recorded on audiotape for use at a more convenient time or more appropriate stage in the curriculum, and the wide range of pre-recorded lessons and lectures that are available on record or audiotape. Self-contained 'audio lessons' of this type – and similar lessons produced 'in-house' by a teacher or instructor – can, on occasions, be a highly effective substitute for a live exposition.

The third main method of using audio materials in mass instructional situations is as a vehicle for enactive learning of some sort. Examples include the use of tape recorders to record simulated interviews, debates, scenes from plays, musical performances, and so on for subsequent replay, discussion or criticism. Other examples include the use of audio materials in language laboratories and similar 'electronic classroom' situations.

Individualized Instruction

If anything, audio materials are capable of playing an even more important role in individualized instruction than in mass instruction, either on their own or in conjunction with visual media of various types. Here they can be used in at least three basic ways. The first is as a vehicle for conveying the actual content of the instruction to the learner, with the learner having a more-or-less passive role and merely having to listen to the material. Most educational radio broadcasts fall into this class, as do many self-instructional audiotapes and records. The second is as a means of managing the instructional process, with the audio material (usually an audiotape) acting as a sort of 'talking study guide' that is used in conjunction with other materials such as textbooks, notes and worksheets. The third is similar to the third role described in the 'mass instruction' section, with the audio materials providing a vehicle for enactive learning in which the learner actually has to interact with the materials themselves. Most self-instructional systems for learning foreign languages fall into this last category, with the audio material being supplied on disc or tape.

Group Learning

Audio materials can also play a useful role in many types of group-learning activity. They can be used in three basic ways:

1.   As a vehicle for supplying information to the group, either of an illustrative or supportive nature or as part of the main content of the exercise.
2.   As a vehicle for managing or guiding the group through the exercise.
3.   By providing a vehicle with or through which the members of the group have to interact.

THE BASIC PRINCIPLES OF SOUND RECORDING AND EDITING

Of the main purely audio media (radio, vinyl discs, compact discs and audiotapes), the only one where it is practical for teachers, instructors and trainers to produce their own materials is the last. We will therefore devote the remainder of this chapter to the production of audiotapes, beginning by taking a fairly detailed look at the basics of audio recording and editing and then showing how to produce audiotape materials for specific instructional purposes.

How Sound is Recorded on Audiotape

The various processes that take place in audiotape recording and playback are shown schematically in Figures 5.1 and 5.2 respectively.

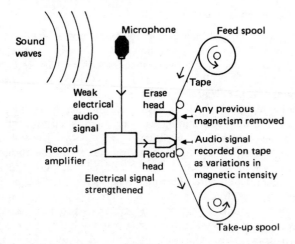

Figure 5.1 **Schematic representation of the various stages of audiotape recording**

In the recording process, the first stage takes place in the *microphone*. Here the incident sound waves cause a membrane of some sort to vibrate, and these mechanical vibrations are converted into a weak electrical signal whose amplitude follows the amplitude of the original sound exactly (a so-called *analogue* signal). Next, the electrical signal is passed into the *record amplifier* of the tape recorder, where it is increased in strength and, in most cases, also has its high frequencies artificially enhanced in order to increase the signal-to-noise ratio in the final recording. The signal is then fed into the *record head*, an electro-magnet that produces between its poles a magnetic field whose intensity varies in exactly the same way as the amplitude of the electrical sound signal. The recording tape is coated with a thin layer of magnetizable iron oxide or chromium oxide powder and, as it passes across the narrow gap between the poles of the record head magnet, has the signal recorded on its surface in the form of a weak magnetic field with the same intensity profile as the original sound.

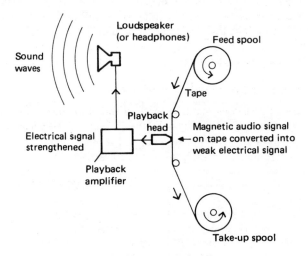

Figure 5.2 **Schematic representation of the various stages of audiotape playback**

In the playback process, exactly the opposite chain of transformations takes place. First, the tape moves across the surface of the *playback head*, an electro-magnet with a similar structure to the record head. Here the variations in magnetic intensity as the tape crosses the gap of the head cause a weak electrical signal to be induced within the head. This is then passed into the *playback amplifier*, where it has its strength greatly increased, and also has any artificial boosting of the high frequencies that was introduced during the recording stage removed. The electrical signal is then passed into a *loudspeaker*, where it is converted into mechanical vibrations of the loudspeaker cone. These, in turn, produce sound waves that are (in a high-quality system) more or less an exact reproduction of the original sound that struck the microphone. Alternatively, the electrical signal can be fed into a set of *headphones*, which are simply two miniature loudspeakers designed for individual listening.

Digital Audio Tape

In 1992, production of vinyl discs has almost entirely been superseded by digital compact discs. The same is likely to happen to tape recording – indeed digital cassette tape recorders are already beginning to appear in various parts of the world. Digital Audio Tape (DAT) uses a completely different principle of recording. The original sound vibrations are analysed in terms of frequency and intensity, and the analysed information is recorded in a digital form on audiotape. When the information is subsequently decoded for playback, the fidelity of the reproduction is extremely high, as the playback no longer depends on the intensity of magnetization of the tape so long as this is sufficient for the coded information to be re-transformed into sound. The digital technique avoids all the losses which occur at the various stages of analogue audio recording, namely:

- distortion on converting the original sound into 'magnetic intensity';

- distortion on reconverting the magnetic intensity into sound on playback.

Additionally, when editing, copying and combining audio recordings, digital recording allows each process to be carried out without any loss of quality whatsoever, and all processes are far less dependent on the precision of tape transport which was so crucial in analogue audio recording.

However, digital audio recording is still (in 1992) mainly confined to professional recording studios, and has not yet appeared in an affordable form on the domestic market – or in educational and training facilities. We can speculate that with the ready existence of a mass market for digital audio recording, it will only be a matter of time before such technology becomes as commonplace as the cassette, and indeed that the only reason why this has not happened already is connected with the difficulty of maintaining copyright arrangements with digital recordings being so eminently 'copyable'. The 'hi-fi' magazines already carry frequent reports of the progress of digital audio developments, and reviews of equipment which is becoming available for using digital technology.

The probability is that digital technology will soon be used for broadcasting, and that it will then be possible to capture very high quality recordings of broadcast material, and copy them faithfully at will. Again, of course, this has serious copyright implications. However, as with audiotape copying, anything which is impossible to police is impossible to prevent. Everyone who has audio recording equipment is likely from time to time to contravene copyright laws (for example by making audio cassette recordings of compact discs, radio or television broadcasts). Similarly, anyone with video recording equipment regularly contravenes copyright on films and documentaries. The only time the law is brought to bear on such 'offenders' tends to be if it is found that the recorded material is being used 'for gain' in one way or another (for example for republication or resale), and a 'blind eye' is turned on domestic copying of original materials. 'For one's own private use' seems to be the key phrase which avoids people facing the full rigour of the law.

Equipment Needed for Audiotape Recording

To record material on audiotape, you require two basic items of equipment: a microphone and a tape recorder. Let us now look at the various types that are available.

Microphones

Microphones come in a wide range of types and, like most other items of audiovisual hardware, vary enormously in quality and price. Thus, when buying a microphone, it is important to choose one that is of a suitable type to do the job that you have in mind and is also of a quality that matches the rest of your equipment. Clearly, buying a cheap, low-fidelity microphone for use with an expensive, high-fidelity tape recorder is a false economy, since any audio system is only as good as its weakest link. Conversely, there is no point in buying an expensive microphone for use with a cheap tape recorder that will not be able to do justice to the signal that it produces.

Microphones differ both in terms of the basic physical principle on which they operate and in terms of their directional characteristics. With regard to the former, there are three main types in common use. *Crystal or ceramic microphones*, in which the *transducer* (the mechanism that converts mechanical vibrations into an electrical signal) consists of a piezo-electric crystal or a layer of piezo-electric ceramic granules. Such microphones are cheap, but are not very rugged, have a limited frequency range, and produce only a low-fidelity signal; they are the sort that are built into many low-cost cassette recorders. *Moving-coil (dynamic) microphones*, in which the transducer is a coil of wire that moves between the poles of the magnet. Such microphones have a wider frequency response than crystal or ceramic microphones, and also produce a higher quality signal; they are, however, more expensive. *Capacitor (condenser) microphones*, in which the transducer is a capacitor of variable gap that produces an electrical signal when one of its plates vibrates in response to incident sound. Such microphones have an even wider frequency response than dynamic microphones, and produce high-quality signals; they can also be made extremely small.

With regard to the different directional qualities of microphones, we can distinguish four main types:

- *Omni-directional microphones*, which are equally sensitive in all directions when suitably mounted. These are suitable for recording group discussions and in other situations where the sound comes from all directions.

- *Bi-directional* (or *figure-of-eight*) *microphones*, which are sensitive in two opposite horizontal directions but not in directions at right angles to these. These are suitable for recording interviews involving two people, with one on either side of the microphone.

Figure 5.3 (a) **A selection of microphones, including a radiomicrophone (left), two general purpose microphones (centre) and a directional microphone (right) together with a sound mixing unit (bottom right)**

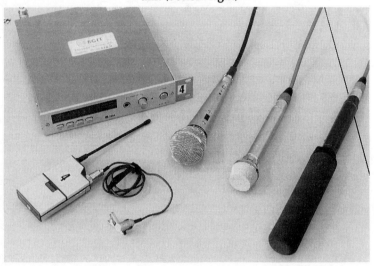

(b) **The relative sizes of the microphones in more detail**

- *Cardioid microphones*, which are highly sensitive in one direction, less sensitive in directions at right angles to this, and not sensitive at all in the opposite direction. These are suitable for recording a single speaker, a choir, or any other sound source where the sound effectively comes from a single direction.

- *Gun (or rifle) microphones*, which are highly directional in their sensitivity, only picking up sound within a narrow cone. These are suitable for picking up sound from a single source located some distance away.

The differing directional properties of these four types are shown in Figure 5.4, which shows polar diagrams of their sensitivity in different directions.

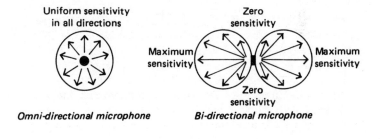

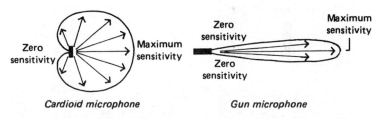

Figure 5.4 **Polar response diagrams of different types of microphone**

Tape Recorders

These are of two basic types: *open-reel recorders* and *cassette recorders*. The former make use of detachable open reels as feed and take-up spools, and, generally, the tape has to be threaded manually through the tape head and drive mechanisms before use. The latter make use of sealed tape cassettes that contain both the feed and take-up spools, and are loaded simply by fitting the cassette into place in the machine. Apart from this, however, the two types of recorder work in exactly the same way, and can be used to do more or less the same things.

The other main way in which the tape recorders differ is in terms of the track configuration of the tapes that they use. In the case of open-reel machines, there are five main configurations that you are likely to come across. These are shown schematically in Figure 5.5. In all cases, the tape is ¼ of an inch wide.

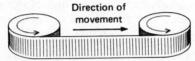

Full-track monophonic: only one recording track, covering virtually the entire width of the tape, so that such tapes cannot be turned over in order to record on 'the other side'. (Note: this system is only used in highly expensive tape recorders of 'broadcast' quality – the type that are used by professional sound engineers and broadcasters.)

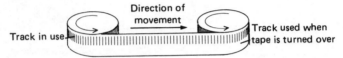

Half-track monophonic: two recording tracks, one on each half of the tape, with only one being used at a time; reversing the tape (ie turning it round so that the take-up spool becomes the feed spool) brings the other track into use. (This is the system that is used in most high-quality single-channel audio work.)

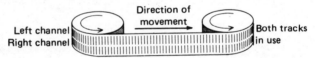

Half-track (two-track) stereophonic: two recording tracks, with one being used to record each channel of a stereophonic signal (or separate signals).

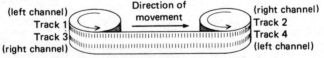

Quarter track (four track) stereophonic: four recording tracks, with tracks 1 and 3 being used when the tape is used as shown and tracks 2 and 4 being used when it is turned over.

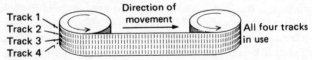

Multi-track: four or more separate tracks, each used to carry a separate sound signal.

Figure 5.5 **The five main track configurations used with open-reel audiotape recorders**

In the case of cassette machines, there are two main configurations. These are shown schematically in Figure 5.6. In the case of the compact cassettes that are now almost universally used, the tape is 4mm wide.

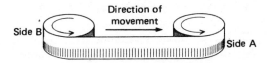

Monophonic: two recording tracks, one on each half of the tape, with the bottom track shown in the figure being used when side A of the cassette is used and the top track when side B is used.

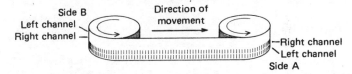

Quarter-track (four-track) stereophonic: four recording tracks, with the bottom two tracks shown in the figure being used when side A of the cassette is used and the top two tracks being used when side B is used; note the difference between this and the corresponding open-reel configuration.

Figure 5.6 **The two main track configurations used with compact cassette recorders**

When choosing a tape recorder for a particular response, you should be aware of these different track configurations and select a machine that is capable of doing the job you have in mind. For making original recordings, it is strongly advisable to use an open-reel machine, since these not only produce better quality recordings than cassette machines of a similar price but also make editing much easier, as we will see later. For making master tapes, either an open-reel or cassette machine may be used, but it is again important to choose one of reasonable quality, otherwise fidelity will be lost during the transfer process. If you already have a good open-reel machine, it would probably be best to buy a general-purpose four-track stereophonic cassette recorder for this purpose, preferably one with pulsing facilities, so that you can use it for tape-slide work. For playing a recording back to a class or group, it is again advisable to use a machine of reasonably high quality – preferably one with an external loudspeaker, since machines with built-in speakers can be difficult to hear clearly from the back of a room. When choosing machines for individual use, on the other hand, cheap cassette players (costing as little as £10 each) may well be all that is required, since quality of reproduction is normally not nearly so important when tapes – particularly ones carrying spoken material – are being listened to through headphones. Such machines can be used to play both monophonic and stereophonic tapes. With the latter, the mono head simply picks up the signals from the two stereo tracks (which occupy the same area as a mono track) and reproduce them as a single combined signal.

Figure 5.7 **A Wollensak cassette recorder being used to add pulses to an audio tape**

The Different Types of Tape

The magnetic tape used in audio recording consists of an insulating base material (usually some form of plastic, mylar or polyester) coated with a thin layer of magnetizable powder. In most tapes, the latter consists of particles of ferrous oxide, but some high-quality tapes use the more expensive chromium dioxide, since this produces less background noise (tape hiss) and gives a higher sound output level and a higher fidelity recording (but causes the tape heads to wear out more rapidly). Most high-quality tape recorders incorporate a switch that enables circuits suitable for use with the two different types of tape to be selected.

In the case of open-reel tapes, three different grades of tape are available: standard of 1.5 mil tape (tape with a thickness of 1.5 thousandths of an inch), long-play or 1.0 mil tape, and extra long-play or 0.5 mil tape. Clearly, the length of tape that can be wound on a spool of a given size (and hence the playing time at a given speed) depends on this thickness, with a 1.0 mil tape giving 50 per cent more playing time than a 1.5 mil tape on a reel of the same size and a 0.5 mil tape giving 100 per cent more. On the other hand, thicker tapes produce better-quality recordings with less print through (unwanted transfer of the signal from one layer of the tape to the next), and also tend to last longer. Thus, it is advisable to use 1.5 mil tapes for original and master recordings, although 1.0 mil tape can be used in the case of long programmes. 0.5 mil tape is not recommended for high-quality work; indeed, some tape recorders cannot handle such tape at all. Figure 5.8 shows the playing times that are available with different sizes of spool of the three thicknesses of tape at different tape speeds (measured in inches per second). Note that these times are for one pass of the tape only, and should be doubled if both sides of the tape are used.

Type of tape	Diameter of reel (inches)	Length of tape (feet)	Playing time at 7½ ips	Playing time at 3¾ ips
Standard	5	600	15 min.	30 min.
(1.5 mil)	7	1200	30 min.	60 min.
Long-play	5	900	22½ min.	45 min.
(1.0 mil)	7	1800	45 min.	90 min.
Extra-long play	5	1200	30 min.	60 min.
(0.5 mil)	7	2400	60 min.	120 min.

Figure 5.8 **Playing times for different types and lengths of open-reel tape**

In the case of compact cassettes, the cassette is designated with a number that shows its total playing time in minutes if both sides are used. The most common sizes are as follows:

C30 – playing time 15 min. per side.
C45 – playing time 22½ min. per side.
C60 – playing time 30 min. per side.
C90 – playing time 45 min. per side.
C100 – playing time 50 min. per side.
C120 – playing time 60 min. per side.

As in the case of open-reel tapes, the thickness of the tape in cassettes with very long playing times is less than for shorter-play cassettes, with an associated reduction both in quality and in durability. Indeed, C120 tape is so thin that it tends to jam or stretch in many machines, and is not recommended for instructional use.

One final word of warning about buying tapes. It is seldom advisable to try to economize by buying cheap tapes, since these not only produce a lower quality of recording and are, in many cases, prone to jamming, but can also cause excessive wear and fouling up of the recorder heads. Thus, always buy good-quality tapes from a reputable supplier; it will pay you in the long run. The Consumers' Association magazine *Which?*, regularly gives tables comparing the qualities, characteristics and prices of branded cassette tapes.

How to Make a Recording

The way in which you set about making a recording on audiotape will obviously depend to a large extent on the nature of the material to be recorded and the purpose for which it is to be used. There are, however, some general rules that should always be observed.

1. *Make sure that what you are recording is of the highest possible quality*
    This is a fairly obvious point, but one that is all too often neglected. In most cases, the key to producing high-quality original material is careful preparation, both in terms of planning and writing the materials and in terms of making sure that the presenter(s) or performer(s) are thoroughly briefed and rehearsed. If you are record-ing spoken material, it is also important to use a presenter with a good, clear delivery – preferably someone who has had training in and/or experience of such work. If at all possible, we strongly recommend the use of a professional presenter (eg an obliging local radio announcer) for any particularly important recording work, since this can make a tremendous difference to the quality of the final product.

2. *Try to optimize the recording environment*
    If you want to produce a good-quality recording, it is essential to carry out the recording work in a suitable environment. First (and most important) it *must* be free from extraneous noise. Remember that the brain of a human listener automatically 'filters out' un-wanted background noise by concentrating exclusively on what the person wants to hear, but that a tape recorder does not, faithfully recording every sound that falls on its microphone. Thus, back-ground noise that is hardly noticed at the time a recording is being made can prove intolerable when the resulting recording is played back. Second, the environment should have appropriate acoustic properties, being neither too reverberant (as in a swimming pool) nor too 'dead' (as in a heavily carpeted and curtained room full of soft furniture). If you are not sure whether the environment is satisfac-tory, carry out a trial recording and, if something is obviously wrong, try to improve matters by judicious use of acoustic screens, absorb-ent materials, and so on. Even a few coats hung in strategic positions round a microphone can sometimes make all the difference, as can the siting of the microphone in an open-ended box lined with absorbent materials such as felt or foam rubber. In some cases, of course, it may be better to move to a completely different location, eg by recording narrative material in a quiet room at home rather than trying to compete with the inevitable background noise that is present in most working environments.

3. *Use appropriate equipment and materials*
   This, of course, is fundamental, for if you use inappropriate equipment or unsuitable tape, the resulting recording will invariably turn
   out to be not as good as it might be. Thus, you should always:

   ▪ Use an external microphone (*not* one built into the tape recorder)
     of sufficient quality to do justice to the rest of the equipment –
     preferably one with directional properties suitable for the job you
     want it to do (an omni-directional microphone for group work, a
     bi-directional microphone for interviews, a cardioid microphone
     for a single speaker or uni-directional sound source, and so
     on).

   ▪ Use the best tape recorder available, assuming it is suitable for
     the job in hand and bearing in mind that open-reel machines
     are generally much more suitable for making original recordings
     than cassette machines.

   ▪ Use a good quality tape of suitable grade and of sufficient length
     to give the required playing time at the tape speed you intend
     using.

4. *Get the most out of your equipment and materials*
   Even if you buy the finest recording equipment on the market, you
   will only obtain good results if you use the equipment correctly.
   Thus, if you want to get the most out of your equipment and
   materials, you should:

   ▪ Select a tape speed that is sufficiently high to produce the quality
     of recording you require. With compact cassette recorders, the
     tape speed is fixed (at $1^7/8$ ips), but with open-reel machines, it can
     be set at various values (usually $1^7/8$ ips, $3^3/4$ ips, $7^1/2$ ips and 15
     ips). With such machines, the quality of the resulting record-
     ing increases as the tape speed increases, especially in terms of
     high-frequency response, so you should always make sure that
     this speed is high enough to produce satisfactory results. When
     recording speech, you will probably find that one of the lower
     speeds is perfectly adequate, but you will probably have to use a
     higher speed when recording music if you want the fidelity of the
     recording to be high. Also, you will probably find that you need
     to employ higher tape speeds with older tape recorders than with
     more modern machines; the latter have smaller gaps in their
     heads, and thus give a better frequency response at a given tape
     speed.

   ▪ Set the recording level correctly. Some machines have a facility
     that allows this level to be controlled automatically, but this
     should *never* be used when recording speech or any other
     material that has periods of silence; during such quiet periods,
     the machine increases the gain of its input amplifier in order to

try to bring the signal strength up to the required level, thus causing the background noise level to increase sharply. To prevent this, the recording level should always be set manually, using the relevant meter(s) or indicator(s) for guidance (these are incorporated in all but the cheapest machines). In most cases, the best setting is to have the average level just below the 'overload' area, so that the level only enters this area during peaks (see Figure 5.9). If the level is much lower than this, the recorded signal will be too weak; if it is higher, you will probably find that the peaks are distorted.

Recording level too low   Recording level about right   Recording level too high

Figure 5.9 **How to set the recording level**

- Use the 'pause' control for starting and stopping the tape during recording rather than the 'play' and 'stop' controls. Use of the latter almost invariably introduces unpleasant clicks and other forms of transient distortion into the recording, whereas use of the 'pause' control is (in the case of a good recorder) virtually unnoticeable.

How to Edit Tapes

Once material has been recorded on audiotape, it is often necessary to carry out some form of editing before the tape can be used, eg in order to remove bad takes, coughs and other unwanted sections, to insert pauses, or to rearrange the material in a different order. Such editing can be carried out in two ways: by physically cutting up and rejoining the tape (*mechanical editing*) and by dubbing the signal from one tape to another (*electronic editing*). Let us examine the two methods in turn.

Mechanical Editing

Clearly, this form of editing can only be carried out with precision on an open-reel tape (hence one of the reasons for using open-reel machines for original recording work), and only on tapes that carry a single re-corded track. It is also much easier to carry out on tapes that are recorded at a fairly high tape speed.

The method involves listening carefully to the recorded tape, noting the approximate positions where cuts have to be made with the aid of the index counter on the recorder. The exact position of each cut should then be found by moving the tape manually backwards and forwards through the playback head and marking its position on the tape using a felt pen or chinagraph pencil. The final cutting and rejoining should be made using a *tape splicing block*, a cradle of non-ferrous metal that holds the ends of the tape precisely in position during the cutting and splicing process. The various stages in the process are shown in Figure 5.10.

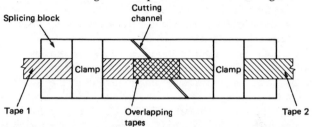

Stage 1 Clamp the two pieces of tape to be joined in the splicing block, base (ie shiny) side up, so that they just overlap across the 45° cutting channel.

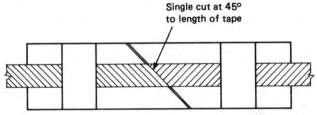

Stage 2 Use a razor blade or sharp knife (or the knife incorporated in the block if there is one) to make a 45° cut across the two tapes. Remove the two waste ends, so that the cut ends butt on to each other.

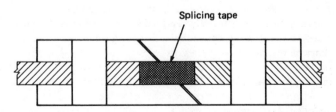

Stage 3 Cut a 1-inch length of splicing tape, and place it over the join. Rub it firmly down using a fingernail or non-metallic burnisher. Trim away any excess splicing tape that extends beyond the normal width of the tape. Unclamp the tape and test the join for strength.

Figure 5.10 **How to splice two lengths of audiotape together**

Although a basic splicing block can be bought quite cheaply, it may well be worth your while paying more for a more sophisticated block that carries out the splicing virtually automatically. If you have to carry out a lot of mechanical editing, such a device can pay for itself quickly in terms of time saved, and also produces a perfect join every time.

Electronic Editing

Electronic editing should be carried out using two tape recorders, with the output signal of the one on which the original tape is being played being fed directly into the input of the one on which the edited tape is being recorded. Such editing should *never* be carried out by using a microphone to pick up the sound from the first machine, since this invariably causes loss of fidelity and reduction of the signal-to-noise ratio. Needless to say, the two recorders used should also be of fairly high quality. When carrying out such editing, it is usual to record from an open-reel machine on to a good cassette machine, particularly if the edited tape is to take the form of a master cassette from which copies are to be made.

When carrying out electronic editing, the output level of the first machine and the recording level of the second machine should be adjusted manually so as to produce a satisfactorily strong signal on the edited tape; the automatic recording level facility on the latter should *not* be used, since this leads to unacceptably high noise levels during silent or quiet sections. The two machines should also be started and stopped during the dubbing process by means of their 'pause' controls, since this avoids the clicks and transient distortions that can result from the use of the 'play' and 'stop' controls.

Mixing sounds from different sources One advantage that electronic editing has over mechanical editing is that two or more separate sound signals can be simultaneously recorded on the final tape if necessary. This is usually done by feeding the separate signals into a *mixer*, an electronic device that enables their relative volumes to be adjusted, and then feeding the output signal from the mixer into the actual recording machine. Such a system can be used to add background music, sound effects, etc to a basic narrative.

Use a variable speed recording Another modification that can be made to recorded speech during electronic editing is alteration of the word rate. The normal speaking rate is roughly 150-200 words per minute (wpm), but research has shown that most people are capable of assimilating spoken information at a much higher rate than this without difficulty. By using a technique known as speech compression, such increases in word rate can be achieved without the rise in pitch and 'Donald Duck' distortion that result if the tape is simply speeded up. This involves passing the sound signal through special electronic circuits that remove tiny fragments from the sound at regular intervals and then join the remaining sections up to produce a shorter signal in which the words are presented at a greater rate. The process is illustrated in Figure 5.11.

By using this technique, it is possible to increase the speed of most recordings by up to 50 per cent without any appreciable loss of comprehension, although a smaller increase is probably advisable if the material is highly technical or otherwise intrinsically difficult or demanding. Clearly, use of speech compression can enable a greater amount of material to be covered in a given time or on a tape of given length. It can prove particularly useful in the preparation of material for individual listening.

A similar technique can be used to reduce the word rate of recorded speech. This involves chopping the original sound into short sections, moving these apart, and filling each gap with an extension of the previous section.

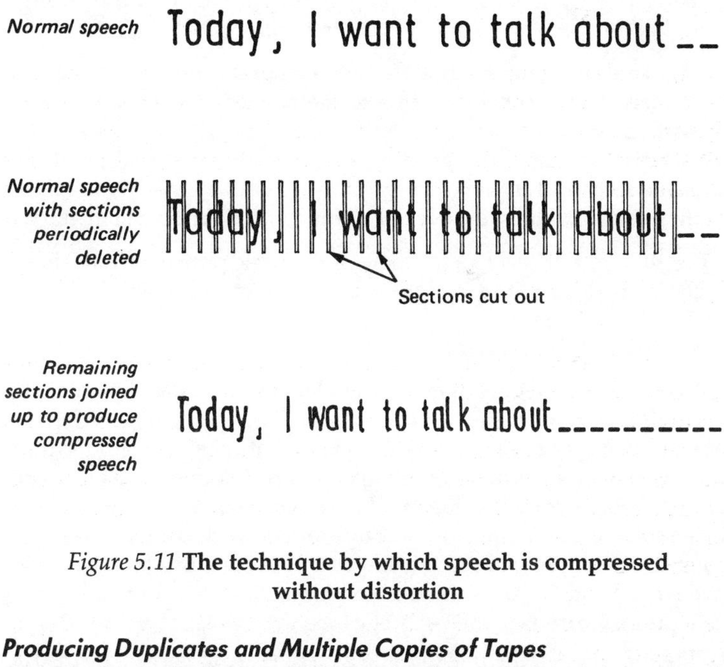

Normal speech **Today, I want to talk about __**

Normal speech with sections periodically deleted

Sections cut out

Remaining sections joined up to produce compressed speech **Today, I want to talk about_____**

Figure 5.11 **The technique by which speech is compressed without distortion**

Producing Duplicates and Multiple Copies of Tapes

Once the final edited version of a tape has been produced, it is generally advisable to use it as a master for the production of one or more copies, preferably in cassette form. Such copies can be produced in two ways. The first involves playing the master tape on one tape recorder and feeding the signal into a second recorder – a similar process to the electronic editing described above. This method can be used if only a small number of copies is required. The second method involves making use of special high-speed copying equipment that enables several copies of the tape to be made simultaneously. Use of such equipment is obviously advisable if a large number of copies is required.

When making copies of cassette tapes for use by individual listeners, it is, incidentally, often a good idea to record the material on both sides of the cassette; this saves the user (or the next user!) from having to rewind the tape.

Many of the above aspects of audiotape recording are covered in an excellent series of leaflets written by N Nichol and published by the Scottish Council of Educational Technology (see Bibliography).

HOW TO DESIGN AND PRODUCE AUDIO MATERIALS FOR SPECIFIC PURPOSES

Now that we have dealt with the technical aspects of audiotape recording and editing, let us end this chapter by looking at how to design audio materials for specific purposes. As we saw earlier, such materials can be used in a large number of ways in different types of instructional situations, but it is possible to divide them into four broad categories:

1. Materials used for illustrative or background purposes.
2. Materials that constitute an expository mediated lesson of some sort.
3. Materials that are designed to *manage* an instructional process of some sort.
4. Materials that provide a vehicle with which learners can interact.

Let us therefore take a look at some of the basic principles that should underlie the design of each of these categories of materials.

Illustrative and Background Materials

Materials in this category, usually intended for use in mass instructional or group-learning situations, come in a wide range of types. They can include such things as recordings of pieces of music, poems, extracts from plays and speeches – anything, in fact, that a teacher or instructor feels will enhance the quality of a particular learning experience for a particular group of people. Because of the wide-ranging nature of materials of this type, it is clearly impossible to lay down highly detailed guidelines for their design and production. As with all other types of instructional materials, the key stages are:

- Identification of the role that the materials are to play in the instructional situation.

- Planning and/or design of materials best suited for carrying out this role, including the preparation of a detailed script, if necessary.

- Production of the actual materials.

Let us illustrate this process by considering a specific example – namely, an English teacher who wants to produce recordings of certain poems for use in a lesson on literary criticism.

Stage 1: Identification of Instructional Role of Materials
Let us assume that our hypothetical teacher is planning to give a lesson on (say) the different styles of a given poet at different periods in his career, or on the contrasting styles of different poets in treating similar subjects. He decides that the best way to introduce the class to the poems would be to have them recited, and feels that the impact of the verse would be much greater if the recitations were polished and 'professional'; hence the decision to pre-record them rather than to try to read or recite them 'from cold' at the actual time of the lesson.

Stage 2: Planning of Materials
Clearly, the main thing that our teacher has to do here is decide exactly which poems (or extracts from poems) would be most suitable for use in the particular situation in mind, and also decide on the sequence in which they should be presented. Next, it is necessary to decide who will carry out the recitations, some of the available options being:

– To perform all the recitations himself or herself.
– To get someone else to perform all the recitations (a colleague who has a particularly good speaking voice or a training in drama, for example).
– To get different people to recite different poems or extracts.

Whichever course of action is adopted, it is then obviously necessary to make sure that the presenter(s) is (are) thoroughly briefed and, if necessary, rehearsed so that the actual recording will run smoothly.

Stage 3: Producing the Materials
This should be done in the way described in the previous section, the various stages being:

■ Selection of appropriate equipment and materials (microphone, tape recorder and tape).

■ Selection of a suitable environment in which the recording can take place and, if necessary, modification of that environment in order to improve its acoustic properties.

■ Making original recordings of the various items.

■ Editing these original recordings into a master tape, and, if this is felt necessary, preparation of a copy of the same.

Expository Materials

This category includes all the various audio materials that present a complete lesson, lecture or instructional sequence without reference to other materials such as textbooks or notes. In other words, the material conveys the actual *content* of the lesson, lecture or sequence to the learner as well as structuring and pacing the learning process.

When designing such materials, whether for use in mass instruction, individualized instruction or group learning, the main thing to remember is that the material will be *listened to*, not read. Thus it is necessary to adopt a different style of writing to that which would be appropriate for (say) a set of handout notes. The style should be conversational rather than formal, avoiding the use of long, convoluted sentences and complicated phraseology, which can make spoken material virtually impossible to follow. Try to make the material easy for the listener to understand, repeating or reinforcing key points wherever possible, and making maximum use of illustrations and examples. Also, never forget that the material must be *completely self-contained*, incorporating *all* the content that you want to get across to the listener. Needless to say, this is particularly important in the case of audio materials designed for use in self-instructional situations, where there is no teacher or instructor on hand to amplify or explain what has been covered.

The planning and production of expository audio materials should be carried out in the same three stages as were described above for illustrative and background materials, namely (i) identification of their instructional role, (ii) planning and design of the materials, including (in this case) the preparation of a detailed script, and (iii) the actual production of the materials.

An example of a script prepared for a typical expository audiotape – the start of a 'tape lecture' on alternative energy – is given in Figure 5.12. This shows the sort of style that should be used when writing such material.

'In this tape, we will discuss the subject of "alternative energy". We will do so in four stages. First, we will explain exactly what is meant by the term "alternative energy", since it often means different things to different people. Second, we will look at some of the reasons why people are now taking an increasing interest in alternative energy. Third, we will take a detailed look at some of the more important forms of alternative energy that are currently being developed or appraised. In this section, we will pay particular attention to alternative methods of generating electricity — probably the most important application of alternative energy. Finally, we will try to make a realistic assessment of the contribution that alternative energy sources are likely to make to our future energy needs — both in the short term and in the long term.'

(four second pause)

'Let us now begin our examination of alternative energy by trying to establish exactly what is meant by the term. You probably have your own ideas about this already. For example, you have probably seen water mills and windmills — both of which rely on alternative forms of energy — wind energy and water energy — to produce their power. Also, you have probably seen the solar panels that many people are now fitting on their roofs in order to heat water. These, too, rely on an alternative source of energy — in this case, the sun. What, then, is the thing that distinguishes these forms of energy — and all the other so-called "alternative" sources of energy — from "conventional" energy sources? The answer is really quite simple. Basically ....'

and so on

Figure 5.12 **The start of the script of a typical tape lecture**

Management of Learning Materials

In practice, this category of materials overlaps with the other categories to a considerable extent, since many audio materials whose main function is to manage or structure an instructional process also contain illustrative or background material, expository material or materials with which the learners have to interact. Such materials are mainly used in individualized instructional situations, although they are sometimes also used in group learning.

One of the most important uses of audio materials in the management of instruction is in the so-called *audio-tutorial* (or AT) system. Here, an audiotape serves as the central, managerial component of a multi-media, multi-activity study unit or module, and can perform a wide range of different functions, depending on the exact nature of the unit or module. These include:

- Providing information of one form or another.

- Directing the learner to various learning activities – reading sections of textbooks, examining materials, making observations, performing experiments, completing worksheets, and so on.

- Providing questions to which the learner has to reply, together with feedback on the answers.

- Providing 'extension material' that builds upon what has been learned from the other materials and activities in the unit, eg in the form of an in-depth discussion of important points.

The planning, design and production of the audio components of instructional systems of this type must obviously be carried out within the overall context of the design of the whole system. Again, the work should be carried out in the three basic stages described in the section

---

'In this unit of the course, we will look at the subject of "alternative energy". The objectives of the unit are listed on page one of the accompanying text. Please stop the tape and read these when you hear the signal, starting the tape again once you have finished.

    (Bleep, followed by five second pause)

'As you have seen, the first objective of the unit is to enable you to explain exactly what is meant by the term "alternative energy". You probably have your own ideas about this even now, so would you please stop the tape when you hear the signal and write down, in not more than 50 words, what you think it is that distinguishes the so-called "alternative" forms of energy from the so-called "conventional" forms. Start the tape again once you have finished.'

    (Bleep, followed by five second pause)

    and so on

Figure 5.13 **The start of the script of a typical audio-tutorial**

on expository materials: (i) identification of the instructional role (or roles) of the audio component: (ii) the planning and design of the audio materials, including the writing of a highly detailed script; and (iii) the actual production of the materials.

Specific examples of the use of audio materials in conjunction with other materials will be discussed in detail in the next chapter but, in the meantime, a specimen script is given in Figure 5.13. This is the start of an audio-tutorial on alternative energy, and should be compared with the tape-lecture script on the same subject that is given in Figure 5.12.

Materials With Which Learners Can Interact

In this category, we include all the different audio materials that themselves provide a vehicle with which learners can interact. Probably the most important type are the various materials that are used as software in language laboratories and similar audio-electronic classrooms, so we shall concentrate on these in this section.

The Different Types of Language Laboratory

Before discussing the design and preparation of language laboratory materials, it would probably be useful to explain exactly what a language laboratory is and describe the main types that are currently in use. Essentially a language laboratory is a facility that enables individual learners (working either alone or as part of a class or group) to listen to and respond to spoken material of various forms through the medium of a headset linked to a central or individual tape recorder. Three types of laboratory are in common use.

Audio-Active Comparative (AAC) Laboratories: These are full-scale class systems containing up to 30 individual carrels, each linked to a master console operated by the teacher or instructor in charge of the laboratory (see Figure 5.14). Each carrel has its own tape recorder, as has the master console, from which all the individual carrels can be monitored or controlled, either singly or in groups. Such laboratories enable individual learners to work at their own pace, to rewind their own tapes and repeat sections if necessary, and – most important – to record and listen to their own responses (hence the word 'comparative' in the name).

Audio-Active (AA) Laboratories: These are again full-class systems comprising individual carrels linked to a master console, but differ from AAC laboratories in that the carrels are not equipped with their own tape recorders. Instead, the students receive their material from the master console. In such systems, the students can listen to and respond to material and can also hear their responses via their microphone and headphones; they cannot record their responses, however, and also have to work in lockstep at a pace controlled by the person operating the master console. Audio-active laboratories are cheaper to install and

Figure 5.14 **A typical audio-active comparative language laboratory**

operate than audio-active comparative laboratories, and appear to be almost as effective for most purposes.

Mini-Laboratories: A mini-laboratory consists of a single study unit, usually audio-active comparative and portable. Such units can be used independently, for individual instruction, or can be linked with similar units to form a full-scale AAC laboratory controlled from a suitable master console. Flexible systems of this type are now becoming increasingly widely used.

Producing Software for Language Laboratories

The design and preparation of software for use in language laboratories is a highly specialized business and, in a general book of this nature, it is not possible to do any more than offer a few general guidelines.

First, it is important not to regard a language laboratory merely as a tool for polishing pronunciation, practising grammar and similar routine and uninspiring activities. When properly used, such laboratories can provide learners with an interesting and highly motivating means of improving their oral and aural performance, extending their vocabulary, and reinforcing general principles learned in open class. By individualizing the learning process, they also tend to improve concentration and, of course, provide each learner with great opportunities for personal language practice than would be possible in a conventional classroom. In too many cases, however, the use of poorly-designed software and excessive use of 'drill and practice' at the expense of more interesting and demanding activities lead to student boredom and failure to get the most out of the system. Thus, it is vital that all language laboratory software should be carefully planned and designed, taking full account of the role that it is intended to play in the instruction process. Some of the basic activities that can be built into such software are given below.

- Pronunciation practice, in which the student is provided with a series of spoken exemplars to try to imitate. Some sort of four-phrase pattern is probably best (exemplar, student imitation, repeat of exemplar, repeat of imitation).

- Structured pattern drills, in which the student is presented with a standard pattern (eg *il a mangé une orange*) and then has to repeat it with different subjects (*elle, nous, vous,* etc) or objects, use the same structure with different verbs, and so on.

- Sentence-building exercises, in which the learner is presented with different pieces of information or phrases that have to be structured into complete sentences.

- Questions and answers, ranging from simple questions in a highly structured situation where the answer is fairly obvious to more open-ended questions where a variety of answers are possible (proper structuring of the debriefing section is vital here).

- Aural comprehension, eg giving the learners some questions in advance, with the answers being contained in a taped passage that they then have to listen to; letting them listen to a taped passage first and then asking questions; making them summarize a passage to which they have listened; and so on.

- Role-playing exercises, eg exercises in which the learner first has to listen to a section of dialogue (preferably twice), this then being replayed with one of the roles missing so that the learner can participate.

- Games, eg quizzes based on true/false responses or multiple-choice answers, or guessing games in which the learner is given a series of clues and then has to supply the answer.

- Specific linguistic activities, eg asking the learner to persuade someone to do something, explain something, complain about something, and so on.

- Changing passages from direct to indirect speech.

No doubt readers can think of many other ways in which language laboratories and similar facilities can be used.

When it comes to the actual production of materials for language laboratories, one of the most important things to remember is that the *pauses* are just as important as the *spoken content*, both in terms of their position and in terms of their length. It is probably best to start by recording all the spoken material, without pauses, and then to edit this material on to a master tape, incorporating the pauses as you do so. This will enable you to concentrate on one thing at a time.

In the case of an audio-active laboratory, it is normally only necessary to prepare a single copy of the master tape. In the case of an audio-active comparative laboratory, on the other hand, there will be many occasions when it is necessary to provide the students with their own copies of the recorded material. This can either be done in advance, by preparing multiple copies from the master tape, or can be done at the time of the lesson, by playing the relevant section(s) of the master tape at the master console and having the students record the material on their individual machines.

BIBLIOGRAPHY

Anderson, R H (1976) *Selection and Developing Media for Instruction.* Van Nostrand Reinhold, Cincinnati (Chapter 7).

Baent, L *et al* (eds) (1988) *Digital Audio and Compact Disc.* Heinemann-Newnes.

Hill, B (1976) *Teaching Aids and Resources.* In *Teaching Languages*, British Broadcasting Corporation, London.

Jones, J G (1972) *Teaching With Tape.* Focal Press, London and New York.

Kemp, J E (1980) *Planning and Producing Audiovisual Materials.* Harper and Row, New York (Chapter 17).

Mee, C D and Daniel, E D (1988) *Magnetic Recording: Video Audio and Instrumentation.* McGraw-Hill, Maidenhead.

Nichol, N *SCET Guidelines on Audiorecording* (a series of leaflets) Scottish Council for Educational Technology, Glasgow.

Postlethwaite, S N, Novak, J and Murray, H (1972) *The Audio-Tutorial Approach to Learning.* Burgess, Minneapolis.

Romiszowski, A J (1988) *The Selection and Use of Instructional Media.* Kogan Page, London (Chapter 6).

Wittich, W A and Schuller, C F (1979) *Instructional Technology – Its Nature and Use.* Harper and Row, New York (Chapter 6).

Chapter Six

How to Produce Linked Audio and Still Visual Materials

INTRODUCTION

In Chapters 2 to 4, we examined the three basic classes of still visual display materials, looking first at printed and duplicated materials, then at non-projected materials and finally at projected materials, while in Chapter 5 we discussed simple audio materials. In this chapter, we will turn our attention to the various hybrid systems that use audio materials in conjunction with these different types of still visual materials, thus enabling multi-sensory stimulation of the learner to take place.

As in previous chapters, we will begin by examining the various ways in which linked audio and still visual materials can be used in mass instruction, individualized learning and group learning – the three basic types of instructional situation that were identified in Chapter 1. Then, we will examine some of the most important types of system, looking first at systems that link audiotapes with textual materials, then at systems that link tape with series of slides or photographic prints, and finally at various other combinations such as 'tape-model', 'tape-microscope' and 'tape-realia'. In each case, we will identify the main uses of the system and then show how the materials can be designed and produced.

HOW LINKED AUDIO AND STILL VISUAL MATERIALS CAN BE USED IN DIFFERENT TEACHING/LEARNING SITUATIONS

Like all the other types of materials discussed so far, linked audio and still visual materials can be used in a wide range of instructional situations. Let us now see what roles they are capable of playing in each of the three basic classes we have divided such situations into.

Mass Instruction

Linked audio and still visual materials have two main roles in mass instruction. First, they can be used to provide background and illustrative material within the context of a conventional 'live' expository lesson, media such as tape-slide programmes and filmstrips-with-sound being ideal for these purposes. Second, they can be used to provide mediated presentations to a class, tape-slide programmes and filmstrips-with-sound again being ideal media for this, together with radio-vision programmes. In both cases, the use of such media can introduce welcome variety into a course.

Individualized Instruction

Until the advent of computer-based learning, the various systems that use audio and still visual materials in combination were probably the most effective tool available to anyone designing an individualized instruction course of practically any type. Indeed, there are a large number of cases where such systems are still the best medium for individualized instruction, as we will see later in this chapter. Systems such as tape-slide and filmstrips-with-sound have long been used in this role, and the great potential of other linked audio and still visual media such as 'tape-text', 'tape-model', 'tape-microscope' and 'tape-realia' is only now beginning to be fully realized.

Group Learning

Here, the main role of linked audio and still visual materials is probably the provision of illustrative and background material, although there is also scope for the use of such materials as a vehicle for small-group activities. Media such as 'tape-model' and 'tape-realia' certainly have potential here.

LINKED TAPE AND TEXTUAL MATERIALS

As we saw in the last chapter, audiotapes linked with textual materials in an integrated audio-tutorial system constitute a useful vehicle for individualized instruction (see page 169). Here, the tape forms the central 'managerial' component of the instructional system, providing the learners with information, directing them to various activities (reading passages from books or notes, examining materials, carrying out exercises, etc) and providing aural back-up to and extension of these activities. Such systems can be used in the teaching of virtually any subject, and have the great advantage of getting the learner actively involved rather than simply being a passive receiver of information.

Another way of using tape in conjunction with text is to link it directly with a specific worksheet or workbook, so that the two media – audio and textual – are fully integrated. In such systems, the role of the tape may be to introduce the topic to be covered, explain and/or describe the content, periodically direct the learner to activities in the worksheet or workbook, and provide aural back-up and extension material related to these activities. The main role of the worksheet or workbook will probably be to provide questions, exercises, problems, etc, although it may also be used to give the student a permanent 'personal copy' of the material covered by the system, provide self-assessment tests, provide 'further reading' lists, and so on.

How to Plan and Design Tape-Text Materials

When planning tape-text materials – or, indeed, any materials that make use of more than one sense or medium – the primary aim should be to produce a fully integrated instructional system that makes optimum use of the different media being employed. Thus, each of the media should be used in a role that takes full advantage of its particular characteristics, and, most importantly, the different components should *complement* one another. When planning such a system, you will probably find it useful to go through the following stages:

- Establish a clear set of instructional objectives for the system, preferably couched in behavioural terms, or in terms of the competences which it is intended for learners to develop.

- Taking full account of the relevant circumstances (target population, overall role of materials, etc), decide on the basic content of the whole system.

- Decide what activities would be appropriate for covering this content and overtaking the instructional objectives, and establish the role of the different media in each activity. Prepare an outline description of the whole system, clearly defining these activities and roles.

- Write the various textual components of the system, always bearing in mind the role that the accompanying audiotape is going to play when they are being used.

- Produce a detailed script for the audiotape, including pauses and recording instructions.

- Record the spoken material for the tape without pauses, preferably using an open-reel machine (see page 160).

- Dub the spoken material on to a master tape (either open-reel or cassette), editing in the pauses and any other sound(s) required as you do so (see page 164).

- Produce as many copies of the tape as are required by copying the master tape on to one or more compact cassettes, preferably recording the material on both sides of the cassette (see page 165).

- Produce copies of the textual materials after making any changes found necessary in the course of producing the tape.

An example of a script for the audiotape component of an audio-tutorial (on alternative energy) was given in Figure 5.13, and a further example of tape-text material is given in Figure 6.1. This is the start of the outline description that was prepared when planning an audio-workbook on writing instructional objectives.

Writing Instructional Objectives — An Audio-Workbook	
Audiotape	*Workbook*
	Title; instructions to start tape
Introduction to audio-workbook, stating overall aims and outlining content *(roughly two minutes)*. Instructions to study detailed objectives in workbook and to re-start tape when finished. *(Bleep, followed by five second pause)*.	
	Full statement of instructional objectives of audio-workbook expressed in behavioural terms.
Recapitulation of first objective, relating to the role of objectives in a systematic approach to course or curriculum design; referral to schematic diagram of such an approach in workbook. *(roughly three minutes)*. Instructions to summarize three key functions of objectives just described in spaces provided in workbook, rewinding tape and replaying section if necessary, and to re-start tape when finished. *(Bleep, followed by five second pause)*.	Block diagram showing role of objectives in course or curriculum design process.
	Labelled spaces for writing in three key function of objectives.
Recapitulation of second objective, relating to the distinction between *aims* and *objectives*. Instructions to study examples given in workbook and to re-start tape when finished. *(Bleep, followed by five second pause)*.	
	Example of a typical aim (from the section of a secondary school chemistry course dealing with chemical bonding) followed by the start of the list of detailed objectives associated with that aim.

Figure 6.1 **The start of the outline of a typical audio-workbook**

Audiotape	Workbook
Discussion of the distinction between aims and objectives, with reference to the illustrative material in the text *(roughly two minutes)*. Instructions to summarize distinctions between aims and objectives in spaces provided in workbook, rewinding tape and replaying section if necessary, and to re-start tape when finished. *(Bleep, followed by five second pause)*.	
	Labelled spaces for writing in distinguishing features of aims and objectives.
Recapitulation of third objective . . . and so on	

Figure 6.1 (continued)

The way in which the audio and textual components of an audio-workbook can be used to support and complement one another is clearly illustrated in this example.

LINKED TAPE AND PHOTOGRAPHIC MATERIALS

The various systems that link audiotapes with sequences of photographic images are among the most widely used of all audiovisual media – particularly as vehicles for individualized instruction. Of the various types of system, the two that can most easily be produced 'in-house' by practising teachers, instructors and trainers are tape-slide programmes and tape-photograph programmes, so we will concentrate on these in this section.

Tape-Slide Programmes

Tape-slide programmes consist of linked sequences of photographic slides, usually of the compact 2 inch × 2 inch variety, that are accompanied by synchronized commentaries recorded on audiotape, usually on compact cassettes. In some cases, synchronization of the advance of the slides with the sound is achieved by incorporating audible 'bleeps' in the actual sound signal, so that the user knows when to advance the slides manually. In more sophisticated programmes designed for display on fully automatic equipment, the advance cues are recorded on a separate track of the tape, consisting of pulses of sound that trigger the 'advance' mechanism on the slide projection or viewing system. Both forms of programme can be used in virtually all types of instructional situation by using appropriate equipment. For showing a tape-slide programme to a class or large group, this usually consists of a slide projector and separate audiotape player, with the two being linked by an electronic synchronizing unit if the programme is an 'automatic' one with inaudible advance cues. For individual or small-group use, the equipment can range from a simple manual slide viewer and cheap cassette player to a fully automatic tape-slide unit incorporating linked audio playback and back-projection slide viewing facilities.

Instructional Uses of Tape-Slide Programmes

As we have seen, tape-slide programmes can be used in virtually all types of instructional situation, both as self-contained units of mediated instruction and also in a secondary or supportive role (providing illustrative material, background material, and so on). When used in the former role, such programmes can be just as effective as a well-prepared, well-delivered lecture or expository lesson in helping students to understand the subject matter. Like the latter, however, they constitute an essentially 'one-way' channel of communication in which the learner has no opportunity for active participation, so that long-term retention of the material tends to be low. Thus it is now generally agreed that tape-slide programmes are most useful as a vehicle for giving a general introduction to a topic, or of stimulating interest and providing motivation for further or more detailed study, rather than as a vehicle for presenting the detailed content of a course. To teach this detailed content effectively, it is advisable to use methods that incorporate higher learner involvement. A more detailed discussion of the strengths and weaknesses of tape-slide programmes as instructional vehicles is given in the book by Romiszowski listed in the Bibliography, and interested readers are referred to this.

How to Design and Produce Tape-Slide Programmes

General guidelines: When designing a tape-slide programme for a specific educational or training purpose, it is obviously necessary to be quite clear what this purpose is, and to be satisfied that use of a tape-slide programme is likely to be an effective way of achieving it. Assuming that this is the case, we would offer readers the following general guidelines.

- Keep the programme simple. As we have seen, the tape-slide medium is best suited to providing general introductions to topics rather than to providing detailed coverage of their content.

- Keep the programme comparatively short – certainly no longer than the 80 slides that can be contained in the standard carousel-type magazines that are used with most automatic tape-slide equipment.

- Make sure that the programme has a clearly defined structure, making appropriate use of 'signposts' and 'links' to ensure that the user has no difficulty in seeing what this structure is.

- Make sure that the visual and audio elements complement each other at all times (this is probably the most important rule of all).

- Do not compromise on quality; a tape-slide programme is only as good as its weakest component, so try to make sure that the photographs, the graphic slides, the narration, and (most important of all) the synchronization are all of the same equally high standard.

The detailed design of the programme: This is best carried out by first producing a skeleton outline, listing the main sections of the programme, and then writing a detailed script for the programme – either in the form of a 'story board' (sketches of the individual frames with the accompanying text alongside) or as a double-column script with the visual component described on one side and the audio element on the other.

Whichever form of script you decide to employ, you should try to make full and effective use of the different types of basic 'building bricks' that can be used to construct tape-slide programmes. It is helpful to classify these as follows:

Visual 'building bricks'

- Signposts and links (main title slides, titles for sections and sub-sections, and so on).

- Photographs (original or 'second-hand' photographic images of all types).

- Graphic illustrations (schematic diagrams, graphs, bar charts, pie charts, tables, and so on).

- Verbal illustrations (slides carrying simple verbal material designed to support or complement the narrative).

Audio 'building bricks'

- Narrative (the main component of the audio element of all tape-slide programmes).

- Silence (the pauses between frames, and any other deliberate pauses or periods of silence).

- Music (introductory or closing music, music used as a link between sections, background music, and so on).

- Special effects (claps of thunder, shots, sounds of machinery, or any other special sound effects thought appropriate at specific points in a programme).

The first six will almost always be used, whereas the last two are only used on special occasions. In the case of music, this is partly because

SEDCO Non-Destructive Testing Appreciation Course
Stage 1: Basic Concepts and Techniques

Slide sequence and commentary for tape-slide programme

Slides	Commentary (pulses signified by •)
1. Main title slide: 'SEDCO Non-Destructive Testing Appreciation Course' Stage 1: basic concepts and techniques	*Silence* (ten seconds) followed by •
2. Photograph of SEDCO personnel (with SEDCO logo clearly visible on helmets) inspecting the flange on the end of a section of pipe-line in their pipe yard prior to carrying out a test for cracks.	'The programme that you are about to see has been specially produced for SEDCO in order to give you and your colleagues an introduction to the field of *non-destructive testing*, or *NDT* as it is commonly called.' (*one second pause;* • ; *one second pause*)
3. Photograph of front cover of self-instructional manual that accompanies programme, showing name of Company.	'You should also have received a copy of the SEDCO self-tuition manual that has been written to accompany the programme, and should read this carefully after you have finished studying the programme itself.' (*one second pause;* • ; *one second pause*)
4. Caption slide listing first set of self-assessment questions in manual.	'At the end of each section of the manual, you will find a number of questions dealing with the material covered. These have been designed to help you tell whether you have mastered the material, or whether you will need to go over some of it again.' (*four second pause;* • ; *one second pause*)
5. Photograph of SEDCO personnel carrying out MPI test on flange on pipeline.	'Once you are satisfied that you can answer *all* the questions in the manual, you will be ready to move on to Stage 2 of the course, which examines some of the ways in which non-destructive testing is actually used by SEDCO.' (*one second pause;* •)
6. Section title slide: 'NDT as a diagnostic tool'	*Silence* (ten seconds) followed by •

Figure 6.2 **The start of the script of a typical instructional tape-slide programme**

Slides	*Commentary* (pulses signified by •)
7. Caption slide 'NDT — examining materials for flaws without impairing their desirable properties'.	'Non-destructive testing has been defined as the science of examining materials or manufactured articles in order to determine their fitness for a certain purpose, *without impairing their desirable properties in any way*.' (*one second pause;* •; *one second pause*)
8. Schematic diagram, showing two possible outcomes of NDT: (1) no serious defects ∴ OK for use. (2) serious defects ∴ unsuitable for use.	'No material or manufactured article is ever *completely* free from flaws or defects, and the object of NDT is to detect any such defects and determine whether they are likely to be sufficiently serious to prevent the item from being able to do the job for which it was designed.' (*three second pause;* •; *one second pause*)
9. Schematic diagram of block of material showing surface and internal defects.	'Defects are of two basic types, namely, those that occur on the surface of an item, and those that are located in the interior, and are thus much more difficult to detect.' (*one second pause;* •; *one second pause*)
10. Caption slide listing three types of NDT tests: — surface tests — sub-surface tests — internal tests.	'We find it convenient to divide non-destructive testing methods into three broad groups, depending on the type of defects that they are designed to detect, namely, *surface tests;* which are used to detect defects that occur on the actual surface; *sub-surface tests*, which are able to detect defects that are located just below the surface; and *internal tests*, which can be used to discover defects that occur deep in the interior.' (*one second pause;* •; *one second pause*)
11. Caption slide listing two main types of NDT methods to be covered in programme: — dye penetrant testing — magnetic particle inspection.	'A large number of different NDT techniques are available, but the ones that you are most likely to make use of in the course of your work are *dye penetrant testing* and *magnetic particle inspection*. We will therefore take a detailed look at each of these methods.' (*one second pause;* •; *one second pause*)

Figure 6.2 (continued)

Slides	Commentary (pulses signified by •)
12. Caption slide listing other four types of NDT methods to be covered: — eddy current testing — ultrasonic testing — X-ray radiography — gamma radiography.	'We will also examine four other important NDT methods with which you should be familiar, even though you are unlikely to have to use them yourself — eddy current testing, ultrasonic testing, X-ray radiography and gamma radiography.' *(one second pause; •)*
13. Section title slide: 'Dye penetrant testing'.	*Silence* (ten seconds) followed by •.
and so on	

Figure 6.2 (continued)

there are generally copyright problems associated with the use of music on tape-slide programmes, and partly because the use of music in such programmes (other than in introductory, linking and closing sequences) can be distracting.

Part of a typical script for a tape-slide programme is given in Figure 6.2. This was written for the South-Eastern Drilling Company (SEDCO) as part of a distance learning package on non-destructive testing that Henry Ellington and Eric Addinall developed for the company in 1982.

The 75-slide programme from which the script extract is presented was used to provide a general introduction to the subject of non-destructive testing, being accompanied by a 68-page self-instructional manual that dealt with the subject in much greater detail. The development of the package is described in detail in the paper by Ellington, Addinall and Blood that is listed in the Bibliography.

Figure 6.2 illustrates many of the basic principles of tape-slide programme design, and readers should note the following specific points:

■ The clear division of the programme into sections using title slides and periods of silence; the latter can, alternatively, be filled with suitable music if this is preferred.

■ The explicit specification of the lengths of the pauses between slides and the timing of the slide changes. These are crucial to the success of the programme, which can easily be ruined if the pauses are too short (or too long), or if the slide changes are badly timed.

■ The way in which the visual elements have been carefully designed to complement the narrative which, in this particular programme, is the main vehicle of communication. Wherever possible, a photograph or schematic diagram is used but, in cases where neither of these would be appropriate, a simple caption slide that reinforces the key points being made in the narrative is employed (see, for example, frames 7, 10, 11 and 12). The later sections of the programme, which deal with the various NDT methods, make use of a similar mixture of photographs, schematic diagrams and 'verbal reinforcement' slides to back up the narrative.

■ The way in which the various visual elements are explicitly described in the script – the verbal equivalent of the sketches in a 'story board' script.

Producing the programme materials: The two processes described above – producing the skeleton outline and producing the detailed script –

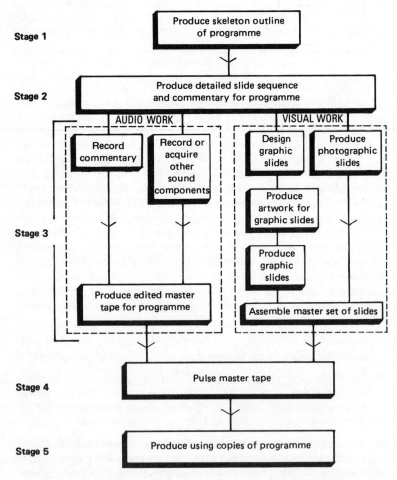

Figure 6.3 **The various stages in the design and production of a tape-slide programme**

constitute the first two stages in the development of a tape-slide programme. As can be seen from Figure 6.3, which shows the complete
development process in a flow diagram form, the next stage consists of
the actual production of the audio and visual components of the programme – two processes that should be carried out in parallel.

The audio side of the work involves three separate processes:

■ Recording the commentary for the programme in the way described
on pages 160 to 162 of Chapter 5. Engage the services of a professional presenter for this work, particularly if the programme is an
important one, but appreciate that this may not always be practicable; if not, make sure that the presenter used is capable of doing
justice to the material (see page 160).

■ Recording or acquiring any other sound components needed for the
programme (music, sound effects, etc). If you do decide to make use
of music, make sure that you have proper copyright clearance, otherwise you could find yourself in severe legal difficulties; by far the
safest way to proceed is to make use of one of the special 'copyright
cleared' recordings that are available for use in such work.

■ Dubbing the commentary and any other sound components on to
a master cassette tape, in the way described on pages 164 to 165 of
Chapter 5, editing in the pauses and periods of silence as you do so.
The easiest way to time such pauses is to 'count in thousands' ('one
thousand', 'two thousand', 'three thousand', and so on) which, with
a little practice, can be used to time multiples of one second with considerable accuracy. Do not edit in the pulses at this stage, since this
is best deferred until you have a complete set of slides available.

The visual side of the work involves five separate processes:

■ Designing all the various graphic slides (main title slides, section title
slides, schematic diagrams, graphs, caption slides, etc). This is best
done by producing a rough version of the material required on each
slide on a separate sheet of paper, using coloured felt pens.

■ Producing the finished artwork for the graphic slides. If you have to
do this yourself, use the various techniques described on pages 94 to
96 of Chapter 3 but, if at all possible, it is obviously better to have the
work done by a specialist graphic artist.

■ Producing the graphic slides, in the way described on pages 135 to
145 of Chapter 4.

■ Producing the photographic slides (ie those slides that consist of
original photographs rather than photographs of artwork). This
should be done in the way described on pages 135 to 138 of
Chapter 4.

■ Assembling the master set of slides. It is best to use one of the display racks in a slide storage/display cabinet for this work (see Figure 4.21), then to transfer the complete set into a carousel-type magazine or transfer storage box. This has the advantage of visually displaying the complete sequence of slides during the assembly process.

Once you have produced the edited master tape and assembled the full slide sequence for the programme, the crucial task of pulsing the master tape can be carried out. This can either be done using a suitable cassette tape recorder that possesses a pulsing facility or using an individual tape-slide playback-viewing machine that possesses a similar facility. Whichever method is used, check that the pulses will operate the equipment that you will be using to show the tape-slide programme, since pulses recorded on one type of equipment do not always work with another.

Finally, run off as many using copies of the programme as are required by producing duplicate copies of the master cassette in the way described on page 165 of Chapter 5 and producing duplicates of the slides in the way described on page 144 of Chapter 4.

Storing tape-slide programmes: One problem that has to be overcome by all users of tape-slide programmes is that of storing the programme materials – especially the slides. If the programme is short, it is possible simply to store the slides in a small box, eg an empty slide binder box, and to load them into the viewing or projection equipment one by one at the time of use. With longer programmes, however, this be-

Figure 6.4 **One of the authors, Henry Ellington, pulsing a dual-projector tape-slide programme**

comes very time-consuming, and it is much better to store the complete slide sequence in such a way that it is immediately ready for use. If the equipment that is to be used to show or view the programme employs a carousel-type magazine, the slides can either be stored in an actual magazine or else in a slide transfer storage box – a circular box that enables an entire programme to be transferred to or from the projector magazine simply by placing one on top of the other and then upending the system.

Tape-Photograph Programmes

A tape-photograph programme is simply a linked sequence of photographic prints with an accompanying audio-tape. Such programmes can be used to do virtually anything that a conventional tape-slide programme can do, and have two advantages over the latter. First, they require no projection or viewing equipment, since photographic prints, unlike slides, are completely 'free standing'. Second, they are in some ways much more flexible and versatile than tape-slide programmes from an instructional point of view. It is, for example, much easier to incorporate textual materials into a tape-photograph programme, and also to build in enactive components such as exercises or worksheets. Indeed an effective way of presenting the photographic component of tape-photograph programmes is to incorporate them into a re-usable workbook.

The principles that underlie the design of tape-photograph programmes are basically the same as those just described for tape-slide programmes, the main difference being in the structuring of the audio-tape narrative. Indeed, the design of the latter is in many ways more like that of the audiotape component of a tape-text system (especially if the programme incorporates textual materials or enactive exercises), incorporating audible cues and instructions rather than the inaudible cues that characterize the tapes used in most tape-slide programmes. The production of the materials for tape-photograph programmes is similar to the process just described for tape-slide programmes, albeit simpler.

OTHER SYSTEMS THAT LINK TAPE AND STILL VISUAL MATERIALS

Although the systems described above are by far the best known of the instructional systems that link audiotapes with still visual materials, they are certainly not the only ones. It is, for example, possible to design a wide range of useful self-instructional systems that make use of audiotapes in conjunction with tools, pieces of equipment, models, microscope slides, items of realia, and so on. Furthermore, such systems often incorporate a high enactive component that makes them much more effective than more passive systems such as tape-slide programmes in achieving certain types of objectives. Some examples of such systems are described below.

Tape-Model

This makes use of an audiotape in conjunction with three-dimensional models or kits from which such models can be constructed. The tape generally plays much the same role as in an audio-tutorial or audio-workbook system, presenting learners with information and guiding them through an appropriate sequence of activities that involve handling and studying the models, and, in the case of systems that use construction kits, actually making up models. Such systems have a wide range of applications, obvious examples being in the teaching of chemistry (work with models of electronic orbital systems, molecules, complexes, crystal structures, and so on), biology (work with models of parts of animals and plants, physiological systems, and so on), physics (work with models of physical systems of various sorts) and engineering (work with models of machines, systems, plant and so on). Figure 6.5 shows a typical tape-model system in use (a student of chemistry using a 'ball and spring' kit to construct and study models of different organic molecules – isomers of simple alkanes, in this case).

Figure 6.5 **A student of chemistry studying the isomers of the simple alkanes using a tape-model system**

Tape-Microscope

When using a microscope, it is obviously difficult to read textual material (instructions, explanatory notes, etc) at the same time. Thus there is obvious scope for the use of audiotapes to supply such information, since this enables learners to work at the same time as they receive the information. Subjects that lend themselves to the use of this technique include all the various branches of biology and medicine, geology and metallurgy.

Tape-Realia

Audiotapes can also be used to provide instructions and information to learners who are studying realia of various forms – eg geological or biological specimens. As in the case of tape-microscopes, use of an audiotape to provide such information can allow complicated enactive processes to be carried out without the distraction of having to refer to textual instructions or notes – obviously a great advantage in an individualized learning situation.

Basic Petrology — Revision Unit: Igneous Rocks	
Contents of audiotape	*Associated activities*
This Unit is designed to help you to recognize hand specimens of the main types of igneous rocks, and to describe their mineralogical compositions as revealed by the study of thin sections of the rocks using a geological microscope. If you require any help with the use of the latter, study the accompanying instruction sheet. We will begin by studying the main types of acid plutonic rocks, ie the *granites*. Please pick up and examine Specimen 1 in the tray of hand specimens when you hear the signal, stopping the tape when you do so. Make a note of what you think are the main characteristics of this specimen, restarting the tape once you have finished. (Bleep, followed by five second pause)	Instruction sheet on geological microscope available if required.
	Study of Specimen 1 (normal granite) and noting down of observed characteristics.

Figure 6.6 **Start of the script of a typical instructional system that uses an audiotape in conjunction with enactive activities (study of geological specimens)**

Contents of audiotape	Associated activities
This is a specimen of normal granite from the Rubislaw Quarry in Aberdeen, its main constituents being quartz (the clear, colourless mineral), feldspar (the grey material) and mica (the black and clear platy materials). Note the relatively coarse texture (indicating the plutonic origins of the rock) and uniform grain size.	Re-examination of Specimen 1 as commentary proceeds.
Now let us take a look at a section of this rock using the geological microscope. Select Slide 1 from the box of slides provided and carry out a thorough examination of it, making a note of all the minerals that you identify in order of relative abundance. Stop the tape when you hear the signal, and re-start it once you have finished the work. (Bleep, followed by five second pause)	
	Study of Slide 1 using geological microscope.
As you should have seen, the predominant mineral in this particular type of granite is *quartz*. This is colourless, free from alteration, shows fluid inclusion, has a low refractive index (close to that of Canada Balsam) and shows low double refraction. Stop the tape until you are satisfied that you can recognize all these features. (Bleep, followed by five second pause)	Re-examination of slide as commentary proceeds.
	Re-examination of slide in order to identify the various features of quartz.
Next in relative abundance are various forms of *feldspar*. Of these, the most important is *orthoclase*, recognizable by its alteration, low refractive index, and low double refraction; some crystals also show Carlsbad twinning. Stop the tape until you are satisfied	Re-examination of slide as commentary proceeds.
and so on	

Figure 6.6 (continued)

No doubt readers can think of many other instructional situations in which audiotapes could usefully be linked with still visual materials of various types.

Designing and Producing the Courseware for Such Systems

The design of the courseware for a system that links an audiotape with the use of materials such as models or realia is basically the same as for an audio-tutorial system (see page 169), except that no textual materials are generally involved. A typical example of the script for such a system is given in Figure 6.6. This is for a self-instructional revision system in basic petrology (the branch of geology that involves the study of rocks), being designed to help students prepare for a practical examination that involves identifying hand specimens of different rocks and describing their compositions as revealed by microscopic study by thin sections cut from them.

The courseware should be produced in the same way as for tape-text materials (see page 176).

BIBLIOGRAPHY

Anderson, R H (1976) *Selecting and Developing Media for Instruction.* Van Nostrand Reinhold, Cincinnati (Chapter 7).

Beaumont-Craggs, R (1975) *Slide-Tape and Dual Projection.* Focal Press, London and New York.

Ellington, H I, Addinall, E and Blood, J (1984) Providing extension training for offshore personnel – an educational technology-based approach. In Shaw, K E (ed) (1983) *Aspects of Educational Technology XVII,* Kogan Page, London, pp 168-73.

Johnstone, A H, Letton, K M and Percival, F (1977) Tape-model: the lecture complement. *Chemistry in Britain,* **13**, 11, pp 423-5.

Kemp, J E (1980) *Planning and Producing Audiovisual Materials.* Harper and Row, New York (Chapter 19).

Langdon, D G (1978) The Audio Workbook, in *The Instructional Design Library* (Vol 3). Educational Technology Press, Englewood Cliffs, NJ.

Postlethwaite, S N, Novak, J and Murray, H (1978) *The Audio-Tutorial Approach to Learning.* Burgess, Minneapolis.

Romiszowski, A J (1988) *The Selection and Use of Instructional Media.* Kogan Page, London (Chapter 6).

Russell, J D (1978) The Audio-Tutorial System. In *The Instructional Design Library* (Vol 3). Educational Technology Press, Englewood Cliffs, NJ.

Chapter Seven

How to Produce Video Materials

INTRODUCTION

The Demise of Cine

In the few years since the first edition of this book, things have changed
a lot regarding video and cine production. In short, video technology has
changed almost beyond recognition, becoming much more versatile,
and, in real terms, much less expensive. Cine technology has changed
little, but the use of cine in education and training has fallen enormously,
as it has become very much simpler to use video. Indeed, the fate of
many a good cine film is now to be turned into an educational video.
The final nail in the coffin of educational cine production has been the
comparative costs. In 1992, cine film is estimated to cost around £3 per
minute, while videotape costs very much less – and is reusable. Editing
cine films was very much an art of cutting and splicing; editing video is
no less an art, but can be done extremely quickly by trained personnel,
and is done electronically (so if it does not work first time, nothing is lost,
it can be tried again and again until perfect results are obtained).

Video as a teaching/learning medium

The main thrust of this chapter will be to take a hard look at the advantages and disadvantages of video as a teaching/learning medium; we
will resist the temptation to go into a lot of detail regarding types of
equipment, costs, and technology. The main reason for this is that the
whole field of educational video is changing day by day, as more sophisticated video recorders and video cameras appear in each new catalogue
of equipment. With video recorders in most homes, there is presently a
flood of relatively inexpensive portable cameras (Camcorders) of various
kinds in shops on every High Street. Even relatively inexpensive Camcorders can deliver video pictures of a quality which could only be obtained in television studios a few years ago.

It is now relatively rare for education and training practitioners to
involve themselves directly in the art and science of editing video
materials. Most education and training organizations have central editing and production facilities, and the work there is done by specialists
who can quickly perform work of very high quality – even on material

created by amateurs. Therefore, the main purpose of this chapter is to help ensure that the ways that video can be used to help learning are kept firmly in mind.

As in previous chapters, we will begin by looking at how moving images can be used in different types of teaching/learning situations. We will then look briefly at the planning and production of video materials, including some explanation of the basics of the technology involved.

HOW VIDEO MATERIALS CAN BE USED IN DIFFERENT TEACHING/LEARNING SITUATIONS

It is probably true to say that video materials can be used in virtually all types of instructional situation, from mass lectures to individualized learning. Video materials can be used at all levels, from primary school classes to Open University learners working at home using household video recorders.

Video materials can be used to provide illustrative material. Equally, video recordings can be the vehicle through which an exposition or instructional sequence is presented. Although an obvious advantage of video is that moving images are directly useful (sometimes indispensable) when there is a need to show movement to learners, video is capable of presenting any kind of visual information. Let us next explore how video can be used in the three broad classes of instructional situations identified throughout this book – mass instruction, individualized instruction and group learning.

Mass Instruction

In education and training establishments, places such as lecture theatres are now usually equipped with facilities to display video recordings. This can be achieved by having video projection facilities which allow a very large image to be projected onto a central screen (usually in a darkened room), or by having television monitors at various points in the room, so that people anywhere in the large group can see a screen relatively easily.

The first use of video materials in large-group situations is to provide illustrative, background or supportive material for use within the context of conventional lectures or demonstrations. Video is particularly suitable where motion needs to be demonstrated, or where elements of 'the world outside' need to be brought into the teaching/learning situation. In many subjects, fine detail such as facial expression and body language are vital to the teaching/learning situation, and video recordings can provide a shared learning experience to a large group, watching intimate details of interviews, role-plays, debates, and human behaviour. Video episodes in large group teaching and training can range from recorded half-hour television broadcasts to short clips lasting minutes or even seconds.

A second use of video materials in mass instruction is to provide self-contained expositions that take the place of a conventional lecture or taught lesson on a given topic. The usefulness of video is by no means restricted to scenes showing movement, however, and sequences of still pictures can be shown just as effectively on video as in a tape-slide programme. For example, a series of illustrations of art or sculpture can be shown, either with commentary and discussion already recorded into the video materials themselves, or added 'live' by the presenter. All kinds of video recordings can be used in this 'mediated lesson' role, including broadcasts recorded from off-air television (with appropriate copyright clearance or payment), video recordings of cine film material, 'home-produced' video sequences, and 'off-the-shelf' educational and training videos, which are often sold with resources to provide handouts and advice to presenters.

A third use of video is as a vehicle enabling learners to interact, even in the context of a mass instructional situation. The use of closed-circuit television systems to record drama, role-playing exercises, debates and so on for subsequent discussion and analysis by a class are examples. Additionally, it is often possible to have a few members of a class acting out (for example) interviews, in another room (or recording studio), while the majority of the class observe 'live' on the screen in a lecture room, and prepare for their turn at contributing to the work in the studio.

Individualized Instruction and Open Learning

Video is an ideal medium for use with individual learners, particularly now that most homes contain one or more video recorders. Only a few years ago, when cine was widely used in mass instructional systems, it was quite impractical to extend its use to individualized learning. With video, the extension is easily made. An individual can derive the same benefits from an expository video sequence as could a large group – with the additional advantages of being able to stop and start the sequence at will, and replay parts whenever this is found necessary or useful.

The Open University has for many years used television broadcasts as an integral part of its provision. Years ago, most Open University students were expected to be in front of their television sets when the broadcasts were transmitted (often at 'unsociable hours' such as round midnight or early on Saturday and Sunday mornings). If you ask present-day Open University students how they access the broadcasts, you will find that they mostly record them on domestic video recorders, and then use the recordings at times and places of their own choice, taking advantage of the ability to stop and play parts again when necessary. Alternatively, the Open University has a service whereby videotape recordings of broadcasts can be supplied to learners by mail, on loan. Many other providers of open learning materials, in both educational and training contexts, now include video recordings as key parts of learning packages.

When the flexibility and impact of video images are coupled to the use of computers, as in interactive video (discussed further in the next chapter), video sequences (and video still images too) can play a very powerful part in highly-responsive teaching/learning situations. Here, individual learners can exercise a great deal of control over the pace and manner in which they learn, with the computer system allowing the learning packages to be accessed in the way that is most suitable to each individual learner, on the basis of the answers learners key in, or the options they select using keyboards, a mouse, light pens, and so on.

Group Learning

Video materials can be used in a supportive role as before, providing visual information of various types for illustrative, background information or extension purposes. Equally easily, video materials can be used by groups as a way of facilitating the interaction of members of the group in role-plays, simulations, and microteaching. Conventional video recordings have already proved to be powerful learning aids for teacher-led and student-led groups alike. It is likely that interactive video packages will prove even more useful in many situations, allowing group discussion and group planning, and with the interactive video package providing responses directly to decisions made by the group (for example, options chosen, data keyed in, and so on).

PROMOTING LEARNING FROM VIDEO RECORDINGS

As we have seen, video recordings can serve a wide range of purposes, and can be used in a variety of learning situations, ranging from mass instruction to individualized learning. When video recordings were first used in education and training, because they were 'new', their impact was high, and the learning experiences were enhanced. Now that broadcast television and video recordings are a basic part of life in the developed world, there is no novelty in using educational videos, whether in a large lecture theatre, or on one's own at home. Familiarity with the medium of video has led to a strong tendency to treat it very passively, detracting from its usefulness as a learning medium.

However, there is much that can be done to help learners and trainees derive greater benefit from video recordings (and indeed from live television broadcasts). Before going any further in this chapter along the lines of helping you decide how you may develop your own educational video materials, we would like you to pause and consider in general terms the usage of video and television in education and training. In other words, we would like you to think about how you have seen existing video and television materials used, and to what extent they contributed to the learning experiences of those viewing them.

Below we have presented twenty questions relating to the way television can be used in education and training, and for each question we have added some suggestions regarding how best to enable learners to maximize the benefits they derive from educational television and video. We should emphasize that the twenty questions below are intended to be employed when it is intended that video is to serve an important role in the overall context of the learning programme – in other words when there are firm objectives that are to be achieved by learners in the process of viewing and following-up the video programme.

Twenty Questions about Educational Television

1. *How are learners' attitudes towards viewing recordings differentiated from 'natural' passive attitudes associated with everyday television? For example, how and when are learners briefed about the expected learning outcomes to be derived from viewing the recording?*

    'Natural' approaches to watching television are passive, due to the prominent role played by television in most homes. It is so often a form of entertainment – or merely 'wallpaper'. With educational video, learners need to be primed to *attend* to viewing a recording in a focused way. Expressing the intended learning outcomes in the form of objectives can help focus the learning. Describing to learners the competences they should acquire from watching the recording can alert them to what they should be trying to extract from it. In short, they should know *why* they're watching it, and what they're expected to be able to do when they have thought about it.

2. *Do the expected learning outcomes fall into the* need to know *category, or the* nice to know *category? Do learners know which?*

    While it is perfectly acceptable to use video for *nice to know* material, it is necessary that learners know that this is the case. This means that when they are watching something more important (ie *need to know*) they can adjust their approach accordingly.

3. *What exactly does the experience of watching the recording do for learners, which could not be done as well by other media? Are they alerted in advance to the reason why video helps in this way?*

    If learners know exactly why video is being used, they have a better idea of what is expected of them. For example, if they are alerted to particular things to watch out for as they view the video, they will approach their task in a much more structured way. It also overcomes the idea that it is simply being used as a relaxation, or that the tutor could not be bothered to produce a 'normal' session on that occasion.

4. *What is a sensible maximum for the duration of a single 'clip'? How is this affected by the nature and purpose of the recording?*

    The sensible maximum duration will depend on what the learners are expected to be extracting from the recording. Concentration spans are short – particularly regarding a medium which has conditioned people to a relaxation approach. Concentration spans are likely to be (as always) shorter in a large group than a small group, or working alone.

5. *How important is it to give learners printed resource materials (eg workbooks) which turn their viewing into structured learning experiences, and provide a frame of reference for their retrospective thinking about the experiences?*
   Something printed can provide a framework for learners to 'hang' their thinking on, especially when the video is being used by small groups of learners or learners working alone. When videos are used in large group instruction, since it will be unlikely that individual learners will have an opportunity to review the recording at will, it is important for them to have something which will later serve as a 'trigger' to the more important aspects of the video, and it is useful to distribute briefing notes to the large group.

6. *How will the learning outcomes be demonstrated? (ie what will constitute* evidence *of the outcomes being successfully achieved?)*
   Working out how the learning outcomes can be demonstrated helps to establish exactly what learners should be deriving from their experience of watching a recording. It helps to 'pin down' learning objectives. If learners are primed that they will indeed be expected to demonstrate things they learned from watching a video, there is a much greater chance that they will be attentive enough to succeed.

7. *When will the learning outcomes be demonstrated? (eg after what time interval?)*
   If the learning outcomes are important, it may be expected that learners will be able to demonstrate them weeks or months after viewing the recording (for example as part of formal assessments such as exams). It could be useful to structure learning outcomes into 'immediate', 'medium-term' and 'long-term' outcomes.

8. *Do the learners know in advance what they will be expected to do? Should they?*
   When learners know exactly what is expected of them, they are better able to deliver it. However, there will be occasions where the element of surprise is desirable – especially as part of a shared learning experience. A balance needs to be sought.

9. *When viewing is directly linked to later assessment, do the learners know the performance criteria which will be used to assess what they have learned from watching a video recording?*
   Letting learners know fine details of the criteria which will be used to assess them gives them the opportunity to adjust their approach so that they maximize the probability that they can live up to the criteria in due course.

10. *Can learners be involved in formulating the performance criteria? Can they be involved in defining the evidence they will be required to demonstrate?*
Where learners have been involved in formulating performance criteria and defining evidence, they establish a sense of 'ownership' of the learning situation. This leads to deeper learning, and a more active approach. If a group of learners has previously prepared descriptors of the competences they are hoping to develop using video recordings as a learning resource, their learning approach will be much more active when they view the recordings.

11. *Do learners know the relative importance of the outcomes they should have derived from watching the programme? (ie how significant are the learning outcomes compared to other parts of the syllabus?)*
For example, if 20 per cent of class-time is used watching video recordings, it may reasonably be expected that the associated learning counts for 20 per cent of forthcoming assessments.

12. *Can the performance criteria be formulated before watching the programme? Should they?*
Unless the elements of surprise and discovery are overriding, learners will benefit by being well prepared regarding how they should structure their approach to viewing the recording.

13. *Can learners be made more receptive by having questions in their minds before watching the programme?*
When learners watch a video recording armed with a list of questions and issues, they are helped to draw more from the experience. It can be worth spending time with large or small groups to provide such an agenda before playing a recording to them.

14. *Can learners be assisted to formulate their own agenda of questions and issues, which will then be addressed by the programme?*
When learners have *their own* questions and issues to hand before watching a recording, their ownership of the experience is greatly enhanced.

15. *Who will measure learners' demonstrations of their learning outcomes?*
When the outcomes are measured by tutors, there are the advantages of objectivity and fairness. However, ownership of the learning experience tends to be reduced, and there is also the danger that feedback to learners is minimal.

16. *Can peer assessment or self assessment be employed, as a means of enhancing and deepening the learning experience?*
Self or peer assessment tends to be slower than tutor assessment, and can be less objective at times. However, self or peer assessment promotes deeper thinking about issues, and peer assessment in particular tends to promote discussion and feedback. If learners know that they are going to apply self and peer assessment in due

course to things that they learn from video programmes, they derive a deeper learning experience both during the viewing and the follow-up work.

17. *When video recordings are used in mass instruction, can learners have later access to the programme at will? (eg in a library or through the availability of personal copies).*
Allowing learners repeated access to recordings can go some way towards addressing the problem that viewing tends to be a 'transient' experience. If the recordings can take a natural place among other resources (textbooks, notes, and so on), learners will pay more attention to them.

18. *To what extent can video recordings be issued to learners as the basis for homework or in-college project work, with self-study directions and a workbook? (ie so learners can work in their own way, at their own pace, and with their own control of repetition).*
Most learning is not directly associated with teaching! When learners can take charge of the way they use video recordings, their learning is likely to be deeper (if perhaps slower).

19. *What sort of feedback is gathered from learners about their learning experience regarding the video recording?*
When structured questionnaires (or interview questions) are used to induce learners to make decisions about what they got out of a learning experience, the experience itself is deepened. This also helps alert teachers to whether or not video is simply being seen by learners as 'a break from real work'.

20. *Is it possible to help learners themselves* make *video recordings to give them a deeper insight into the issues involved, and establish 'ownership' of their learning experiences?*
The act of making a video recording tends to be memorable. Whether operating a camera, or playing a part in the recording, heightened learning outcomes are normally achieved. For example, when helping learners improve their interview skills or presentation skills, asking them to make video recordings of each other exercising these skills leads to 'deep thinking' about the processes involved, and ultimately helps learners develop the respective skills far more effectively than simply watching other people demonstrating them.

You will have gathered from the twenty questions above, and the discussion points we provided for each, that we are concerned about the dangers of using video 'lightly' when it could with a little care be used with much higher learning payoff. We hope that you will find it useful to bear these reservations in mind as you go on to consider how best to use video in your own work in education or training.

QUALITY AND VALIDITY

If you have ever tried making your own videos, and then watched them critically, you will without doubt have looked at your television set with 'different eyes' when watching broadcast television. The quality of broadcast television is very advanced indeed for much of the time. Anyone who has been round broadcasting studios, and seen the sophistication of the studios themselves, and the editing facilities, and the care taken with productions, will appreciate how much expertise and talent lies behind even the simplest broadcasts on television. The consequence is that people have high expectations regarding the quality of television or video sequences, even though these expectations are normally quite subconscious. As a result, when we see something that is obviously an 'amateur' production on our television screens, we are immediately alerted subconsciously that something is 'wrong'. The problem is that our instinctive reaction is likely to be to distrust the 'amateur' video – not only the production itself, but the content of the programme.

If the quality of video recordings used in education and training does not match up to learners' expectations of television, it is logical that the message itself will be devalued. An amateur video may seem to imply that the topic is not important. A clumsy video may cause learners to think more about the faults than the content of the programme. So for video to be used in a way that engenders learners' trust and confidence, the standard needs to be as close to that of good broadcast television as possible. This means that it is probably much safer to seek to use directly (or adapt) high-quality programmes that are already available than to start from scratch and make your own video.

The converse side of the 'quality' issue concerns involving learners in making their own videos. In this case, they will be much more forgiving regarding technical shortcomings in the final product. In addition, because much of their minds is on performance, camera technique, sound levels, lighting and so on, as they make and edit their videos, their learning about the subject itself is 'spread out' – in other words there is plenty of opportunity for them to subconsciously reflect as they work. This can lead to more substantial learning payoffs. In short, it is often much better to give learners time to make a 'bad' video, than to show them one!

THE BASIC PRINCIPLES OF VIDEO RECORDING AND EDITING

How Television Pictures are Produced

Both television and motion-picture films create an illusion of continuous movement by presenting a rapid succession of still images to the eye. In the case of television, these pictures are built up in a series of horizontal lines, British television pictures consisting of 625 such lines and American pictures 525. In order to reduce flicker, a system known as interlaced scanning is employed. In this system, which is shown schematically (in greatly simplified form) in Figure 7.1, a complete scan of the picture (a *frame*) is carried out in two stages (or *fields*). Alternate lines (the solid ones in the figure) are first scanned in succession, then the scanning process is repeated for the remaining lines (the broken ones in the figure). In the British 625 line system, the scanning of the first field begins at A (the start of line 1) and ends at B (half way along line 313); the scanning of the second field starts at C, beginning by completing line 313 and finishing at D (the end of line 625), after which the scanning process starts again at A. In the American 525 line system, the scanning process is similar, with the transition between the two fields of a frame taking place half way along line 263. In both systems, the field scanning rate is equal to the mains frequency, something that is necessary for technical reasons. Thus, in Britain, the scanning rate is 50 fields (25 frames) a second, while in America it is 60 fields (30 frames) a second.

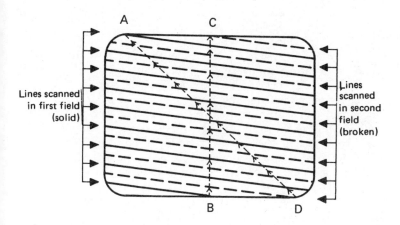

Figure 7.1 **The principle of interlaced scanning**

In a television camera, a system of lenses is used to produce an optical image of the scene being recorded on a mosaic of photo-conductive or photo-emissive cells. This is then scanned by an electronic beam, producing an electrical signal that varies in strength according to the intensity of the light falling on that part of the mosaic. In a colour television camera, three separate scanning processes take place, one for each of the three primary colours used in colour television (red, blue and green).

In a television receiver or monitor, the opposite process takes place, the fluorescent rear surface of the screen being scanned by an electron beam that builds up the picture line by line. In a colour set, three separate scanning systems are again used – one for each of the primary colours – with a special perforated mask being used to ensure that each colour beam strikes the correct parts of the screen.

How Television Signals are Recorded

A television signal consists of three basic components: a high-frequency signal carrying the picture information, a synchronizing signal that controls the scanning process by which this information is converted into a sequence of fields and frames, and an audio signal that carries the sound. The latter two signals can be recorded on magnetic tape in the conventional manner, namely, by using stationary heads to produce tracks running along the length of the tape, but it is not possible to record the picture signal in this way because of the high frequencies that it contains (up to five mega-hertz). The maximum frequency that a tape recording system can handle is proportional to the speed at which the tape moves past the head and inversely proportional to the head gap width. Even using the smallest head gaps possible, it would be necessary to employ tape speeds of several hundred inches per second in order to record the picture components of television signals in the conventional way; this is clearly not practicable. Fortunately, this problem can be overcome by employing a rotating head support system that moves the video head(s) rapidly across the tape as it travels through the machine.

In most of the video recorders used for instructional purposes, some form of *helical scan* system is used. Here, the tape is wound round a cylindrical drum in a manner similar to that shown in Figure 7.2, a drum that rotates at high speed within the loop of moving tape. In the U-wrap system shown in the figure (the configuration used in most video cassette recorders) the drum carries two heads, diametrically opposite one another. Thus, as the drum revolves, these execute a series of parallel scans across the tape as it moves round the drum. The video signal is therefore recorded in a discontinuous series of stripes, which can be joined up electronically to produce a continuous signal when the tape is replayed. These diagonal video tracks take up the entire width of the tape except for narrow strips at the top and bottom edges, which are used to carry the audio and control signals in the form of conventional tracks. With a twin-head U-wrap system of the type shown in Figure 7.2, the head drum rotates 25 times a second when recording 625 line pictures and 30 times a second when recording 525 line pictures. Thus, in each case, one complete frame is recorded during each revolution, with each frame corresponding to two segments of video track on the tape – one for each of the two fields that compose it. As shown in the lower part of the figure, the start of the track segment representing each field is labelled with a field synchronizing pulse. These pulses enable the separate segments of the video signal to be properly integrated during the playback process.

When the tape is played back, the tape moves through the machine in exactly the same way, the video signal being read off the tape by the rotating video heads, the audio signal by the audio head and the control signal by the control track head. The latter is used to synchronize the movement of the tape with the rotation of the video head so that the intermittent video track is scanned in the correct way.

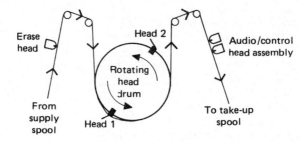

Plan view

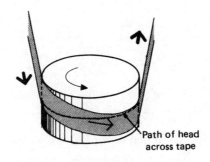

Front view

The configuration of the tape-head system

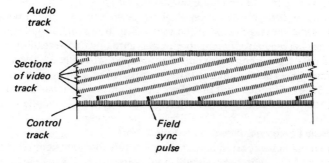

The pattern of tracks on the tape

Figure 7.2 **The principle of helical-scan videotape recording using the U-wrap tape configuration**

The Different Videotape Formats

Like motion picture film, videotape is available in a range of widths, in this case 2 inches, 1 inch, ¾ of an inch, ½ an inch and ¼ of an inch. Of these different widths, however, only two are widely used in instructional television work, namely ¾ of an inch and ½ an inch, with the latter being by far the most popular type. The two largest sizes of tape are only used when the work has to be of broadcast standard, while the smallest is only used with a single small non-standardized type of video recorder.

Half-inch videotape is available both in open-reels (for use with open-reel videotape recorders (VTRs) similar to open-reel audiotape machines) and in sealed cassettes (for use with videocassette recorders (VCRs), which are again similar to their audiotape counterparts). The most widely used videocassette format is VHS, which is primarily designed for domestic use but is perfectly adequate for most educational and training purposes. (An alternative ½-inch format, 'Betamax', has now become obsolete.)

Three-quarter inch videotape is used when higher quality is required, and is again available both in open-reel and cassette form. The most widely used videocassette format is U-matic, which is available in two forms: standard or low-band U-matic and high-band U-matic. As its name suggests, the latter has an extended bandwidth compared with the standard form, and thus produces higher quality results; it is, however, considerably more expensive to work with.

The Equipment Needed for Producing Video Materials

In the early years of video recording, practically all instructional television work was carried out using monochrome (ie black and white) equipment, since (a) colour equipment was prohibitively expensive in comparison, and (b) research had shown that monochrome television was just as effective as colour television for most instructional purposes. (Now that everyone *expects* colour, perhaps monochrome would 'devalue the message'?) Since the mid 1970s, however, colour equipment has become steadily cheaper in real terms, with the result that it has achieved progressively wider use. Indeed, virtually all television equipment now being purchased for educational or training purposes is of this type, with the result that black and white instructional television has, to all intents and purposes, become obsolete.

The Basic Equipment Needed for Video Work

If you work in an educational or training organization, it is probable that it has a central facility through which you can gain access to equipment such as video cameras, editing suites, and maybe even a fully-equipped television studio. Alternatively, it may be your organization's policy to buy in such services as necessary – for example, some organizations without central media facilities choose to hire specialist firms when it is wished to make a video production. Such specialist firms may offer the services of a fully-equipped studio, or may arrange to cost out your planned video production, and do all the filming and editing work to your specifications.

Where your organization already has its own equipment, your first plan of action will be to see how you can proceed with what is available to you. Your organization may offer one or more of the following facilities:

- video filming equipment you can borrow and use yourself;

- technical support for filming: ie technical staff who will do the filming for you, to your specifications;

- editing suites which you yourself can use;

- editing facilities and technician expertise, so that your films can be produced to high standards;

- a fully-equipped television studio for indoor filming, coupled to editing and production facilities, with the options to use the studio yourself, or to have your productions filmed by experienced technical staff.

If you have the benefit of the availability of technical staff experienced in making educational and training videos, it is well worth seeking their advice and cooperation at a very early stage in your planning. The more they know about what you are trying to do, and how you are approaching your task, the more their experience can be channelled to help you.

The advent of camcorders

Alternatively, for one reason or another, you may decide to do it yourself – indeed you may already have some experience of making videos. Gone are the days when you needed to strap a portable videocassette recorder to your back or over your shoulder, and set out with a portable TV camera across your other shoulder, with somewhere your batteries, microphones, and probably lighting gear too. The late 1980s saw the advent of *camcorders*, which are self contained units, comprising a camera, a recorder, and the necessary batteries (usually mains-rechargeable). At the beginning of the 1980s, less than one home in three had a video recorder in the UK, and hardly any homes had a video camera. In the early 1990s, most homes have a video recorder (many homes have more than one!), and High Street shops are full of camcorders. Camcorders have become an established part of the domestic and leisure scenes. People using them are seen at weddings, on holidays, beside children, on family visits, and pursuing every imaginable hobby.

At first sight, camcorders look complicated pieces of machinery, with at least 30 controls of various sorts bristling from them. However, for most purposes the only controls you need to know about are the on/off

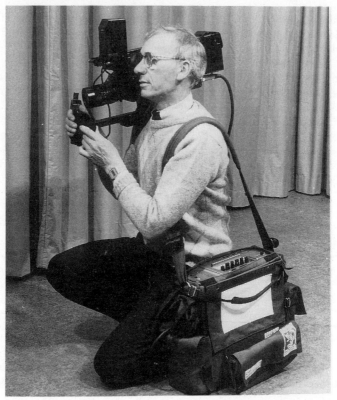

Figure 7.3 **An early portable TV camera and linked videocassette recorder system in use**

Figure 7.4 **A modern camcorder**

button, and the zoom control. Focusing and exposure are almost always done automatically, and acceptable quality can be obtained in a wide range of lighting conditions, making the need for special lighting rare.

These cameras take a full-size VHS videocassette, which after recording can be taken out and inserted directly into the ubiquitous video recorder – at home, or in most teaching and training rooms. These tapes can record one hour, two hours – up to four hours when recorded at the standard speed, and some cameras have double-play facilities by recording at half-speed (with many domestic video recorders offering appropriate compatibility). Alternatively, the camcorders themselves can be connected to any television set, and the recordings replayed directly. Using a video recorder, however, provides the opportunity to edit the tapes, and more and more people are developing the skill of editing their camcorder recordings on domestic video machines.

Thinking of the cost of videotape, it is clear why cine has almost disappeared. Several hours of action can be recorded on a tape costing little more than £2 (and less than £8 for the highest available grades of videotape) at 1992 prices – and the recordings can be copied very easily (albeit with some loss of quality). The videotapes can of course be used many times. The comparative cost of cine film in 1992 is around £3 *per minute!* Need we say more about the demise of cine?

New waves of camcorders

In 1992, the earlier generation of 'full-size' VHS camcorders is already being superseded. The existing generations of camcorders are already considered too heavy – despite the fact that they are less than half as heavy as the portable separates which preceded them. VHS-C machines operate exactly like the heavier camcorders, but use small tapes, enabling the whole assembly to be considerably smaller. The tapes are limited presently to 45 minutes at standard speed (and 90 minutes at long-play speed), and in 1992 cost around £4. The small tapes from VHS-C machines can be played back on home video recorders by paying about £25 for an adaptor. The VHS-C tape is simply slipped into the adaptor, which is then used in a video recorder in exactly the same way as a standard VHS videocassette. Direct playback from camera to television set is still possible, as is direct re-recording and editing onto a video recorder.

8mm video is now also appearing in High Street shops. Camcorders of this type use even smaller cassettes, but can record for 90 minutes at standard speed and three hours at slow speed, with tapes costing around £5 in 1992. An advantage of 8mm video machines is sound quality, which is somewhat better than VHS or VHS-C machines, though the additional quality may be lost in the process of copying the recordings onto VHS cassettes for 'normal' use. However, with the availability (at a price) of hi-fi video recorders, even this disadvantage is removed.

In 1992, VHS camcorders, VHS-C machines and 8mm camcorders range in price from £450 to £800. As is always the case, even higher

Figure 7.5 **The television studio in The Robert Gordon University's Educational Development Unit**

Figure 7.6 **The control room of The Robert Gordon University's television studio**

quality is available at a price. For around £1000, there are *Super VHS-C* camcorders, and also *Hi8* machines. These are similar to their predecessors, but use improved recording formats and higher grades of tape (more expensive at about £9 for a 45 minute S-VHS-C tape, or £16 for a 90-minute Hi8 tape). With these sophisticated machines, picture quality is even better, especially if you are in due course copying or editing to full-sized VHS cassettes. Different machines with all sorts of special features are available, for example, alternative high-speed shutter settings up to 1/10000 sec (normal speed is 1/50 sec) are useful for filming fast moving objects, and then allowing you to see still pictures of the action. If you want to study your golf swing, or your high-jump take-off, such features are invaluable. You will no doubt be able to think of educational uses of such facilities, where students can benefit from seeing very rapid action slowed down.

Even the most expensive camcorders of 1992 cost well over two orders of magnitude *less* per minute of recording than cine film. The quality produced by these sophisticated mass-market machines is considerably greater than the generation of studio machines of only a decade earlier. It is highly likely that the pace of development will continue, and that do-it-yourself video will improve even further in technical quality. However, we mentioned earlier in this chapter the danger of amateurishness – the possibility of the message of the video recording being devalued if the television production seems clumsy or ill-conceived. The danger of amateurishness has moved now away from the technical side of making video recordings, and is firmly located in the production design arena.

Editing video recordings
As we mentioned earlier, it is possible to edit recordings from a camcorder directly onto a videocassette recorder. Similarly, it is possible to edit VHS cassettes by using two VHS recorders. Each editing process tends to cause a reduction in quality – often more noticeable in the quality of sound than that of the images on the screen. In camcorder recordings, especially those made in open-air, sound quality can be the weak link in the chain. However, it is relatively easy to add a new sound-track (for example a commentary or music) to the edited copy, only retaining the original sound when this is essential (for example, people speaking on screen).

Many educational and training institutions have television studios, with several high-quality cameras being fed into a control room containing very sophisticated recording and editing equipment. These facilities normally have computer-aided features, such as caption generators, software for mixing video images, and for showing two or more moving images on the screen at once ('split screen'). It is now very rare for the educational or training practitioner to be the 'hands-on' person at a video-editing or video-recording suite. Highly experienced technicians are usually there, and can give you a great deal of useful advice regarding how to go about filming the programme you are trying to

Figure 7.7 **A videotape editing suite**

make. Such people can do wonders editing together the various good, bad and indifferent parts of recordings you've made.

Even if you've not got the back-up of experienced technical staff, it is possible to go to specialist firms who can turn even quite basic video shots into a well-captioned and well-structured educational video for you. For this to happen, of course, it is necessary for you to be able to explain in as much detail as you can, exactly what the intended purposes are for the video, and how it is intended that learners will use it. We will discuss the planning side of making a video in greater detail shortly.

PLANNING TO MAKE A VIDEO

Establishing the Purpose

The starting point for making an educational or training video should be an analysis of the purposes it is intended to serve, coupled to a logical exploration of how the medium of video is ideally suited to the particular purposes it is to serve in your educational or training programme. If the video is to be an important part of the educational programme, it is useful to work out exactly what the intended learning outcomes will be for your learners. This can be done by expressing them as educational objectives, eg: 'After viewing this video, you should be able to make suggestions indicating how you would choose to redesign the traffic flow in Central Cardiff'. Alternatively, it is sometimes useful to express the intended learning outcomes as competence statements, eg: 'When you have studied this video, you can make your own action plan regarding how you are going to timetable your revision for your exams'. When you are making an expository video programme where the purpose is to facilitate a significant amount of learning, there may well be half-a-dozen such objectives or competence statements for a mere half-hour video.

Of course, not all educational videos are intended to be fundamental parts of the respective learning programmes. There are many 'lesser' reasons for making and using educational and training videos, including:

- as pure entertainment to 'lighten' the learning programme somewhat;

- as a discussion-starter, rather than something to be learned from directly;

- as 'icing on the cake', for example to give learners an idea of things it would not be possible for them to see in person, such as the inside of a nuclear reactor, or far-away geological or geographic phenomena, and so on;

- as a shared-experience, which the group of learners can then react to – for example a political interview, or a drama excerpt, and so on;

- as purely illustrative material, allowing learners to see how the theoretical concepts they are studying relate to everyday industry or life.

As you can see, for some of the purposes listed above, it would be quite unnecessary to go to the trouble of working out educational objectives or competence statements in detail. However, even for 'lighter' purposes, it is useful to at least share with learners the reasoning for using the medium of video.

Planning the Modes of Use

Before going too far with the planning, we recommend that you consider carefully exactly how the programme is intended to be used. There are many possibilities – here are just some of them (for example) for a 30-minute video programme.

- To be played continuously to a large group in a lecture room, as a prelude to discussion and a question-answer session.

- To be used to illustrate a 1-hour large group session, with the 30-minute programme being played as a series of half-a-dozen shorter 'clips' during the hour.

- To be played to a large group in either of the ways outlined above, but also to be available for learners to consult further, either individually or in groups.

- To be used in tutorial groups, either played all at once, or as a series of clips.

- To be given to learners, for them to work through it in groups, armed also with a handout or worksheet intended to help them focus their work using the video.

- To be copied, and given or loaned to individual learners, supported by handout or workbook material.

- To be part of an open learning package, where learners individually (or in groups) use it in their own ways, at their own paces, and so on.

There are many more ways that learners can use videos. Even those above are not mutually exclusive, and you may well decide to produce a video which can be adapted to several of the uses listed above. The adaptation can often be done by varying the supportive print-based material which you design for use with the video.

Making an Outline Plan

Once you have decided to produce a video, it is advisable to draw up some kind of sketch for the film or programme, outlining its content and the basic structure you propose to adopt. This can then be converted into a more detailed plan, specifying the visual and narrative contents of different sections to be incorporated into the finished programme (preferably with notes of what learners are intended to gain from each episode). This sketch plan can be produced in the form of a storyboard or script, in the same way as was discussed for tape-slide programmes. However, you may well prefer to keep the whole plan more of a 'skeleton' as, when going about making a video, the unexpected is often more valuable than your original plans.

Bearing in mind the decisions you will already have taken about the educational purposes, and the planned modes of use, the following suggestions will help you add structure and impact to your plan.

- Limit the planned content. Remember that none of us remembers a great deal of what we see on our television screens. It may well be better to cover a limited amount of material in some depth, than to give a transient coverage of a wide amount of content.

- Remember that while watching a video (whether learners are in a large group or alone) learners cannot ask questions. If you cover too much in a single video, their questions can easily get lost.

- Plan to give the programme or clips a definite structure, and moreover to share this structure with your viewers by using appropriate 'signposts and links' – these can be visual, verbal, or contained in printed briefing materials you design to accompany the video.

- Plan for linear arguments in each section of the programme, avoiding the temptation to go off on diversions or tangents. Particularly if learners will be using the video without you being present, remember that you may not have the 'facial-expression' feedback which helps you check whether the video is achieving the purposes you intended it to.

■ Remember that video is essentially a *visual* medium, and that narrative should play a supportive role rather than a central role. When planning the sequences to be filmed, *think visual* at all times, building the programme around the sequence of images that you have decided to incorporate, rather than simply using the picture to illustrate a narrative (as you may have done in tape-slide programmes).

■ Capitalize on the fact that video is essentially a *moving* medium. This does not mean that there should be hectic motion on the screen at all times, however. Slowly moving the camera can give a realistic sense of motion when filming fixed objects such as paintings or sculptures.

■ Don't get carried away with the technology. You may have brilliant ideas for using split-screen images, 'shock' sudden changes of light and colour, artistic fade-ins and fade-outs, gimmicky shots, and so on. The danger is that the medium can so easily get in the way of the message, and too many 'high-tech' features are likely to distract your learners from the content of the video.

■ Plan to get the continuity right, so that the shots or sequences in due course will follow each other in a logical order (considering, however, that editing is relatively easy with video, there is no necessity to do the filming in the intended order). For example, if your programme is going to illustrate an actual situation (for example a process or a machine) together with a schematic diagram or flowchart of the same thing, try to match them as closely as you can, so the viewer can relate the diagram and the situation it represents as the programme moves backwards and forwards between realia and diagrams. For example, something that moves from right to left in your flowchart, should not move from left to right when you film 'the real thing'!

The Different Types of Shot That Can Be Used in a Video

Let us now explore briefly the different visual 'building bricks' that can be used to construct video programmes, ie the different types of 'shot'.

The three basic types of shot: In all cine and video work, three basic types of shot should form the bulk of most sequences. These are:

1. The *long shot* (LS), which provides a general view of the subject taken from such a distance that the subject is seen in the context of the background or setting in which it is located at the time.

2. The *medium shot* (MS), which provides a closer view of the subject, eliminating most of the background details.

3.   The *close-up* (CU), which provides an even closer view of the subject
or a specific part thereof, excluding everything else from view.

These three types of shot are illustrated in Figure 7.8. Note that the terms
'long shot', 'medium shot' and 'close-up' do not imply that the shot
should be taken from any specific distance, since this will depend entirely on the nature of the subject being shot. A 'long shot', for example,
can be taken from several hundred yards in the case of a large building
and from a few feet in the case of a piece of equipment of relatively small
size. Also different cameramen can interpret the terms in different ways,
so that what is a medium shot to one may well be a close-up to another.
It is also possible to use shots intermediate to the three basic types (eg a
medium close-up (MCU), which is half way between a medium shot and
a close-up), or shots which lie beyond the normal LS-MS-CU sequence
(eg an extreme long shot (ELS) or extreme close-up (ECU) – see Figures
7.9 and 7.10).

Moving camera shots: As we saw above, it is possible to introduce a sense
of movement into a video sequence by moving the camera or changing
the effective distance or angle of viewing during shooting. Some of the
main options available include the following:

■   *Zooming* – where the apparent distance from which the scene is shot
is increased (zooming out) or decreased (zooming in) during the actual shooting by using a zoom lens and varying its focal length in a
continuous manner (not to be confused with dollying).

■   *Panning* – where the camera is rotated about a vertical axis during the
shot, thus causing its effective field of view to sweep across the scene
being shot (not to be confused with crabbing).

■   *Tilting* – where the camera is rotated about a horizontal axis at right
angles to the direction of shooting during the shot, thus causing the
subject to be scanned in a vertical direction.

■   *Dollying* (or tracking) – moving the camera towards or away from the
subject during the shot.

■   *Crabbing* (or trucking) – moving the camera along a line at right angles
to the direction of shooting during the shot.

Angle and position shots: Another way of introducing special effects or
variety into a video sequence is to use different camera angles. Some of
the possibilities are again listed below:

■   *High-angle shots* – where the camera is above normal eye level, looking down on the subject (this effectively places the subject in an 'in-
ferior' position, reducing its size and slowing down any motion that
it may possess).

Long shot

Long shot

Medium shot

Medium shot

Close-up

Close-up

Figure 7.8 **The three basic types of shot used in cine and video work**

Figure 7.9
An extreme long shot

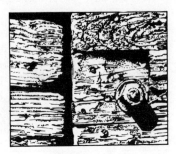

Figure 7.10
An extreme close-up

- *Low-angle shots* – where the camera is below normal eye level, looking up at the subject (this places the subject in a dominant position, exaggerating its height and speeding up any movement).

- *Subjective shots* – where the camera shoots 'over the shoulder' of the person carrying out the operation being filmed, thus giving the impression of seeing the operation from that person's point of view (in most shots, the camera views the scene from the point of view of an objective observer).

Ten Tips on Using Camcorders

These suggestions are not meant for experienced users of modern recording and editing equipment, but may be helpful if you are venturing out on your first mission with a camcorder!

1. Don't be afraid of the machine. You are not going to break it by pressing the wrong button at the wrong time. The worst you can do (unless you drop the machine from a reasonable height) is to make a poor recording.

2. Video tapes are cheap and can be used over and over again. In other words, it costs nothing to practise. As with many other skills, producing good videos is learned better by trial and error than by reading learned treatises on cameramanship.

3. Don't film for three days and only then start to look at what you are recording. Arrange to see the results of your recording as soon as you possibly can, so that you can learn immediately from your mistakes – and your successes. It's useful to have a cable connector which allows your camera to be linked directly to the aerial socket of any television set, so you don't need to wait till you get to a set which can be tuned in to your camera's output.

4. Video cameras are not just for fast moving objects. Indoors or out-

doors, enough is moving without you seeking out motion. Faces, leaves, traffic, etc will bring enough 'lifelikeness' to your recordings.

5. Using a simple tripod can make a great deal of difference to your recordings, especially if you need to use zoom facilities. Remember that at high zoom, even the slightest 'camera shake' will seem like an earthquake on the screen.

6. Try not to use the zoom except when really necessary. It's very tempting to get carried away by the zoom facility, but the higher the zoom, the more you need your steadiness and expertise. Also, if you're having to use high zoom, the chances are that you're not going to be getting a good sound recording of what you are filming.

7. When possible, take close-up shots. These can add impact to a recording, and you may well be surprised at how well details come out in close-up (and of course, any associated sound is likely to be captured with a minimum of stray noises).

8. When you particularly wish to capture sounds, where possible use a suitable separate microphone rather than the one built into the camcorder. Internal microphones always suffer from at least some vibration and machine noises; a well-placed separate microphone can give much better results. Practise microphone positioning as well as practising camerawork, and learn from your successes and failures.

9. When using a camcorder, try to avoid rapid temperature changes. If you move a cold camera into a warm, moist environment, you are likely to risk condensation forming on the cold metal parts of the camera – not least the recording mechanisms. This can cause the tape to stick, or cause deposits to be left from the tape on the intricate innards of the camera. Water is an obvious enemy of camcorders, but remember that sand can be just as dangerous if it gets into the works.

10. When you are ready, show your results to experienced camcorderists! Don't defend your results – regard every criticism as useful feedback. The more criticism you can get, the faster you will build up a useful collection of techniques and wrinkles.

BIBLIOGRAPHY

Choat, E, Griffin, H, and Hobart, D (1987) *Teachers and Television*. Croom Helm, London.

Coombes, P and Tiffin, J (1978) *Television Production for Education*. Hastings House, New York.

DeLuca, S M (1991) *Instructional Video*. Focal Press, London and New York.

Downrick, P W (1991) *Practical Guide to Using Video in the Behavioural Sciences*. Wiley, New York.

Elliott, G (1984) *Video Production in Education and Training*. Croom Helm, London.

Kemp, J E (1980) *Closed-circuit Television Single-Handed*. Pitman Publishing, London.

Kemp, J and Smellie, D (1989) *Planning, Producing and Using Instructional Media (6th edition)*. Harper and Row, New York.

Newble, D and Cannon, R (1991) *A Handbook for Teachers in Universities and Colleges*. Kogan Page, London.

Pinnington, A (1991) *Using Video in Training and Education*. McGraw-Hill, Maidenhead.

Romiszowski, A J (1988) *The Selection and Use of Instructional Media*. Kogan Page, London.

Rowatt, R W (1980) *Video – A Guide to the Use of Portable Video Equipment*. Scottish Council for Educational Technology, Glasgow.

Taylor, M H (1988) *Planning for Video – A Guide to Making Effective Training Videotapes*. Kogan Page, London.

Utz, P (1982) *Video Users Handbook*. Prentice-Hall, Englewood Cliffs, N.J.

Useful Relevant Journals

Educational Media International. Kogan Page, London.

Educational and Training Technology International. Kogan Page, London.

British Journal of Educational Technology. National Council for Educational Technology, Coventry.

International Journal of Instructional Media. New York, USA.

Journal of Information Technology. Kogan Page, London.

Media and Methods. Philadelphia, USA.

Multimedia and Videodisc Monitor. Falls Church, USA.

Videodisc Newsletter. British Universities Film and Video Council, London.

Chapter Eight

An Introduction to Computer-mediated Instructional Materials and Systems

INTRODUCTION

Having completed our examination of the various 'traditional' types of audiovisual educational and training materials, we will now turn our attention to the latest and – in the opinion of many practitioners – the most important type of instructional materials: computer-mediated materials. The terms 'computer-assisted learning' (CAL) and 'computer-based training' (CBT) are now endemic in the education and training literature, and in this chapter we can do no more than alert you to the vast amount of development which is being devoted to this field.

Both of your authors can remember the days when computers were 'new'. We remember large rigs containing thousands of glowing diodes, triodes, pentodes, bristling with resistors and capacitors, and generating several megawatts of heat in confined spaces. Just occasionally, these computers would have one of those moments when every single component was functioning optimally, and the whole thing worked!

With the advent of the microcomputer, within 20 years, as much power could be sitting on the top of a desk – and working correctly for most of the time. Computers have continued to become smaller, cheaper, more versatile and more powerful at a rate which no-one could have foreseen just a couple of decades ago. Computers have pervaded all aspects or society. Computerized bills, invoices, accounts, bank statements, and Reader's Digest Prize Draw documents fall onto every doormat. It is not surprising that computers are just as common in education and training as once was the chalkboard or more recently the overhead projector.

We have noticed the effects of generation gaps on attitudes towards computers. Our own generation tends to be either somewhat shy of computers, or inclined to read the manuals diligently before trying to make a computer do anything. Our children have a quite different approach – they press everything in sight on the keyboard until the machine does what they want it to do. Much to our disgust, the latter technique tends to work much faster than our own – indeed, learning by getting things wrong at first, then getting feedback and then trying again, seems to be the natural way of using computers.

Following our usual pattern, we will begin this chapter by discussing the various ways that computers can be used in different types of instructional situation. Then, however, we will depart from the practice we have been able to adopt hitherto in this book. It is quite impossible in a single chapter (or even in a single book) to set out to write a 'how to do it yourself' treatise. The most we can hope to do is to alert you to some of the possibilities, to some sources of further information, and to help you prepare the instructional side of any development you plan to transpose into computer-assisted learning formats. We have, therefore, included a much more comprehensive bibliography at the end of this chapter than in previous parts of this book, particularly listing relevant specialized journals which interested readers are advised to consult for latest developments.

HOW COMPUTERS CAN BE USED IN DIFFERENT TEACHING/LEARNING SITUATIONS

Let us now see how computers can play their part in the three broad classes of instructional situation that we have discussed throughout this book – mass instruction, individualized instruction, and group learning. It will come as no surprise to you that the situation is much more complex this time.

Mass Instruction

To date, the main use of computers in mass instruction has been in a supportive role during conventional expository lessons rather than as a vehicle for mediated exposition. That said, many of the computer-assisted packages which are employed to support mass instruction are highly interactive in nature (interactive video for example), and the effect can be for members of a large group to 'get the feel of' an interactive learning programme, with which they are later destined to interact individually or in groups. Some of the many ways that computers are being used in large groups include;

- As vehicles for teaching about computers and computing;

- As a method of carrying out complex calculations or data-processing activities in the course of a lecture, lesson or training session, and demonstrating these as a 'shared experience' to the large group;

- As a means of setting up simulations, and demonstrating these to large groups, including the ability to change particular parameters in the simulations at will, and allow the class to see the effects on the simulation of such changes immediately;

- As 'number-crunching' devices, allowing data to be transformed into visual forms such as graphs, pie-charts, histograms, and so on before the eyes of the members of the large group (and with a little planning, with copies of printouts being available to everyone at the end of the lecture);

- As a means of accessing databases of all kinds, at will, in the large group situation; for example, requests 'from the floor' can be keyed in at will, and the resulting data displayed on large-screen (either through linking the computer system to video projection facilities, or by special devices which can be placed on any ordinary over-head projector, transmitting 'screenfuls' of information onto the 'big screen' with even greater clarity and definition);

- In place of handouts – lecturers can have their lecture notes stored on a computer conferencing system, and summon up these notes on 'big screen' in large group sessions, talking through the notes and answering learners' questions. (This is the computer-age equivalent of having a prepared set of overhead transparencies.) The learners can then go to any terminal linked to the computer conference, summon up the lecture notes, edit them, add to them on-screen, and then print out a personalized copy of their own versions of the notes for further study.

Figure 8.1 **A student using an interactive video workstation**

These are just some of the ways we have used computers for large groups we work with but there are many more. It is almost becoming the case that a large group lecture *without* any 'new technology' is 'something different' – and maybe 'chalk and talk' will be so rare as to be memorable shortly!

Individualized Instruction

Although, as we have seen, computers are capable of playing powerful roles in the mass-instruction educational toolkit, their most important potential role in education and training is undoubtedly in the area of individualized instruction. Here they can constitute the most versatile and powerful delivery system yet invented, and are bringing about changes which in the opinion of many commentators are no less than revolutionary. It is by now well established that most learning occurs 'by doing' (experiential learning) – including by getting things wrong as well as by getting them right. It is further well established that a vital adjunct to any learning experience is feedback – the more immediate, the better. Computers are capable of giving almost instant feedback, tirelessly, no matter how many learners 'get it wrong' (it is equally well known that human tutors have limited value when it comes to learners repeatedly getting things wrong!). Below, we give a summary of the ways in which computer-assisted learning systems and resources can be used in individual instruction.

Uses as 'Substitute Tutor', 'Substitute Laboratory', 'Substitute Library', etc.

This sort of computer-assisted learning process is the sort where individual learners using a keyboard (or mouse, or infrared remote controller) carry out an on-line dialogue with the educational or training software, with the computer being programmed by the software to interact with learners in various ways including:

- Asking learners structured questions. For example, multiple-choice questions, with learners choosing options via the keyboard, or using a mouse to move the on-screen cursor to 'option boxes', or by using a light-pen on a touch-sensitive screen.

- Responding to the choices learners make. The computer is programmed to provide direct feedback to each choice learners make, for example letting them know that they chose the correct option, and (more important) explaining to them why any other options they chose were not correct.

- Providing expository information. This can be screenfuls of text, digital graphics frames, moving animated images, and even full-colour video, depending what variety of multimedia software is being used with the computer.

- Testing learners. For example, giving them structured questions, and storing their scores until the end of the test, then giving learners a breakdown of their performance, assistance with issues which caused them to make mistakes, and feedback on areas they need to seek to improve.

- Pretesting learners as a prelude to moving them to the most relevant starting-point in the programmed software. This can save more advanced learners having to go through the basic parts of the learning programme at all, saving their time, and increasing their motivation.

- Allowing learners to access stored data and information in databases of various sorts. Videodiscs, compact discs, computer hard-disks, and even 'floppy disks' can be used to store all sorts of information – still images, moving images, sound commentary, numerical data, and so on.

- Allowing learners to contribute to 'computer conferences' where a series of terminals are connected to a central computer. This allows learners to share data and ideas with each other, and to receive feedback from each other and from tutors. The great advantage of computer conferencing is that it is possible to have the system running for 24 hours a day, 7 days a week, and learners can literally work completely at their own pace, and at times and places (subject to terminal availability) of their choosing. Bournemouth University in the UK has already a large suite of rooms containing computer-assisted learning equipment which is open continuously; the facilities are indeed in use round the clock (though not by many students at 0400 hours – which therefore is a good time not to expect to have to queue for a machine if a deadline makes some work urgent!).

- Allowing learners to perform mathematical and statistical analysis of data. For example, allowing learners to change the variables (temperature, pressure, concentrations) in chemical industrial processes,

Figure 8.2 **A microcomputer being used for computer conferencing**

with the computer very quickly calculating and displaying the result-ing effects on product yields, heat flow, and so on. This sort of computer simulation can be far faster (and far more memorable) than 'manual' manipulation of data. The particular advantage of com-puter-assisted learning here is that learners receive feedback very quickly about the effects of changing the variables in a simulation. They can therefore use trial and error to arrive quickly at the ideal conditions to use in a chemical process, for example. Moreover, they can get a 'feel' of the sensitivity of a complex overall process to the adjustment of the different parameters which effect it. Similar learn-ing benefits apply to a wide range of subject matter. For example, learners sitting at a keyboard can engage in simulations relating to the overall economy of a country, varying at will any of the many factors which contribute to the overall picture.

■ Allowing learners to produce printed outcomes of the products of their work, for example graphs, charts, diagrams, histograms, spreadsheet printouts, and so on. Learners can then use these for traditional 'human' assessment and feedback, or simply as part of their learning resource materials.

Figure 8.3 **Primary school children using a microcomputer in a problem-solving exercise**

Computer-Managed Learning

The discussion so far has used the term computer-assisted learning, but in all such processes the computer is also *managing* the learning process to at least some extent. There are, however, additional ways that com-puters can be used to perform tasks that are essentially 'learning manage-ment' or 'learning administration' roles, including the following.

Figures 8.4(a) and (b) **Typical mainframe computers**

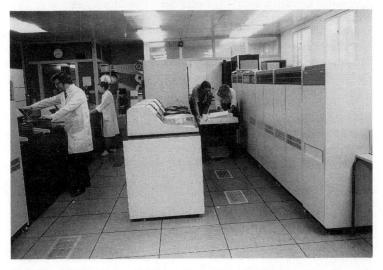

- Computers can be used to administer tests, and keep records of learners' respective performances (not least, including how long they have spent on-line studying a package, and the loops they have chosen in their personal journey through the package.)

- Computers can be used to 'mark' tests at a distance, and to control the generation of printed feedback to learners. In various open and distance learning programmes, learners at home or at work can fill in optically readable cards or sheets, entering their choices of options for multiple choice questions. These sheets can be posted or delivered to the computer facility. Learners' selections are then entered into the computer using an optical reader (saving considerable human time and avoiding the boring job of keyboarding-in learners' choices), and the computer then selects from a bank of 'responses', and can generate a letter responding to each choice that learners may have made, as well as keeping records of scores and progress.

- Computers can be used to keep track of the relative progress of large cohorts of learners, and to gather continuous assessment data. (Readers are reminded, however, that legally we all have a right to access information about us kept on computer records – this applies equally to assessment and progress data kept for learners.)

Group Learning

Computer-assisted learning systems can make a highly significant contribution to a wide range of group-learning activities. Almost everything we have already described above regarding individualized learning can be done by groups of learners – often with more success than when done individually. Learners in groups benefit not only from the feedback they receive from the computer-assisted learning package, but also from feedback from each other.

THE RANGE OF COMPUTER-ASSISTED LEARNING FORMATS

Different Kinds of Computer?

A few years ago, computers were described using terms such as 'mainframe' (for large central machines with terminals wired to them), 'minicomputers' (less expensive versions of mainframe machines, such as were used in small businesses or small colleges, and often for computer-assisted learning programmes), and 'microcomputers' (small desktop machines, used independently by students, trainees, lecturers, trainers and so on). The principal difference between the sorts of machines were the speeds at which they could process data, and their memory capacity. In the early 1980s, many desktop machines had a memory capacity of a mere 32Kb (32000 bytes), and even such machines led to a rapid growth in the educational and training software that they could support. In 1992, for a similar cost to what would have been paid in 1982 for a 32Kb system, one can purchase a 40Mb microcomputer system with 2Mb of processor memory, ie over 1000 times as powerful and very much faster in its operations. So in some ways, the terms 'mainframe', 'minicomputer' and 'microcomputer' are all somewhat irrelevant now.

Mainframe machines remain in larger organizations, continuing to serve many different users at once, usually operating continuously, and being accessible not only by 'wired' terminals, but also from remote terminals using telephone lines and suitable modems. The real revolution has been in microcomputers, with individuals able to use machines with power once only obtainable from mainframe computers, on their desktops. The differences between mainframes and micros are now being even further eroded, as it is increasingly common to find microcomputers linked together by cables (and by telephone lines) to form networks, over which information can be transferred at great speed. Computer networks also allow software to be shared by many users. Even where mainframe computer systems are in use, it is common to find that terminals are now microcomputers in their own right, and only used to connect to the mainframe for particular purposes requiring high processing capacity, or to access centrally-housed software.

Authoring Languages

During the 1980s, large numbers of 'authoring languages' were introduced. Authoring languages are essentially the means for educational and training practitioners to convert their instructional sequences into computer software. It is no longer necessary to have any detailed knowledge of computer programming or computer 'languages' to create interactive educational sequences. Only a few years ago, it was useful to provide an example of the use of an authoring language ('PLATO' was used as an illustration in the first edition of this book). Now, however, there are so many different authoring languages, and their sophistication has increased so dramatically, that to give an illustration would detract rather than help. Indeed, it is increasingly common for educational and training practioners to hand over their requests for the production of computer-assisted learning packages to professional firms or personnel skilled in the selection and use of relevant authoring languages. Readers who wish to follow these issues further are referred to the Bibliography, and particularly to the list of journals which have proliferated in this rapidly-developing field (textbooks on the subject become out of data almost as soon as they are published – sometimes before!).

Hypermedia

As with authoring languages, in this chapter we will only alert you to the fact that more is being published about 'Hypermedia' than any other topic in the vast field of educational and training computing. The best known example of Hypermedia is 'Hypercard', introduced on Apple Macintosh machines during the 1980s. However, the term 'Hypermedia' is now being extended to an ever-growing range of ways of using computers to access other media, such as videodisc, compact disc, and so on.

With Hypercard, it is possible for a relative novice to learn to compose interactive educational software quite quickly. However, the escalation of the production of such software has meant that the standards of presentation have increased dramatically. Professionally produced educational software uses high resolution graphics, a full range of colours, and all sorts of on-screen effects which make amateur productions look decidedly old-fashioned. We advise readers who wish to get involved directly with Hypermedia to consult the literature referred to in the Bibliography – or better still, to find a professional expert or firm who can demonstrate to them just how powerful these media can be.

Electronic Books

With the escalation of advances in the new technologies, it has become possible to store vast amounts of information (text, graphics, sound animated pictures, and video sequences) on a range of storage media (videodiscs, compact discs, computer hard-disks). The term 'Electronic Books' has come into common usage for such resources. Professor Philip Barker has contributed much to the literature on computer-based training resources. The following extract from a presentation he made at the 1991 AETT Conference gives a useful picture of the scope of electronic books (now published as Barker, P G and Giller, S (1992) listed in the Bibliography).

Definitions of Electronic Books
The simplest type of electronic book consists of a computer-controlled data source along with a sophisticated data retrieval system. The retrieval system allows users to access the stored information using a number of different methods. Several categories of electronic book currently exist (Manji 1990).

An electronic book can be defined in a variety of different ways. One of the simplest approaches is to liken it to a traditional paper-based book. One of the main design objectives of an electronic book is to capture some of the attractive properties of conventional books but also to offer 'dynamic user control' over available information. Users are able to control navigation and make access choices according to their individual needs. In addition, an electronic book may also offer a number of extra features. Amongst the more important of these we include: high quality images; animated pictures; sound; TV quality moving pictures; user interaction; reactive pages; editing and annotation facilities; end-user testing and assessment facilities; hypertext; hypermedia and simulations. Not all books will contain all of the facilities listed above. Those facilities which are included will depend upon the type of book that is required and the purpose for which it is to be used.

Classification of Electronic Books

A variety of different classifications of electronic books currently exists. In this paper we use a taxonomy which involves four different functional classes. These are: archival; informational; instructional and interrogational.

Archival

This category of book offers a method of storing large volumes of information relating to some particular subject area. Within such books the user interface will normally be designed in such a way that it will permit a variety of different methods of information retrieval. Examples of such books include large catalogue systems and databases of records and data. The Grolier Encyclopedia (Grolier 1988) and Compton's Multimedia Encyclopedia (Britannica Software 1990) are two such examples of this category.

Informational

In many ways, this type of electronic book overlaps with the previous type. However, the stored information is less comprehensive and more specific. One example of this category of book is the Oxford Textbook of Medicine on compact disc (Weatherall, Ledingham and Warrell 1989). Another example – of a multimedia electronic book (containing pictures, sound and text) – is the Nimbus 'Music Catalog' (Nimbus Information Systems 1989).

Instructional

The design of this type of electronic book is intended to achieve a highly efficient and effective knowledge and skill transfer mechanism to support learning activities. Users are given the opportunity to learn at their own pace and in their own style. Some electronic books in this category will actually assess and adapt to the user's personal learning style. Such books automatically re-configure the material presented to accommodate the user's preferred approach to learning.

Interrogational

The intention of this category of book is to support testing, quizzing and assessment activities which will enable readers to gauge their depth of knowledge about a particular topic. This type of book contains three basic components: a question bank; a testing and assessment package; and an expert system. The latter is used to analyse a reader's responses and deduce an appropriate grade or level of competence based on these responses.

It seems likely that the use of compact discs in particular to store a wide range of information will increase, and that the ways in which computers will be used to allow learners to interact with such information will continue to advance rapidly. Readers wishing to follow up this technology are referred to a wide range of published material, listed in the Bibliography, and in particular to the various journals which carry the latest reports and researches.

Compact Disc Interactive

Most readers will think of compact disc technology as something they have on their domestic hi-fi sound equipment. From around 1950 to the early 1980s, vinyl gramophone records were the most common music medium, with 'long play' records capable of holding 40 minutes per side of recorded sound (though it was much more common for side-lengths to be 25 minutes or so, and as low as 15 minutes in the field of popular music). LPs were known for their 'snap, crackle and pop' – an array of background surface noise which pervaded quiet passages of music. They were also known for their 'clicks', and the ease with which they could be scratched by rough handling. When compact discs came onto the scene, it was at first thought that they would be unlikely to catch on, as the market for recorded vinyl discs and for cassette tapes was so established. However, in 1992, very few vinyl discs are manufactured, and compact disc sales are rapidly overtaking cassette tapes in music shops.

The compact disc uses digitally stored information, which is read using a low-power laser, then transformed into sound with no discernible loss of quality in either the recording or the playback stages. 'Snap, crackle and pop' were abolished at a stroke, and compact discs are so robust they can be handled quite carelessly and still produce perfect sound quality. For music reproduction, it is now common to find compact discs containing well over 70 minutes of recorded sound. What is more, the 'tracks' can be digitally selected, and you can programme your playback equipment regarding which tracks to select, and in which order.

Compact disc technology has, however, potential far beyond domestic audio reproduction. In 1992, the first training and educational programmes to use the medium of compact disc were launched in Britain (following successful introduction of the technology in the United States in 1991). *Philips Interactive Media Systems* launched the technology into the UK consumer market.

CD-I integrated digital video, digital audio, graphics and text onto a 5-inch optical disc. A CD-I player is similar in size and technology to an ordinary domestic CD player (and can play ordinary CDs as well). The CD-I machine is connected to a television set, through which it delivers sound and pictures as controlled by the user of the CD-I educational software being used. Visual scenarios can feature colourful graphic images, animated sequences, full-motion video, and using a computer keyboard (or mouse, or light pen) the user interacts with information on the screen. For example, users can select from alternative choices to questions or situations posed on the screen, then immediately receive constructive feedback on the implications of their choices. In other words, the pathway through which the training package is delivered is completely responsive to each individual user's choices, needs and wishes.

It is thought that this technology is set to become the 'next generation' medium for training and education, and also for the distribution of entertainment and information. The technology is backed by the world's largest suppliers of consumer electronics: Philips, Sony and Matsushita, JVC and Panasonic, all of whom have adopted an agreed international standard, making global compatibility a reality.

CD-I technology is quite inexpensive, with a CD-I player including colour TV or monitor ranging (in 1992) from £800-£1600. The system can use 16 simultaneous soundtracks. This means that (for example) the sound commentary in a training programme can be recorded in several languages, and providing translated versions of accompanying workbooks and assignments are made, a good training resource from one country can be used directly in several other countries. The technology is particularly user friendly, and it is claimed that it appeals to computerphobes. Most of the control is exercised with either a mouse, or with a remote-control very similar to those which are endemic in homes already, for televisions and videorecorders. SPIN UK (a Philips subsidiary company – see contact address listed in the Bibliography) is the UK's first producer of CD-I education and training software, and claims that during the remainder of the 1990s CD-I is likely to become as commonplace in the office and the school as CD audio already is in homes. Among the advantages claimed for CD-I are that it is easily transportable from room to room (ie can be used anywhere where there is a suitable TV set), and that there is no need to waste time training learners how to use the equipment. The first four CD-I packages launched in the UK by SPIN UK are:

- The Complete Manager (a training package approved by the Management Charter Initiative, and supported by the National Council for Vocational Qualifications (NCVQ), which includes guidance and assessment towards a BTEC Certificate in Management);

- Developing Competence through Coaching, Mentoring and Assessing;

- Welcome to Work (an induction training package).

- No Need to Shout (an assertiveness training package).

An ever-increasing flow of such training packages is planned. As with the other high-tech developments referred to in the preceding sections of this chapter, we refer readers who wish to use these formats and resources to the wide range of publications currently appearing in specialized journals (please see the Bibliography at the end of this chapter).

TWO CASE STUDIES

As we have explained, it is not wise to try to provide a 'how to do it yourself' element to this chapter. Nor is it feasible to illustrate adequately in the medium of print just how interactive and stimulating the new multimedia computer-assisted learning packages can be, with their colourful graphic displays, on-screen effects, instant referencing to massive databases, and highly sophisticated interaction with learners at keyboards. However, we would like to end this chapter by giving two examples of uses of interactive computer-assisted learning formats, namely a computer conferencing system, and the development of one particular interactive video package. Our illustration is necessarily confined here to print. Moreover, the printed examples which follow in our illustrated account of these developments necessarily lack all the colour and drama of the on-screen displays, particularly in the case of the interactive video development. Nevertheless, we hope that our attempts to show the types of information which learners can interact with on their screens will give you an idea of the power and range of these media. We also hope that our basic descriptions of the respective development of the case studies may tempt readers to develop their own ideas for using interactive media for education and training, and that our case studies go some way to compensate for the impossibility of providing a sensible 'how to do it' section.

CASE STUDY 1: COMPUTER CONFERENCING

Educational computer conferencing at the University of Glamorgan (formerly Polytechnic of Wales) was largely the result of the work of Bob Hall in the University's Information Technology Centre. The following summary of the way the system works in general, and the ways that students can interact with it, is from a conference paper he presented at the AETT Conference in 1991 (see Bibliography).

There are various different varieties of computer conferencing software. The two most popular in the UK appear to be VAX Notes from Digital Equipment Corporation and Caucus from X-On Software.

Advantages of Computer Conferencing

- A wide variety of information can be passed quickly and easily between large (even very large) numbers of people who may be widely geographically dispersed. All contributions are immediately available to all participants.

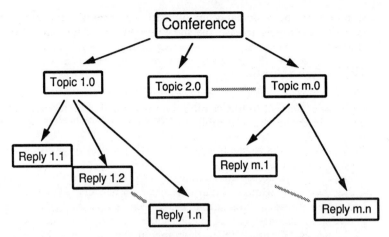

Figure 8.5 **Schematic diagram of a computer conference**

- Computer conferencing is time efficient: all users can access the conference at times to suit themselves; reading from a conference is much quicker than hearing people speak; if users don't want to read a piece of text they can skip on to the next message without delay; a record is kept of which messages an individual user has read and he/she will automatically only see new messages unless the software is requested to display the others.

- It is possible to participate in a number of conferences on a variety of subjects whilst sitting at the same terminal/microcomputer.

- All participants have the same opportunity to have their thoughts and ideas taken into account and listened to in a way that is often impossible in a face-to-face meeting.

- It is possible for contributors to consider carefully their contribution before adding it to the conference.

- Technical problems can be discussed with a higher probability of solution since there are likely to be larger numbers of people participating. A further benefit is that the solution is automatically made available to others immediately.

In the last three years, computer conferencing has become widely used by students at the University of Glamorgan, both informally (conferences on all manner of topics from 'Restaurants' to 'Sport') and formally (where 'class' conferences are set up for particular groups of students, and lecturers contribute to the conferences as appropriate).

The following pages give 'raw' details of one particular use of the computer conferencing system. It should be noted that we have reproduced students' entries (and those of the course leader) exactly as they appeared on-screen – with idiosyncrasies of spelling and grammar as and when they occurred. This is an example of a 'class' conference, rather than a 'public' one – in other words, entry to this conference was restricted to the 45 members of a particular class (the Science, Engineering and Technology Foundation Year – 'SETFY'). These students were all intending to go on to various courses in their respective disciplines, and were already studying a variety of options, therefore one of the purposes of the computer conference was to give them a forum wherein to discuss their experiences of their studies. The 'Foundation' conference was set up as part of a 'Learning Strategies' module run by Phil Race.

Students could access the conference from various terminals in any of their home departments, or from public terminals in the Information Technology Centre, or from terminals located in the Learning Resources Centre of the University (these being available from 0830 till midnight on weekdays, and for most of Saturdays and Sundays as well). This meant that students could contribute in their own way, at times of their own choosing, and could participate singly, or in small groups.

Entries to the conference range from serious contributions and questions, to lighthearted banter and repartee (the students used the conference – among other things – to arrange nightclub trips into Cardiff, and to explore the possibility of setting up a Foundation Year Rugby Football team).

The first hurdle was for the students to obtain their computer passwords, and master the process of logging in to the system. The first entry they saw on logging in was the page shown in Figure 8.6.

At first, many of the replies were relatively trivial, as the main intention was for students to find out how to interact with the conference. It

```
=====================================================================
Note 1.0            Yes, you've found it            21 replies
V8800::WPRACE "Phil Race, Ed.Dev. L309 tel.2018"    15 lines  30-SEP-1991
    16:50
    ------------------------------------------------------------

    Well done - you've found "Found_Conf" - that was the first hurdle!

    The aim of this Conference is that it should be YOUR class conference -
    a sounding-board for all aspects of your experience of this course, a
    chance to practise your skills at working with computers, a chance to
    develop your keyboard skills, a chance to practise your skills of
    expressing yourselves - - - and on and on!

    This conference enables each of you to talk to everyone else in your
    group (and to me) any time you choose.

    I look forward to seeing your Conference grow.

    Cheers - over to you now -
    Phil
=====================================================================
```

Figure 8.6 **The 'starter page' for the 'Foundation' conference**

was not long, however, until students started to enter more serious contributions, for example Figure 8.7.

```
===============================================================
Note 1.3              Yes, you've found it             3 of 21
V8800::MRBUNN                          5 lines  4-OCT-1991 15:11
        -< I got more brain cells than "CJRYDER+LMATTWOO" >-
---------------------------------------------------------------
    It looks as though this is the only reply that hasn't been written by
    some simpletons who have left their brain in a box at home!
    Q) After completion of the (setfy) could we change degree courses?
    Q) also, could we change inst. at a later date?
    Q) what do i do about
===============================================================
```

Figure 8.7 **An example of a more serious question**

One member of the group (a mature student, Nick Jay) was already familiar with the computer conferencing system, and he quickly became a very useful resource to the group as a whole. For example, when one or two students began to ask questions regarding the computing elements of the course (which were to follow next term), he entered a very detailed response as shown in Figure 8.9, overleaf.

The computer conferencing system was soon the vehicle for all sorts of general questions about the course, the structure of its modules, the possibilities of progression from the course, and even the transferability of the programme to other institutions of higher education. In this way, the computer conference provided a ready helpline to students with a

```
===============================================================
Note 1.17             Yes, you've found it            17 of 21
V8800::AGPOWEL1                        5 lines  28-OCT-1991 15:24
            -< A CHANGE OF SCENERY >-
---------------------------------------------------------------
    Dear Phil,I would like to know whether or not it is possible to change
    institution at the end of the foundation year.Would there be any sort
    of credit system whereby we could show another poly or uni that we
    are'nt (or at least I'm not )completely useless just because I failed
    all my A levels.Could you possibly clarify this point for me please.
===============================================================
Note 1.18             Yes, you've found it            18 of 21
V8800::WPRACE "Phil Race, Ed.Dev. L309 tel.2018"   10 lines  30-OCT-1991 08:58
---------------------------------------------------------------
    There isn't a "formal" way as far as I know, but if you go somewhere
    else carrying a batch of wonderful grades for all your topics, I'm sure
    that it would be clear to everyone that you'd made up for A-level
    deficiencies.

    Also, your course leader could write a letter to state the sort of
    course SEFTY is, and give an opinion about your (eminent) suitability
    to join a degree course elsewhere.

    Phil
===============================================================
```

Figure 8.8 **Typical 'question and answer' uses of the computer conference**

```
===============================================================
Note 1.12              Yes, you've found it          12 of 21
V8800::NMJAY                      55 lines  17-OCT-1991 11:22
           -< Computer Module for 2nd Semester. >-
---------------------------------------------------------------
  Computing will replace the current learning strategies module in
  semester 2. For those interested in the sylabus it will be as follows:-
  (Information taken from SETFY factsheet, as supplied by Mr Lee).

  24 scheduled lectures and 28 practicals.
  Students will study one module of computing.

  AIMS
  1 To provide a broad outline of the nature of computing and its
  application to Science and Engineering.

  2 To introduce students to the application of computer databases in the
  field of engineering.

  3 To introduce students to the facilities of a typical wordprocessing
  package.

  4 To introduce a range of computer applications so as to provide a
  comprehension of the power and versatility of the computer and the
  benefits of its use in the scientific study area.

  Introduction to Computing
  What is a computer and what can it do. Introduction to computer
  application areas with emphasis on Engineering. Explanation of the
  various forms of hardware and software.

  Introduction to Databases
  Use of databases, facilities of a database package, the generation of
  simple databases for use in engineering.

  Wordprocessing
  The benefits of a word processing package, facilities of a typical word
  processor, the generation of reports and documentation.

  Scientific Software Packages
  The use of software packages in the engineering/scientific environment.
  Computer aided design packages for engineering, spreadsheets and their
  usefulness for statistical analysis. Statistical analysis packages for
  the manipulation of numerical data.

  Assessment
  2 Assignments and continuous assessment for 100%

  Essential reading
  Microcomputers in Engineering Applications, B A Scheffler, R W Lewis,
  Wiley, 1987

  Computing for Engineers, Fenner, R T., Addison Wesley. 1988


  I hope that answers your questions for those who were asking about the
  computer course.

  Nick
===============================================================
```

Figure 8.9 **A detailed reply from one of the students**

variety of questions or worries. Often, other course members would furnish replies, or the programme leader could give more authoritative guidance when needed. Figure 8.8 shows a typical question and reply.

Experienced students soon came to the fore in the conferencing, and Figure 8.10 shows one of these volunteering his help for anyone who was finding difficulty with system.

```
================================================================ =

Note 3.0            Help or Advice Wanted?         3 replies
V8800::NMJAY                          13 lines  1-OCT-1991 13:15
----------------------------------------------------------------
Although I'm no VAX expert, nor do I proclaim to be, I have managed to
get well-aquainted with the POWCON area and mail, amongst others. If
anyone is having troubles or problems and can't find the solution,
please feel free to put them up here and I, or anyone else, may be able
to point you in the right direction. Or else grab me when I am on
campus and, as long as I'm not rushing off to a lecture myself, I will
be pleased to accompany you to one of the VAX terminals and point you
in the direction, hopefully. Any time, please feel free to ask!

Good luck to everyone and happy conferencing.

Nick.

================================================================ =
```

Figure 8.10 **A student offering his services to help others**

```
===============================================================
Note 20.10         AN INTERESTING QUESTION?        10 of 10
V8800::RMEDWARDS "Robert Edwards, Computer Studies"  19 lines  30-OCT-1991
    15:10
          -< Assessing conference contributions >-
-------------------------------------------------------------
Dear Foundationers,

Will you forgive a stranger butting in here?

This course sounds very interesting and well run, as far as I can
tell from the conference. Actually I am ashamed to say I don't
know much else about it!  Could you enlighten me, privately,
Phil?

I joined in here just to tell you about an American University
course I have just read about (on a conferenciong system, of
course!).  The course was about the use of computers in peoples'
lives, and involved practical work on conferencing sytems.  The
students' contribution to a conference was used as part of their
assessment.  The course leader seemed to have tackled the obvious
problems in doing this in a clear-headed way.  So perhaps it is
possible.

Robert

===========================================================
```

Figure 8.11 **A spontaneous contribution from another lecturer who had been observing the conference**

Other lecturers who were interested could view the conference, and one (Dr Robert Edwards) offered the above useful contribution, as thoughts began to be directed to the assessment of the Learning Strategies module, and to the computer conference itself in particular. The suggestion he made (see Figure 8.11) was indeed used, and the students' contributions to the conference were assessed in due course, using criteria that had been agreed by the whole group.

The computer conference, among other things, became the main vehicle for exchanging information with the class regarding assessed tasks on the Learning Strategies module. Each assessed task was presented as briefing information in the conference, and students could enquire if they needed further clarification or detail. Figure 8.12 shows the guidance given for a typical assessed task, including the deadline.

```
==========================================================================
V8800::WPRACE "Phil Race, Ed.Dev. L309 tel.2018"   27 lines  22-OCT-1991 08:44
--------------------------------------------------------------------
  Syndicate SWOT Analysis

  Due to be handed in for assessment, at L309 before 0915 on 25 October
  for up to 100% of the 20 marks for it, after 0915 for up to 50% of the
  20 marks for it (which will be part of your official mark for the
  "Learning Strategies" module.

  Guidance:

  STRENGTHS: discuss the strengths the syndicate has: talents,chances to
  do things you could not do so well on your own, etc.

  WEAKNESSES: what are the weaknesses of the GROUP? (You don't have to
  say who they belong to specifically).

  OPPORTUNITIES: the things the syndicate intends to do to help all its
  members succeed in their studies

  THREATS: an objective appraisal of the things that could get in the way
  of your hopes and plans.

  Don't forget to add the GROUNDRULES that you come up with as a
  syndicate, and the NAMES of the members who have contributed to
  the SWOT analysis andthe groundrules.

  Look forward to assessing these starting at 0916 on Friday 25 October.
  Phil
==========================================================================
```

Figure 8.12 **A screen showing details of an assessed task**

One of the fundamental purposes of the Learning Strategies module was to help students develop organization and method in their approaches to studying. Another purpose was to help them improve their written communication skills. A further assessed task aimed to help them achieve both of these objectives at the same time. They had already been issued with booklets 'Organising your Studies' and 'Revision Strategies' written by the Course Leader some weeks ago, and each booklet had already been the basis of an interactive workshop with the class. Next, each member of the class was asked to review either of the booklets, and to enter his or her review into the computer conference, so that all students could see and compare the reviews. The main aim of asking the students to review the booklets was to get them thinking about the issues involved in organizing their studies, and also to give them practice at entering a longer piece of written communication into the conference. While some of the entries were perhaps rather more 'congratulatory' about the booklet than was warranted, the exercise seemed to achieve its aims. Figure 8.13 shows the way the task was set.

```
==========================================================================
Note 60.0       START YOUR PERSONAL (ASSESSABLE) FILE NOW        1 reply
V8800::WPRACE "Phil Race, Ed.Dev. L309 tel.2018"    22 lines   6-NOV-1991 08:46
--------------------------------------------------------------------------

   Now that you've all got used to working the system, it's time to start
   doing something "assessable".

   I suggest that each of you opens your own file as a NAMED file. I.e.
   make your full name the TITLE so it can easily be tracked down in the
   directory. This file will then be for your serious contributions to the
   conference.

   For your first task, I'm going to ask you to do a short review: either
   of the booklet "Organising your Studies" that I gave out on Monday, or
   of the booklet "Revision Strategies".

   In your review, I'd like you to include:

   * the two things you like most about the booklet
   * the two things you like least about the booklet
   * how the particular booklet has helped you personally
   * any other comments.

   Make it a critical review though. You'll get just as much credit for
   your review if it's critical as if it is all positive (crawley!!).
   Phil
==========================================================
```

Figure 8.13 **Briefing for a written review**

Figure 8.14 shows one of the reviews. Many of the students took up the invitation to offer suggestions for improving the booklets, and the whole exercise was at least as useful to the author of the booklets as to the students.

The final assessed task in the Learning Strategies module was a short presentation, given by each of the students to the whole group. The exercise was peer-assessed, with a set of criteria generated by the group being used by each member of the group to assess each of the presentations. It had been agreed that 8 out of the 20 marks for the presentations should be earned simply by starting – this was because one or two members of the group were particularly nervous about giving presentations, as they had not done so before. Figure 8.15 shows a conference entry reminding students of the date and time of their presentations.

```
================================================================
Note 69.0           MWRADFORD              No replies
V8800::MWRADFOR                    38 lines  18-NOV-1991 17:35
----------------------------------------------------------------
BOOK REVIEW - ORGANISING YOUR STUDIES BY PROFESSOR PHIL RACE
----------------------------------------------------------------

I think that the Organising Your Studies booklet is a very good idea,
in respect of making students analyis their study techniques and doing
something about them. The way that the book is layed out is a very good
idea, because the book asks the reader questions about their studying
and then compares their answers with the correct method.

This is far better than just reading a book, because if you are just
reading a book then it is very hard to take much in, unless you are
doing something like takeing notes about the book. By the book being
layed out in an reader interactive way, the reader can learn and
correct oneself about their attitudes towards studying.

It's good, because the book guides you through the questions, and tries
to make the whole thing interesting and fun. Once you have answered a
certain set of questions then you can look them up in the other half of
the book and compare your answers with the answers there. This way you
can learn where you go wrong in organising your studies, and correct
yourself.

I think that the Action Plan, is a very good idea, because this enables
the reader to make sure that some sort off action is taken to correct
their learning techniques rather than forget about what has been
learned in the book.

By reading and answering the questions in this book I have learnt allot
about my own learning Organisation, and have decided to make an action
plan of what to do to correct myself. I have decided that instead of
copying up my notes, I should do neatish notes in lectures and then
underline important notes later with a highlight pen. Also to summarize
my notes in blocks of sylabus areas for different areas. I have also
decided to do a number of other tasks to enable me organise my studying
in a more effective manner.

Organising Your Studies - Reviewed by M.W.RADFORD (Setfy - M group).

================================================================
```

Figure 8.14 **A typical review from one of the students**

```
================================================================
Note 73.0        ASSESSED PRESENTATIONS 2.12.91        6 replies
V8800::WPRACE "Phil Race, Ed.Dev. L309 tel.2018"   17 lines  25-NOV-1991 16:27
----------------------------------------------------------------

Monday 2 December  1300-1700 (with breaks)

PRESENTATIONS

The moment you've all been waiting for - your 5-minute presentation.

As suggested this afternoon, please prepare handout material and/or OHP
to reinforce your presentation.

The topic? Anything (respectable!).

the marks: 20, 8 just for getting up and starting.

The benefits: a start towards the skills you'll need many times in your
future life, convincing other people by the power and style of the way
you talk about things.
Phil
================================================================
```

Figure 8.15 **A conference entry reminding students of their presentations**

CASE STUDY 2: 'SECRETS OF STUDY'

In a chapter in a book like this, it is entirely impossible to give you any real indication of how lively and stimulating media such as interactive video or even just interactive computer-based training can be. We can, however, give an example of some material we have worked with and outline the preparation of such resources, leaving it to your imagination to picture the graphics, and the degrees of interaction achieved by the final media-based packages.

'Secrets of Study' was a project developed in 1988 by Mast Learning Systems (London), funded by the Manpower Services Commission (now the Employment Department of the British Government). Mast Learning Systems already had a proven track record regarding the production of highly professional training packages, and worked with many multinational companies, custom-designing training packages for such companies. Among the media in which Mast had developed expertise were computer-based training, interactive video, and interactive audio (similar to interactive video, but using sound and still images rather than moving images).

Mark Harrison of Mast Learning Systems had the idea of creating an entirely novel package to help people develop their study skills. This would indeed contain advice on many standard aspects of study skills, but set in a 'game' situation. The idea that Mark Harrison developed was to devise a spy thriller story, in which the user of the interactive packages could participate.

The story can be summarized as follows. The user plays the part of a spy, being sent to a conference on 'Vulcanology' (the study of volcanoes) to try to track down previous agents who have disappeared. To successfully avoid being found out at the conference, the user needs to acquire very quickly a considerable range of knowledge about volcanoes. This information is available as a briefing paper, and various briefing episodes are done on-screen using full video sequences. By the end of the briefing, the user has a considerable 'feel' for the mission, and a strong impression of the people involved in the mission (for example the training officer, the 'boss' and so on).

Six study-skills modules are available to the user, to help him (or her) to learn the information on vulcanology successfully. These modules can be accessed via an on-screen menu at any time while using the package (and similarly, the user can return to the story at any time from within any of the six study-skills modules). The entire package is designed to be as flexible as possible regarding how it is used. Learners can choose simply to play their way through the 'story' (and almost invariably end up being arrested in due course, as their ignorance about some particular piece of vulcanology is revealed to enemy agents). The story sequences themselves were filmed on video, using actors, at a Scottish country house, providing all the moving-image sequences and briefings which users can receive at various parts of the 'story' programme.

Alternatively, learners can sit down at the keyboard, and completely ignore the story, simply selecting one or more of the study skills modules, and working through it in their own way. The titles of the study-skills modules speak for themselves:

- Getting Down to It (largely on target setting and motivation)
- Reading (including speed reading)
- Writing (including essay writing)
- Memory
- Making Notes
- Preparing for and Taking Exams

Phil Race came into this project as a consultant to help Mark Harrison fine-tune the content and nature of these six modules. Between them, they devised hundreds of questions which would in various parts of the modules be thrown up on the screen, with learners selecting options or choices using a mouse or the keyboard, and then receiving feedback responses on the options they had chosen.

The following extracts from the wording used for the screens simply give an idea of the words, not the drama or colour with which the final package was presented.

MODULE 1: GETTING DOWN TO IT

Welcome to the first of our Study-Skills modules. (Of course, you may not be reading this one first - you may already have delved into others - that's exactly the sort of freedom we intended you to have when using these Modules).

The title "Getting Down to It" was chosen because so often people say "If only I could get down to some studying!". We hope we've found some convincing suggestions for you.

This module has 5 main sections:

Section 1: Target Setting

Section 2: Snowballing

Section 3: Motivation

Section 4: Timetabling

Section 5: Learning the Rules

It doesn't matter which of these sections you try first, nor does it matter at all if at the moment you don't know what we mean by some of the terms above!

When you've explored the module you'll know exactly what we mean - and we hope you'll have picked up many useful tips about getting down to your studies.

So - on you go - and good luck!!

Figure 8.16 **The lead-in text to the 'Getting Down to It' module in 'Secrets of Study'**

Section 1: Target Setting

For a moment, imagine you're a bit of an athlete! Imagine you're going in for the high-jump in a competition.

Let's say you're aiming for a record jump of 1.80 m, and your personal best so far is 1.60 m.

You're allowed three jumps at each height you choose, until you get eliminated from the competition!

Self Assessment Question

Which of the following heights would you choose to START on?

(a) 1.00 m

(b) 1.20 m

(c) 1.40 m

(d) 1.60 m

(e) 1.80 m

Figure 8.17 **A small extract of text, then a self-assessment question for users to try**

Response

(a)	Well, you probably won't fail to reach this height! But you may well take a lot of time - AND A LOT OF ENERGY - working up to the target height. Your target is achievable, but probably not challenging enough.
(b)	Indeed, you should manage this height comfortably enough. But you may still take a lot of time and energy working up to the target height. Your target is achievable, but probably not quite challenging enough.
(c)	That's a good decision. If you started at your personal best (or more) you'd probably fail at the first hurdle. And if you went for too easy a start, you'd spend a lot of time and energy working towards your ultimate target.
(d)	Going for your personal best right away is probably a bit risky. It would have been more advisable to start with a height which is more achievable, but still challenging - e.g. 1.40 m.
(e)	Going well beyond your personal best is surely a bit too ambitious for a first attempt. It would have been more advisable to start with a height which is more achievable, but still challenging - e.g. 1.40 m.

Figure 8.18 **The responses to the self-assessment question. Note that on-screen, users would only be given one of the five responses shown above, depending which option they had chosen initially (though of course they could return to the question and choose alternative options if they wished to see what the alternative responses would be)**

The Revision Process: One Approach

- look at syllabus and past exam questions;

- look through ALL your notes, study materials, lecture notes, etc.

- decide what you NEED TO KNOW, and what it would simply be NICE TO KNOW. (See the difference?)

- plan a revision timetable; keep it sensible - keep healthy!

- in each revision session:

1. Read some notes:
   ask yourself questions
   be active
   walk around the room now and then
   speak to a recorder (as a change from writing answers)

2. When you feel you've understood some material: CLOSE THE BOOKS, PUT THE NOTES OUT OF SIGHT.

3. RECALL the main points of the notes - write them down on a card or SMALL piece of paper - keep it short!

4. CHECK against your original study materials;
   - if OK use the card or small piece of paper as a future revision aid.
   - if not OK, REPEAT the above processes till it is OK.

Figure 8.19 **Some discussion material on revision processes presented in an expository way on screen near the start of the 'Preparing for and Taking Exams' module of 'Secrets of Study'**

Self Assessment Question

How closely does the process you've been looking at match your own personal approach to revision?

(a) Very like mine.

(b) Quite like mine.

(c) Not much like mine.

(d) Not at all like mine.

Figure 8.20 **A self-assessment question asking users to decide whether their own approaches to revision resemble the appraoch they have just been shown on-screen**

Mast Learning Systems initially produced 'Secrets of Study' in three formats:

- Interactive video (moving film sequences, particularly relating to the spy story, stored on videodisc);

- Interactive audio (still digitized images relating to the film story, with digitally stored audio material from the soundtrack or the video sequences, giving almost as much 'sense of reality' as the moving images);

Response

(a)   Good. You'll have found that a key element of successful revision is practice at recalling things - answering questions. After all that's exactly what you need to be able to do in any exam.

(b)   Good, you've at least made an effort to organise your revision in a systematic way. Remember that a key element of successful revision is practice at recalling things - answering questions. After all that's exactly what you need to be able to do in any exam.

(c)   If your existing method serves you well, by all means continue to use it. But remember that a key element of successful revision is practice at recalling things - answering questions. After all that's exactly what you need to be able to do in any exam.

(d)   It seems that you already have a quite definite method of doing your revision, even if it's quite unlike the one you've been looking at here. But remember that a key element of successful revision is practice at recalling things - answering questions. After all that's exactly what you need to be able to do in any exam.

Figure 8.21 **The response text which would be given on screen for each of the options in the question about revision practices (users would as before only see one of (a) to (d) unless they chose to explore the whole range of possibilities by selecting each option in turn)**

■   Computer-based version, without sound, and with the story being presented on-screen as episodes of text and graphics.

The study skills modules themselves were almost identical in the three versions, as they did not require many moving video sequences. Students' preferences were explored during piloting. As expected, the interactive video version (although necessarily more expensive) was the one which most users preferred, and the interactive audio version was soon discarded.

Speed Reading

One of the most interesting parts of the study skills modules turned out to be the section dealing with speed reading. This works along the following lines.

■   Learners are shown two or three screens of information, for example from the story 'Three Men in a Boat' by Jerome K Jerome.

■   They read the information at their own comfortable pace.

■   When they finish (ie move on from the information screen) the computer gives them a figure for their reading rate measured in words-per-minute (by timing the length of time the information screens were shown).

■   Learners then do a short multiple-choice test on the information they have been reading, receive feedback on each answer, and receive a total score for the test (which the computer stores for further processing).

■   Learners are then given some on-screen suggestions regarding ways of increasing their reading speeds – some more information, another test, further analysis of progress (or regression).

- Learners are then given something that can only be done using an interactive computer system. More information appears, with a coloured square cursor, which learners are asked to control at their maximum reading speed. For this, two keys on the keyboard serve as 'accelerator' and 'brake', and learners have considerable fun trying to read as fast as possible. The computer then confirms just how fast they have been reading, and compares their performance to their earlier attempts.

- Similar processes continue, with further advice, and a final practice-piece (as always followed by a comprehension test).

- At the end of the section, the computer displays the speeds and the scores for the respective episodes and tests, and it is quite normal for learners to find that they have retained more (and read at a much higher speed) at the end of the module than when they began.

BIBLIOGRAPHY

Barker, J and Tucker, R N (1990) *The Interactive Learning Revolution: Multi-media in Education and Training.* Kogan Page, London.

Barker, P G (1987) *Author Languages for CAL.* Kogan Page, London.

Barker, P G (1989a) *Multi-media Computer-assisted Learning.* Kogan Page, London.

Barker, P G (1989b) *Basic Principles of Human-computer Interface Design.* Century-Hutchinson, London.

Barker, P G and Giller, S (1990) *An electronic book for early learners – a CDROM design exercise, The CTISS File* Issue 10, 13–18.

Barker, P G and Giller, S (1992) Electronic books, in *Developing and Measuring Competence,* Saunders, D and Race, P (eds), Kogan Page, London.

Barker, P G and Manji, K (1989) Designing electronic books, *Journal of Artificial Intelligence in Education* 1(2), 31–42.

Barker, P G (1990a) Designing interactive learning systems, *Educational and Training Technology International,* 27(2) 125–45.

Barker, P G (1990b) Electronic books, *Learning Resources Journal* 6(3), 62–8.

Barker, P G (1990c) Automating the production of courseware, 203-208 in *Aspects of Educational and Training Technology – Vol. XXXIII: Making Systems Work,* Farmer, B, Eastcott, D and Matz, B (eds), Kogan Page, London.

Barker, P G (1991a) Interactive electronic books, *Interactive multi-media* 2(1), 11–28.

Barker, P G (1991b) *An object orientated approach to hypermedia authoring,* paper to be presented at Advanced NATO workshop on Multimedia

Design, Laval University, Quebec, Canada.

Barrett, E (ed) (1989) *The Society of Text: Hypertext, Hypermedia and the Social Construction of Information.* MIT Press, Cambridge, Ma, USA.

Bates, A W (ed) (1985) *The Role of Technology in Distance Education.* Croom Helm, London.

Bostock, S J and Seifert, R V (1986) *Microcomputers in Adult Education.* Croom Helm, London.

Boyd-Barrett, O and Scanlon, E (eds) (1991) *Computers and Learning.* Addison-Wesley/Open University, Milton Keynes.

Britannica Software (1990) *Compton's Multi-Media Encyclopedia – User's Guide,* Britannic Software, San Francisco, CA, USA.

Burns, H, Parlett, J W and Redfield, C L (1991) *Intelligent Tutoring Systems – Evolutions in Design.* Lawrence Erlbaum, New Jersey and London.

CD-I (Compact Disk Interactive): for information: Weil, Stephen; Sales and Marketing Manager, SPIN UK Ltd, Lombard House, 2 Purley Way, Croydon, CR0 3JP.

Dean, C and Whitlock, Q (1988) *A Handbook of Computer Based Training (2nd Ed).* Kogan Page, London.

Flegg, D and McHale, J (1991) *Selecting and Using Training Aids.* Kogan Page, London.

Gerver, E (1986) *Humanizing Technology: Computers in Community Use and Adult Education.* Plenum, New York / London.

Grolier Inc. (1988) *The New Grolier Electronic Encyclopedia – User's Guide and Compact Disk.* Grolier Electronic Publishing, Sherman Turnpike, Danbury, USA.

Hall, R M (1992) Using Computer Conferencing to Develop Competence, in *Developing and Measuring Competence,* Saunders, D and Race, P (eds), Kogan Page, London.

Harrison, N (1990) *How to Design Effective Computer Based Training.* McGraw-Hill, Maidenhead.

Hawkridge, D (1983) *New Information Technology in Education.* Croom Helm, London.

Kist, J (1987) *Electronic Publishing.* Croom Helm, London.

Luther, A C (1989) *Digital Video in the PC Environment.* McGraw-Hill, New York.

Manji, K A (1990) *Pictorial communication with computers.* PhD Dissertation, Teesside Polytechnic, Cleveland, UK.

Mason, R and Kay, A (eds) (1989) *Mindweave: Communication, Computers, and Distance Education.* Pergamon, London.

Mast Learning Systems (1988) *Secrets of Study.* Mast Learning Systems, 3 Wetherby Mews, London, SW5.

McAleese, R (ed) (1989) *Hypertext: Theory into Practice.* Intellect, Oxford.

McAleese, R and Green, C (eds) (1990) *Hypertext: State of Art.* Intellect, Oxford.

Nielsen, J (1990) *Hypertext and Hypermedia.* Academic Press, London.

Nimbus Information Systems (1989) *Music Catalog on CDROM.*

Wyastone Leys, Monmouth, UK.

Picciotto, M et al. (1989) *Interactivity, Designing and Using Interactive Video.* Kogan Page, London.

Question Mark Computing (1990) *Objective Testing on a Computer.* Question Mark Computing, London.

Race, P (1989) *Teaching and Learning in Higher Education: Series 3 (A suite of 9 booklets on study-skills topics).* CICED Publications, Aberdeen.

Romiszowski, A J (1986) *Developing Auto-Instructional Materials from Programmed Texts to CAL and Interactive Video.* Kogan Page, London.

Romiszowski, A J (1988) *The Selection and Use of Instructional Media.* Kogan Page, London.

Roth, J P (ed) (1991) *Rewritable Optical Storage Technology.* Meckler, Westport and London.

Roth, J P (ed) (1991) *Case Studies of Optical Storage Applications* Meckler, Westport and London.

Schneiderman, B and Kearsley, G (1989) *Hypertext Hands-On – A New Way of Organising and Accessing Information,* Addison-Wesley, Reading, Ma, USA.

Steinberg, E R (1991) *Teaching Computers to Teach.* Lawrence Erlbaum, New Jersey and London.

Terry, C (1984) *Using Microcomputers in Schools.* Croom Helm, London.

Weatherall, D J, Ledingham, J G G and Warrell, D A (1989) *Oxford Textbook of Medicine on Compact Disk (2nd ed).* Oxford University Press, Oxford.

A Selection of Relevant Journals

Artificial Intelligence Review. Blackwell Scientific Publications, Oxford.

British Journal of Educational Technology. National Council for Educational Technology, Coventry.

Classroom Computer Learning. Peter Li, Dayton, USA.

Computers and Education. Pergamon, Oxford.

Educational Technology. Educational Technology Inc., New Jersey, USA.

Educational Media International. Kogan Page, London.

Educational Technology Abstracts. Carfax, Abingdon.

Hypermedia. Taylor Graham, London.

Intelligent Tutoring Media. Learned Information Ltd, Oxford.

International Journal of Computers in Adult Education and Training. Kogan Page, London.

International Journal of Instructional Media. New York, USA.

Journal of Artificial Intelligence in Education. Charlottesville, USA.

Journal of Computer Assisted Learning. Blackwell Scientific Publications, Oxford.

Journal of Educational Multimedia and Hypermedia. Charlottesville, USA.

Journal of Educational Research. Washington, USA.

Journal of Information Systems. Blackwell Scientific Publications, Oxford.

Journal of Information Technology. Kogan Page, London.

Media and Methods. Philadelphia, USA.
Multimedia and Videodisc Monitor. Falls Church, USA.
Videodisc Newsletter. British Universities Film and Video Council, London.

Keyword Index

(This index refers only to the main text of the book, not to the references or the Bibliographies. Where topics have been dealt with in depth, **bold type** indicates the page on which discussion of respective topics begins)